Eliot Ness

The Real Story

by

Paul W. Heimel

Copyright © 1997 by Paul W. Heimel

Published by:

Knox Books
407 Mill Street
Coudersport PA 16915

ISBN: 0-9655824-0-X

First Edition, January 1997
Printed in the United States of America

Cover design by:
Piet Sawvel
Cable Television Services, Inc.

Foreword

Who was Eliot Ness?

The purpose of this book is to explore that question with a degree of thoroughness never before attempted by the hundreds of journalists, authors, historians and other researchers who have pondered it over a span of more than a half-century.

Americans love a hero; they're fascinated by a villain. Stories pitting good against evil captivate them. That could explain their fascination with Eliot Ness.

The elevation of Eliot Ness to the status of a legend was inevitable, irresistible, and altogether fitting. Yet, people have a distorted view of the man who bashed the breweries of Al Capone in Chicago, fearlessly battled organized crime and official corruption in Cleveland, and refused to compromise his principles, even when to resist temptation meant certain personal sacrifice.

Though the familiar character presented on the television screen and movie reel is a myth, Eliot Ness's actual accomplishments were legitimate. Ness deserves his image as a champion of law and order; a symbol of honesty, integrity and bravery.

This book is an attempt to separate the man from the legend. It is a story of good against evil that is complex and uniquely American.

Acknowledgments

This has been a much more difficult task than I had expected. The vast majority of what has been written and said about Eliot Ness is exaggerated, distorted, sensationalized or fabricated. Most of those who could have helped to fill the gaps are deceased. Others who were acquainted with Ness, or have information about him, acknowledge gaps in their recollections. Separating fact from fiction or speculation was a major challenge. I was buoyed by the interest, support and encouragement of others who wanted to know the whole story.

As I neared the completion of this book and investigated publishing options, certain incentives were dangled in front of me if only I would commit further crimes against history and the true legacy of Eliot Ness by fabricating events and creating fictitious dialogue. I refused.

This book is the product of exhaustive research, countless interviews, and three rewrites, each involving the extraction of information or episodes that could not be substantiated.

Eliot Ness: The Real Story never would have been completed without the help of many people who shared my "sense of mission." I have listed these acknowledgments alphabetically, with apologies to anyone whose name has been inadvertently omitted:

Lou Abraham, John Adduci, Maggie Allison, Fred Anderson, William Ayers, Bill Bogart, D. Bruce Cahilly, Larry DelGrosso, Jim Devlin, Jill Diamond, Alan Dickerson, Jack Dorfeld, Katharine Dorfeld, Leslie Easton, Bill Grabe, John Graves, Sue Gunn, Barbara Heimel, Chris L. Heimel, Lugene Heimel, Steve Heimel, Rodney Heymann, Christina Hice, Michael Husain, John O. Jones, Dawk Knox, Shirlee Leete, Jeannette Libonati, the Rev. Robert Loughborough, Carl Lindahl, Joseph A. Majot, Matthew Mangino, Rebecca McFarland, the Rev. Robert B. Merten, Jane Metzger, Gerri Miller, Dan T. Moore, Scott Morris, Dr. George Mosch, William Olson, Brian Pekarski, Joe Phelps Jr., Rick Porrello, John Rigas, Piet Sawvel, B. Mark Schmerling, Michael Schneider, Lynne Skinner, Robert Stack, Steve Talkington, Mary Taylor, Gerry Wallerstein, Lewis Wilkinson, Al Wolff.

Paul W. Heimel
Coudersport, Pennsylvania
October 1996

About The Author

Paul W. Heimel has more than twenty years' experience as a professional writer. He has been published in dozens of magazines and has worked as a stringer for Associated Press since the mid-1970s. He has also served as managing editor of two newspapers. Heimel's publishing credits include four other nonfiction books: *No Longer Any Danger* (Enterprise Publishing Company), which focused on a nationally-publicized double murder case involving attorney F. Lee Bailey; *Always A Danger* (Leader Publishing), a follow-up to the first book; *Shattered Dreams* (Leader Publishing), which traced the life of Norwegian violin virtuoso Ole Bull and his efforts to establish a colony in northern Pennsylvania; and *High Wire Angel* (Piccadilly Books), the authorized biography of aerialist Angel Wallenda. Heimel was born and raised in Coudersport, Pennsylvania, the small community where Eliot Ness spent the final two years of his life.

Table of Contents

	Page
Chapter One: Bye, Bye Snorky	11
Chapter Two: 'Elegant Mess'	15
Chapter Three: Big Jim & Little John	21
Chapter Four: When Tommy Guns Ruled	27
Chapter Five: It Was His Funeral	34
Chapter Six: The Law Is The Law	42
Chapter Seven: Only A Matter Of Time	51
Chapter Eight: Sending A Message	58
Chapter Nine: Inside Connections	65
Chapter Ten: Nobody's Legit	71
Chapter Eleven: The Untouchables	81
Chapter Twelve: Crumbling Empire	92
Chapter Thirteen: Marked Man	98
Chapter Fourteen: Federal Convict No. 40886	107
Chapter Fifteen: Making A Difference	118
Chapter Sixteen: Cleveland: One Tough Town	127
Chapter Seventeen: Crooked Cops Pay The Price	135
Chapter Eighteen: A Better Cleveland	143
Chapter Nineteen: Troubled Times	152
Chapter Twenty: Social Protection	160
Chapter Twenty-One: 'I'm Sure Having Fun'	167
Chapter Twenty-Two: What Might Have Been...	177
Chapter Twenty-Three: Beginning Of The End	188
Chapter Twenty-Four: 'You Should Write A Book'	194
Chapter Twenty-Five: Symbol of Courage & Decency	206
Chapter Twenty-Six: Eliot Ness, The Myth	216
Epilogue	222

CHAPTER ONE

Bye, Bye Snorky

"Did you ever think you wanted something more than anything else in the world and then, after you got it, it wasn't half as good as you expected? Has that ever happened to you?"

It took a while for Eliot Ness's words to sink in to his fellow "Untouchable," Paul Robsky, who stood beside him on the dock at Chicago's Dearborn Station. Robsky avoided eye contact as he digested his boss's words. The deafening roar of the train engine made a response unnecessary.

"What could he mean by that?" Robsky thought to himself. "Can't this man, just once, savor the moment?"

Hundreds of curious Chicagoans had gathered at the train station on this cool spring night in 1932, hoping to catch a glimpse of an American hero—not Eliot Ness, but his archenemy of the Prohibition era, Alphonse "Scarface" Capone. Through the work of several federal agents—Ness among them—Capone had been toppled from his seat atop one of the most brutal, efficient and lucrative organizations in the history of American crime. Crooked cops, politicians and judges had looked the other way while gang wars strewed Chicago's streets with corpses. They were not about to stand in Capone's way; they were on his payroll.

Capone had emerged as a combination public enemy/folk hero. But now, this mastermind of a criminal empire built on bootlegging, prostitution, gambling and racketeering was bound for the federal penitentiary in Atlanta.

Handcuffed and linked to another inmate by a three-foot-long chain, Capone wore a ragged gray topcoat as he awkwardly climbed out of the U.S. Marshal's car. He and his prison mate huddled behind a phalanx of police officers, detectives and deputies who bulled their way toward the loading platform. Cameramen protested as the circle of officers pushed past them. Capone looked up briefly, then squinted from the glare of photographers' flashbulbs.

"Damn it, come on!" he barked to the other inmate, who stumbled as he tried to keep up. "Let's get the hell out of this!"

Capone then directed his ire at the newspaper reporters. "Go to hell, you lousy rats!"

Among the group of onlookers were many friends and family members who gathered to bid him a silent farewell. The officers stopped at the foot of a stairway leading to the passenger car entrance. Capone stood silently, looking downward, as Eliot Ness and some other federal officers scampered up the steps and fanned out for a quick inspection of the "Dixie Flyer," a regularly-scheduled Pullman train bound for Atlanta.

Once the signal went out that all was clear, Capone and the other prisoner were led up the steps and through the doorway. The crowd pushed forward for one last look at "Public Enemy Number One" as the group moved down the center aisles to the second car from the end. Photographers flashed away as Capone buried his face deeper into his left shoulder, concealing the scars that gave him the nickname he detested. This disfigurement was the ugly aftereffect of a New York street fight when Capone was in his teens.

Federal guards poured into the cars on either end. Ness, trailing the others, watched through the doorway as a uniformed officer helped Capone remove his overcoat and lit the prisoner's cigar before locking him into leg irons. Capone leaned back and closed his eyes, no longer concerned that the left side of his face was fully exposed to the photographers on the platform outside. At long last, he seemed to have resigned himself to his fate.

Ness slipped between the guards and watched in silence as Capone forced a slight smile for the half-dozen reporters who began firing questions at him.

"I don't know much about Atlanta," Capone said, his voice barely audible. "I guess, for one thing, it's gonna be hot. I figure I'll lose some weight, maybe play on the prison baseball team.

Hey, I'm a pretty good pitcher and first baseman, if I do say so myself."

Federal marshals ordered the reporters out, but Ness remained in the doorway, waiting for Capone to acknowledge his presence. Finally, Capone looked up at the man who had worked so hard to cripple his lucrative bootlegging business. This may have been their only face-to-face encounter.

"Well, I'm on my way to do eleven years," he said flatly, glancing up at Ness and then peering out the window into the Chicago sky. "I've got to do it. I'm not sore at anybody. Some people are lucky. I wasn't." He paused. "There was too much overhead in my business anyhow, paying off all the time and replacing trucks and breweries. They ought to make it legitimate."

"That's a strange idea coming from you," Ness retorted. "If it was legitimate, you certainly wouldn't want anything to do with it."

Capone glared at his young antagonist, but said nothing. Ness backed away, feeling triumphant, and the door slammed shut. By the time Capone regained his freedom, he would be a mere shell of the dynamic force that ruled Chicago with an iron fist. Syphilis, already eating away at his central nervous system, would force him to spend his final years as a bloated paranoiac who could recall nothing of his Chicago days and sometimes failed to recognize his own wife and son.

President Herbert Hoover and law enforcement personnel nationwide celebrated the downfall of Al Capone. Equally elated were rival gang leaders who were positioned to pick up the spoils of the Chicago crime wars and continue Capone's self-proclaimed mission of "giving the public what the public wants."

Eliot Ness was in no mood to celebrate. He stood rigidly on the dock, raising his shoulders to shield his neck from the cold wind as he tucked his hands into the deep pockets of his overcoat. A long, piercing whistle silenced the crowd. "Bye, bye, Snorky," Ness whispered to no one in particular.

Thick, grey coal smoke poured into the air as the wheels began to turn. The engine's chug became a loud roar, quickly dispersing the crowd.

Ness and Robsky were the last officers to leave the platform. They walked slowly toward the parking lot in silence before Robsky broke the ice. "Something buggin' you?" he asked, looking into the eyes of his fellow agent.

"I can't put my finger on it," Ness replied, looking away. "I just wonder if it really makes any difference that old Snorky is riding out of town on a rail, or whether we're just fooling ourselves."

"Yeah, I know what you mean," Robsky sighed. "You know damned well there are plenty more thugs who've moved in on most of the rackets already. I don't think anything is really gonna change."

"That's my point. What's there to celebrate?" Ness said, slipping into the passenger's seat of the black sedan. "It's kind of an empty feeling. First thing tomorrow, let's all sit down and figure out where we go from here."

"Fine with me," Robsky replied, "But let's enjoy it tonight. I think we both could use a beer. We'll have a toast to our old friend, Scarface Al."

The two agents glanced out the side window, just in time to see a pair of red lights from the back of the Dixie Flyer glowing like rubies as the train disappeared into the night.

"We've still got a lot of work to do," Ness said. "A hell of a lot of work to do."

CHAPTER TWO

'Elegant Mess'

Hard work came naturally to Eliot Ness. By the time he was age nine, Eliot was cleaning the floors and doing other odd jobs at his father's bakery in suburban Chicago, always eager to please his parents. Peter and Emma Ness marveled at their youngest son's cooperation.

They were among the thousands of Norwegians who came to America in the late 1800s, seeking a better life in a land where economic opportunities were said to be limitless. Their arrival coincided with the assassination of President James Garfield, not that either of them realized it at the time. "I knew that something big was going on," Peter Ness said of his first few days in America. "But I didn't speak English and nobody around me spoke Norwegian, so I didn't know what."

A master baker, Peter made arrangements with an elderly couple to take over their Scandinavian bakery in Kensington, a cohesive ethnic conclave on Chicago's South Side. Emma Ness, the daughter of a Norwegian dressmaker and an English engineer, split her time between tending to the couple's three daughters and helping her husband manage his business. Eliot would later tell a newspaper reporter, "I'm so proud to be the son of two people who built a successful business and raised a large family while never cheating anyone out of a nickel."

Ness Bakery served a growing customer base in the Chicago Scandinavian community. Eventually, Peter Ness opened a second retail outlet in Kensington. A third and fourth would follow.

The Nesses were never wealthy, but not poor by neighborhood standards. Their first son, Charles, was born in 1890. Eliot did not arrive until thirteen years later, on April 19, 1903. The fact that they named him after George Eliot, the British novelist, suggests that his parents were not aware they had bestowed on their youngest child the pen name of Mary Ann Evans.

The role models for Eliot—those people with whom he interacted the most—were female. Peter Ness was often away from home, tending to his bakeries for upwards of eighty hours per week, so the responsibility for raising Eliot fell to Emma. This close, dependent relationship with his mother helped to shape Ness's gentle personality in early adulthood. She sometimes behaved as if her son could do no wrong, and instilled the same attitude in him.

"He was so terribly good that he never got a spanking," she recalled in a newspaper interview conducted during the peak of her son's prominence as a crimefighter in the early 1930s. "I never saw a boy like him."

As close as he was to his mother, Eliot respected his father and craved his attention.

"What I now appreciate most about my father is the way he took the time to give quiet lectures separating right from wrong," Ness told one interviewer. "He made sure I recognized the importance of hard work, honesty and compassion. He never had a lot to say, but when he did speak, I knew it was something worth listening to. I always took it to heart because I didn't see him all that much... I just wish I had gotten to know him better before he died."

Exhausted by their daily routines, Eliot's aging parents too often gave in to their youngest son's demands. A freckle-faced lad with a winning smile, but quiet manner, Eliot spent much of his early childhood with neighborhood pals, gathering at the Palmer Park playground or visiting the nearby soda fountain for ice cream sundaes and penny candy.

"We used to tease him for playing with girls, but he didn't seem to mind," said William Olson, who grew up two doors down from the Nesses. "We'd play army, or baseball, or other games that were just for boys. We'd invite him to play, too, and he would just look away and say, 'Naw, no thanks.' He seemed uncomfortable; nervous, I guess. After a while, we quit asking him."

One of Ness's few male friends was Wallace Jamie, the son of Eliot's sister Clara and her husband, Alexander Jamie, an agent with the United States Justice Department. Whenever Jamie shared his tales of adventure, a fascinated Eliot hung on his every word.

Eliot was a bright and attentive student at Pullman Elementary School, reluctant to speak out in class unless encouraged by his teachers. He could sometimes be found reading detective novels or comic books off in a corner by himself while classmates played nearby. After school and during the summer, Eliot pedaled his bicycle to his father's bakery and begged to help. He particularly enjoyed riding along on delivery routes, pocketing tips for later use at the soda fountain.

Childhood acquaintances recall how Ness attacked every task, no matter how menial, with determination and total commitment, often at the expense of personal friendships.

"We used to call him 'Elegant Mess,' which was really a put-down," recalled Jeannette Libonati, a classmate of Ness's at Fenger High School. The nickname stemmed from Eliot's often spotless appearance and his inability, or unwillingness, to fit in with any of the high school cliques.

"It seemed like he always had something on his mind," Libonati said. "I guess he was daydreaming, or nervous. Some people considered him arrogant, like he thought he was better than everybody else, but I think he was just uneasy in social settings. Once you started talking to him, he loosened right up and was fine. He just didn't ever take the first step."

Among the many ironies of Eliot Ness's life is the fact that Jeannette, his classmate, became the wife of Roland Libonati, one of Al Capone's closest associates and a Chicago politician of some renown.

By the time he reached his senior year in high school, Eliot had matured from a gangly adolescent to a solid, square-shouldered adult. He seemed taller than his six feet because he was so slender, but that slimness belied his powerful arms and shoulders. His brown hair, neatly parted in the middle, and his soft gray eyes offset a slight pug nose. A fashionable, well-fitting wardrobe complemented this natural attractiveness. The former Elegant Mess, now considered a "catch" by his female classmates, found it easy to open up to girls, though he was more interested in friendships than romance.

Graduating near the top of his class, Ness had his choice of colleges, but he instead went to work for a Chicago South Side auto plant. Within a matter of weeks, he grew tired of dipping radiators and accepted a job as a real estate office clerk.

His mother urged Eliot to continue his education, but it was only after Peter Ness took his son aside for a heart-to-heart conversation about his future that Eliot agreed to enroll at the University of Chicago.

"He said he hadn't worked day and night so that his youngest child would be a failure and have to work just as hard," Ness would relate many years later.

After declaring multiple majors in pre-law, commerce and political science, Eliot switched to accounting. In the classroom, he dressed in stylish sport coats. Women were naturally attracted to this quiet, handsome Norwegian, intrigued perhaps by an inner sadness that lurked beneath his pleasant exterior.

As Ness began to seek out more intimate feminine companionship, he developed an interest in Edna Staley, the daughter of a Chicago factory worker. Edna was an attractive young woman whose dark blond hair, light blue eyes and heart-shaped face reflected her Scandinavian heritage. She and Eliot met in elementary school, but attended separate high schools and barely knew each other as children. Ness had seen Edna in passing while visiting the office of Alexander Jamie, where she worked as a secretary, and finally summoned the courage to ask her for a date. From that moment on, Edna once said, she knew that Eliot Ness was the man with whom she wanted to spend the rest of her life.

Ness pledged the Sigma Alpha Epsilon fraternity, much to the chagrin of his parents, but was never active in the group's affairs. More often than not, he declined invitations to attend beer parties. Instead, Ness concentrated on tennis, which he played with such intensity that some schoolmates considered him a show-off. What he lacked in physical coordination, he made up for with technique, strategy and endurance.

Ness also began studying martial arts. Three nights a week, he attended classes in jujitsu, developing a strong passion for both the sport and the mental discipline that it required.

Eliot was filled with boundless energy. Despite the demands of his studies, his involvement with women, his affinity for tennis and martial arts, and his fraternity connections, he still worked part-time at his father's bakery.

During his final year of college, Ness became more comfortable participating in classroom discussions and impressed his teachers with his emerging leadership qualities and persuasive manner. He remained a compulsive reader, immersing himself in every mystery novel or American history book he could find.

In 1925, Ness was awarded a bachelor's degree in business administration and political science. With industrial development all around him, numerous business firms courted the 22-year-old Ness. He flirted with the idea of enrolling in law school. Instead, Ness became a field officer for the Retail Credit Company, an Atlanta-based firm that investigated people who applied for insurance coverage.

The "investigation" work he had been promised consisted of checking credit ratings and verifying the accuracy of insurance claims, a far cry from the exciting adventures another "investigator," Alexander Jamie, had described. By that time, Jamie had been promoted to Chief Investigator for the Justice Department's Prohibition Bureau.

Eliot's days were spent in the field, his nights devoted to paperwork, all for a salary that would not even allow him to rent a modest apartment. He continued to spend what little spare time he had with Edna, or with Alexander Jamie. If nothing else, the two-year stint with Retail Credit showed Eliot Ness what he didn't want to do for a living.

Jamie was becoming a key figure in the federal government's enforcement of Prohibition laws throughout the greater Chicago area. His role was the collection of evidence demonstrating conspiracies between the producers and sellers of the illicit alcoholic beverages. Jamie also headed a secret task force charged with investigating corruption within the Prohibition Bureau itself.

As their relationship evolved, Eliot Ness, although not on the government's payroll, began working hand-in-hand with Jamie. Ness persuaded his brother-in-law to take him along during a variety of surveillance missions and undercover operations. After regular lessons at the FBI firing range, Eliot became a crack shot with a pistol. This growing interest in law enforcement prompted Ness to enroll in a criminology course at the University of Chicago, studying under August Volmar, a noted expert in field.

In 1927, with those credits added to his resume, Ness was hired as a trainee with the U.S. Treasury Department's Chicago Division. Just a few weeks later, Jamie used his influence to have his nephew transferred to the Prohibition Bureau, one of 300 agents charged with drying up Chicago.

The Prohibition agent was held in wide and profound contempt by the average wet citizen, who disliked his function and indiscriminate toughness, and by the bootlegger, who saw him as a dishonest and expensive nuisance. With no Civil Service requirements in place for Prohibition agents, the bureau rapidly filled with incompetents, political appointees and even gangsters. Enough agents lived far above their $50-a-week means to support the widely-held assumption that they were on the take, which many were.

In a speech he delivered several years after his service in Chicago, Ness recalled how disturbed his mother was when she learned her son would be associated with such a group:

"So many of them are dishonest men," she said, protesting with a searching look at him.

"Not me," Eliot soothed her. "If there's anything you taught me, mother, it's to be honest."

Peter Ness intervened. Pulling his wife close, he said, "A man needs a set of values and an education, and then he has to set his own course."

Emma Ness nodded her agreement and never again protested her son's choice of a career.

CHAPTER THREE

Big Jim & Little John

Individual states had been outlawing alcoholic beverages since the middle of the 19th century. Not satisfied by this crazy quilt of liquor control measures, politically powerful groups such as the Women's Christian Temperance Union and the Anti-Saloon League of America pressed their case that alcohol was, if not the root of all evil, at least responsible for the vast majority of the nation's social ills.

In 1919, the necessary three-fourths of the states ratified a congressional resolution that became the 18th Amendment to the Constitution. The measure, known as the Volstead Act, was named for a Republican representative from Minnesota who proclaimed that one of the main functions of government was to legislate morality.

President Woodrow Wilson opposed Volstead, but Congress overrode his veto. Thus, effective January 17, 1920, the federal government was in the business of enforcing Prohibition. The vice lords of New York, Chicago and other major U.S. cities couldn't have been happier.

When alcohol was legal and its production regulated, quality standards had to be met, while market forces kept a close check on profits. With these barriers removed, the underworld could dictate the quality, price and distribution of alcoholic beverages throughout the nation.

No sooner had the ink dried on the federal legislation than the crime organizations began turning out millions of gallons in illicit beer and a variety of liquors. They also opened routes to funnel high-quality Canadian alcohol into the domestic distribution network.

Brewers had three options. They could convert to the manufacture of legal "near beer," first brewing the standard product with its alcohol content of three to four percent, and then dealcoholizing it to 0.5 percent. They could lease or sell their breweries for legitimate enterprises. Or, they could continue producing beer in defiance of the law, under the management and protection of gangsters.

The "Great Social Experiment" of Prohibition was doomed from the start. It was disregarded and flouted by most Americans, many of whom resorted to producing their own home brew. Flavoring extracts, bay rum and medicinal preparations were widely used for beverage purposes, often with harmful consequences.

In most cities, anyone who wanted liquor could get it delivered right to his doorstep by a bootlegger. For anything from a quiet drink with friends to a wild night on the town, he could take his pick from a variety of speakeasies that operated with little interference by law enforcement authorities. The finer hotels gave their guests mixers such as club soda and ginger ale, then insisted that their patrons sign an affidavit stating that they would not use the beverages for highballs.

In less populated areas, most of which were already "dry" by local ordinance or custom, many a farmer continued distilling whiskey solely for his own family and neighbors— the traditional "still on the hill." Drugstore and cafe owners sold alcohol under the counter for "medicinal purposes." On college campuses, fraternity brothers—Eliot Ness sometimes included—found great adventure in imbibing.

As the illegal liquor trade flourished, it gave rise to its own vocabulary. The term "moonshine," used since the 18th century to describe the phantom presence of spirits distilled at night, hidden from inquisitive eyes, became a part of everyday parlance. Anyone who produced and peddled moonshine was labeled a "bootlegger," a term that originally referred to drinkers' tendency to hide their spirits in the upper part of the boot. Far from the sinister figures these labels might suggest, the moonshiners and bootleggers of the 1920s enjoyed widespread popularity, if not respect, from a thirsty populace.

Class distinctions developed, as described at the time by Federal Prohibition Administrator Maurice Campbell:

"First we have the night club and extravagant 'private clubs' patronized by visitors bent on seeing night life. Next in order is the bar patronized by the businessman. Often he thinks it is clever to drink his cocktail in defiance of the law. I am sorry to say that a considerable section of the business community likes a sly drink. Then we have the bohemian place in the cellar or the garret, supposedly patronized by artists or people who would like to be. After them there is a great gap in the social order of the speakeasy. Finally there is the criminal gathering of the lowest order. In these places it is possible to buy any kind of drink, occasionally genuine but generally diluted or poisonous. No matter who says it 'just came from the boat,' it usually just came from some nearby still or bathtub."

Each of these speakeasies of the early 1920s was regarded by its patrons as somewhat of a private club, not wide open to the public, but not very hard to enter either. Welding everyone together into a common brotherhood was the knowledge that all present were engaged in a conspiracy to flout a very unpopular law.

Prohibition agents were not prepared for the danger and drama that their job entailed. Officers could make more money and avoid the hazards of their job by accepting bribes. Local law enforcement officials were of little help. Most of them opposed Prohibition, and many regularly violated the law themselves.

As racketeers' fortunes increased, they expanded their operations, muscling into control of gambling casinos, brothels, numbers games, slot machines, horse books, and phony labor unions. Dry laws also stripped the state and federal governments of a huge source of tax revenue.

The 18th Amendment sparked a brutal turf war among gangsters across the country to meet the demand for alcohol. Of even deeper concern to many law enforcement officials and government policymakers was the growing sentiment among Americans that the law of the land was misguided and, therefore, could be ignored.

Nowhere in the nation was the violation of Prohibition laws and the spread of corruption more evident than in Chicago.

"Ske-kag-ong," or "wild onion place," was the name given by the Ojibwa Indians to the river which branches out from Lake Michigan and divides into two parts about one mile inland. By the time of the American Revolution, both the river and the surrounding settlement were firmly established as Chicago.

Separate monolithic ethnic neighborhoods developed, few of them overlapping. About 500,000 Poles settled in neighborhoods on the sprawling South Side. Southern Italian immigrants were concentrated in two areas, the crowded "Little Italy" section and Chicago Heights, a separate city about one hour south of Chicago. The wealthy congregated in the relatively compact North Side, while Chicago's industries sprang up on the west side.

These regions all intersected at the "Loop," the city's central business district. The seamier side of Chicago was the "Levee District," between Clark Street and Wabash Avenue, where brothels and speakeasies were everywhere, and where youth gangs and pickpockets roamed the streets.

By the beginning of the 20th century, Chicago, known as "Queen of the Lake," had become the hussy of America. Its open display of raw vice and spectacular mayhem was appalling to outsiders, and to many of its own inhabitants. The colorful names of the South Side neighborhoods—Satan's Mile, Dead Man's Alley and Hell's Half-Acre—spoke volumes. The red light district stretched for block after block, lined with whores, pimps, pickpockets and hoodlums.

Chicago replaced New York as the nerve center for the country's bootlegging and organized criminal activities. By the late 1920s, an estimated 20,000 speakeasies were flourishing in the Windy City. Chicago came to symbolize the Roaring Twenties, a violent, colorful decade in which people lived fast, thumbing their noses at authority and openly enjoying those vices that formed the foundation of criminal syndicates.

Among the major crime figures learning their trade in Chicago was James "Big Jim" Colosimo. The son of an immigrant from Consenza, Italy, Colosimo spent his early adulthood as a pimp, extortionist and precinct captain on the South Side. His big break came in 1902, when he married brothel keeper Victoria Moresco and assumed control of many bordellos and ancillary saloons throughout Chicago.

Before Prohibition, Colosimo had built his trade with prostitutes and young "white slaves." His nightclub, the popular Colosimo's Cafe at 2128 South Wabash Avenue, became the unofficial headquarters of the Chicago underworld. Celebrities, policemen and politicians all rubbed shoulders with gangsters at Big Jim's establishment, which was adorned with green velvet walls, gold and crystal chandeliers and an immense mahogany and glass bar. Expensive tapestries and murals depicting tropical vistas hung on the walls. Beautiful chorus girls performed on a stage controlled by hydraulic lifts. The bar was stocked with the largest selection of imported wines in all of Chicago.

Upstairs, customers could find gambling tables of almost unlimited stakes, as well as a large variety of female companions. Colosimo's Cafe would rock until dawn or beyond, with Big Jim himself in the midst of it all, complete with massive diamonds and other symbols flaunting his considerable wealth.

It was inevitable that he would receive a visit from the Black Hand, a Sicilian society that specialized in extortion. The Black Handers insisted that the generosity he regularly showed to aldermen and cops also be extended to his fellow Italian-Americans. Colosimo caved in to the demands for some time, but then stubbornly resisted. Further pressured, he turned to the powerful New York crime boss, Johnny Torrio, for protection and business advice.

Behind the gentle manner and diminutive appearance of "Little John" Torrio lurked a ruthless villain who exercised near-total control of the New York rackets. In his 1930 book, *Al Capone: The Biography of a Self-Made Man*, Chicago journalist Fred D. Pasley wrote: "Torrio was one of the elder fuglemen of the powerful New York Five Points gang. The Five Pointers are dark fellows— cosmopolites of crime. He who rises to leadership with them is no ordinary ruffian, and Torrio rated a vice-presidency. He had executive ability, business sagacity, and a practical imagination.

He was skilled in the duplicity of politics, proficient in the civilities, smooth of tongue and adroit of manner. He had a plausible front and he was young—only 29 and ambitious."

Torrio saw Chicago as a fertile field for his criminal enterprises. After arranging for the extermination of three Black Handers who had attempted to extort money from Colosimo, Torrio joined forces with Big Jim to consolidate Chicago's prostitution, gambling and alcohol rackets.

This coincided with Chicago voters' elevation of the bombastic William Hale Thompson Jr. to the Mayor's office in 1915. Thompson was a husky ex-athlete who rose in Republican ranks by bullying those around him and exploiting the prejudices of ethnic and national groups. Despite promises to rid Chicago of crime and corruption, Thompson sent word that he was eager to play ball with the underworld. Naturally, Colosimo and Torrio turned their forces loose to assure that Thompson was elected.

It did not take Torrio long to decide that Colosimo lacked the administrative skills and self-discipline necessary to manage the rackets effectively. In 1918, Torrio acquired a four-story brick building in the Levee District at 2222 South Wabash Avenue, just a block from Colosimo's, and turned it into his own headquarters, which became known as the "Four Deuces."

On the ground floor was a nightclub with a long mahogany bar where local whiskey sold for a quarter. Canadian whiskey and rum imported from the Bahamas cost 75 cents. The upper floors contained Torrio's business offices; a posh gambling hall where roulette, poker, faro and blackjack were featured; a horse-betting parlor; and a brothel that was a cut above the typical flophouses that dotted the South Side.

The Four Deuces became a huge melting pot for a wide assortment of criminals from the Windy City. Among the clientele were the soft-spoken, smiling florist, Dion O'Banion; "Little Hymie" Weiss; the trigger-happy Genna brothers; the blustering Colorado Cowboy, Louis Alterie; and any number of lesser-known gangsters of Italian, Sicilian, Irish, Polish or Jewish descent.

In 1921, Torrio returned to New York to meet with some of his former colleagues and invite them to become part of the action in Chicago. Among those who agreed to join him was Al Capone.

CHAPTER FOUR

When Tommy Guns Ruled

No one symbolized the wanton disregard for the law more than Al Capone. One of nine children born to Neapolitan immigrants, Alphonse often bristled when his Italian connections were mentioned. "I'm no Italian," he would snap. "I was born in Brooklyn."

Big and strong for his age, Capone was quick to anger. When he was fourteen, he dropped out of school after assaulting a teacher who scolded him for playing hooky. This was his first formal rebuff from an American institution and, by extension, the mainstream of American life.

While kicking around the streets of New York, Capone fell in with members of adolescent neighborhood gangs who practiced turf warfare, random mischief and professional crime. As the American establishment rejected them, many immigrant children, Capone included, found refuge and a sense of identity in the gangs. Capone was arrested at least three times as a teenager, twice on suspicion of murder and once for disorderly conduct, but none of the charges stuck.

Brooklyn's famous Calabrian gangster, Francesco Ioele, alias Frankie Yale, installed Capone as a bouncer and bartender at the Harvard Inn, a modest Coney Island dance hall and underworld hangout. Effective with his huge fists or with a club, the hulking, hard-knuckled 18-year-old kept peace and gained immediate favor with Yale. He perfected "the look," a gangsters' gaze designed to strike mortal fear into the hearts of men.

Capone did not always come out on top. One night, while tending bar, he poured drinks for a small-time criminal, Frank Galluccio, and Galluccio's sister. When Capone made a remark that Galluccio took as an insult to the woman, he pulled a switch-blade from his pocket, vaulted the bar and slashed at Capone's face. The attack produced a wound near Capone's left ear and another down his cheek, earning him the nickname he detested: "Scarface." Ironically, Galluccio went to work for Capone many years later in Chicago as a $100-a-week bodyguard. Many others who crossed the path of Al Capone were not so fortunate.

The syphilis that shortened Capone's life was probably contracted while he was under Yale's employ. One of the job's fringe benefits was the service of prostitutes, which Capone frequently enjoyed. He did curb many of his promiscuous activities when he became romantically involved with Mary "Mae" Coughlin, an Irish woman Capone met at a Brooklyn cellar club. Their only child, Albert "Sonny" Francis Capone, was born on December 4, 1918, about a month before Al and Mae were married.

In 1919, Capone moved his family to Baltimore to work as a clerk for a construction firm. He became familiar with accounting procedures and learned to read balance sheets— skills he would use later in life. However, the money he craved to pamper his wife and son eluded him. Capone accepted an invitation from Johnny Torrio to join him in Chicago.

He served as a bartender, pimp, chauffeur and bodyguard, steadily rising in an organization that was rapidly expanding its domain. Journalist Courtney Ryley painted this picture of Capone in the book, *Capone: The Life and World of Al Capone* (Putnam, 1971), by John Kobler: "I saw him in front of the Four Deuces a dozen times, coat collar turned up on winter nights, hands deep in his pockets as he fell in step with a passerby and mumbled, 'Got some nice-looking girls inside'."

Capone summoned other family members to join him at the 15-room red brick house he bought on the South Side. He turned the building into a fortress, with armed guards at each entrance and iron bars on the windows.

With Prohibition sweetening the pot for the best-run criminal organizations, Big Jim Colosimo became the victim of his own success. On the afternoon of May 11, 1920, he arrived at his cafe shortly before 4:00, chatted briefly with his secretary and walked to a hallway next to the cloak room. Two shots rang out. The secretary rushed out to discover Colosimo's body lying face down on the porcelain floor, blood streaming from a bullet wound behind his right ear.

Police never made an arrest for this "piece of work," but the evidence pointed to Frankie Yale as the killer. Historians who have studied the evolution of organized crime in Chicago have concluded that Yale was hoping to move in on the city's lucrative vice trade by knocking off Colosimo. If that was the case, his strategy backfired. Big Jim's death consolidated Torrio's organization, effectively locking Yale out of the Chicago scene.

Torrio expanded the bootlegging operations and established trade agreements that guaranteed territorial sovereignty. Rivals warmed to Torrio's plan to eliminate wasteful hostilities. The frightening prophecy of Chicago Crime Commission Director Henry Barrett Chamberlin was coming true: "Modern crime, like modern business, is tending toward centralization, organization and commercialization. The men and women of evil have formed trusts."

Torrio recognized that beer was the beverage of choice for the Chicago working class, a big moneymaker even at small profit margins, and what better place to produce it than a brewery that was already up and running? Beer producers in Chicago, believing that Prohibition would probably be repealed in a year or two, were not inclined to sell their properties. A few tried to meet the government's regulations for "near-beer," but the public was not interested in this substitute brew. Torrio cornered the lion's share of the beer business by making the manufacturers offers they could not refuse. His gangsters would front as company officials, making the payoffs to police officers and Prohibition agents, and fight highjackers or territorial invaders. They would also take the fall in the unlikely event of a raid. In return, brewers furnished the equipment, the technical skills and administrative expertise.

Under agreements with Chicago's leading gangs, nearly every speakeasy, brothel and cabaret in the metropolitan area was forced to buy its supplies from mob sources.

For hard liquor, they turned to Dion O'Banion, chief of an organization that controlled the "Gold Coast," where townhouses and apartments of the city's wealth and fashion overlooked Lake Michigan. Reared in poverty as an Irish plasterer's son, O'Banion became a skilled florist. His round face wore a habitual grin, but under the tailored clothes on his small frame he carried an assortment of revolvers. "Dino" filled orders at his flower shop on State Street, while his operatives ran Canadian whiskey into Chicago, cut it with cheap dilutants, and shipped it off to retailers at highly-inflated prices.

The Genna gang reigned supreme in Little Italy, thanks in large part to a government license they had secured to handle industrial alcohol. Most of this was redistilled, colored, and then flavored to imitate whiskey, brandy or another forbidden beverage. The Gennas' legal plant could not begin to supply the demand, so they persuaded hundreds of tenement dwellers and shopkeepers to let them install portable copper stills in kitchens.

Capone helped Torrio plot these developments from his new position in Chicago's dominant crime syndicate: manager of the Four Deuces. He also summoned his brother, Ralph "Bottles" Capone, from New York to join the organization.

For three years there was peace in gangland as the power of Torrio's organization swelled. Resistance from policemen or politicians was overcome by bribery, intimidation, or a combination of the two. Once Torrio was convinced Al Capone could handle more authority, he elevated his young recruit to a full partnership and assigned Ralph Capone to manage the Four Deuces.

It was only a matter of time before rivals would seek a greater share of the action. The most brazen of these was the O'Donnell gang from Chicago's far South Side, who began running beer into territories that were supposed to be the exclusive domains of the Torrio/Capone organization. Fortified by hired guns imported from New York City, the O'Donnells strong-armed speakeasy owners and began hijacking the Torrio/Capone delivery trucks.

In September 1923, the O'Donnell gang felt the first sting of retaliation. Hours after a half-dozen gang members went on a violent spree, assaulting uncooperative tavern owners and smashing furniture, the group was reposing at one of its own outposts, a saloon on South Lincoln Street. Suddenly, three avengers burst through the doors. They wrestled one of the O'Donnell gang members, Jerry O'Connor, to the ground. Then they marched him out onto the sidewalk, where one of the avengers put a sawed-off shotgun to O'Connor's temple and pulled the trigger.

This was the opening shot of Chicago's bloody "beer wars," during which the O'Donnell forces—and all other challengers, for that matter—were no match for the Torrio/Capone machine. As the body count rose, witnesses placed Capone at the scene of several slayings. However, none of them would repeat these observations under oath.

Battle tactics were changing as a new weapon, the Thompson submachine gun, or "tommy gun," arrived in Chicago. This high-powered military weapon, capable of firing 800 rounds per minute, commanded a price of $2,000 on the black market. Once the gangsters acquired tommy guns, Chicago area policemen followed suit.

By the mid-1920s, Chicago was paying a stiff price for its gang violence and political corruption. The city was no longer being considered as a site for manufacturing plants and corporate headquarters. All of the news reports about rampant gang murders were also scaring away tourists.

The street warfare shocked most Chicagoans, but many took solace in the notion that "they're only killing each other." They greeted spicy newspaper reports more with curiosity than with outrage.

The public became fascinated with the gangsters' vocabulary. A five-dollar bill was a fin; the $10, a sawbuck; and the $100 a C-note. One thousand dollars was a gran'. A man shadowed was tailed or cased. A hoodlum was a hood (the "oo" pronounced like mood). An indictment or complaint was a rap; a pretty woman, a broad; a revolver, a heater; and a cop was the law.

One who talked too frequently was a squawker. If a criminal confessed, he sang. There wasn't much singing, since most gangsters obeyed *Omerta*, a sacred Sicilian code of confidentiality translated as "silence beyond death."

Stopping the wars in the streets was one thing, and much of the Chicago populace rallied behind that cause, but shutting off the flow of alcohol did not have nearly as much public support. Federal agents fell into disfavor for their overzealous enforcement of Prohibition laws, which included raids of private residences and high-profile arrests for possession of as little as a single bottle of liquor.

Chicago voters finally sickened of the bootleggers' best friend, Mayor Bill Thompson, and elected a reform-minded municipal judge, William Dever, to replace him. Torrio and Capone took their cue from the election and moved across the city border to the community of Cicero, thirty minutes west of the Loop and a safe distance from the city Police Department's jurisdiction.

About 80 percent of Cicero's 40,000 inhabitants were from Bohemia in Central Europe, or their parents were. They were quiet, submissive folks who wanted their daily beer, a heavy, robust brew. Residents of Cicero resented Prohibition and all but ignored it.

After plotting the ambush of Cicero, Torrio left for an extended vacation in Europe. Unleashed, Capone struck with a vengeance. He and his oldest brother, Frank Capone, opened dozens of speakeasies and nightclubs while taking over most of those already in operation.

Challengers from Cicero who emerged to take on the corrupt incumbents in the 1924 election never stood a chance. The Capones recruited about 200 thugs to patrol each voting district and ensure success for compliant officeholders.

Author John Kobler described the election day tactics as follows: "As a voter waited in line to cast his ballot, a menacing, slouch-hatted figure would sidle up to him and ask how he intended to vote. If the reply was unsatisfactory, the hooligan would snatch the ballot, mark it himself, hand it back, and stand by, fingering the revolver in his coat pocket until the voter had dropped the ballot into the box. Defiant voters were slugged, honest poll watchers and election officials kidnapped and held captive until the polls closed."

Capone's forces also seized ballot boxes and replaced votes that were not cast in favor of the preferred candidates.

Law enforcement officials mounted an eleventh-hour counter-offensive. Over 100 specially-deputized Chicago police officers and detectives were dispatched to Cicero to restore order. A squad of four officers and a detective pulled up at the corner of 22nd Street and Cicero Avenue, where the Capone brothers and another man were intimidating voters. The trio apparently mistook the officers for rival gangsters. Frank Capone reached for his gun, but before he could pull it out of his pocket, two of the officers blasted him with both barrels of their shotguns. He fell dead on the sidewalk.

His brother's death was a turning point for Al Capone. He would, from that day forward, be a dedicated outlaw.

CHAPTER FIVE

It Was His Funeral

Not surprisingly, a slate of politicians sympathetic to organized crime was swept into office in Cicero. Within six months, more than 150 gambling establishments and 100 speakeasies were running round-the-clock. A new state-of-the-art gambling house, the Hawthorne Smoke Shop, offered handbook play totaling as much as $50,000 a day. Capone also took control of the Hawthorne Race Track, which presented fixed horse races.

Despite Mayor Dever's best intentions, most of Chicago's rackets continued unabated, although less visible. With the Four Deuces temporarily padlocked, Capone opened a new Chicago outpost at 2146 South Michigan Avenue. He hung a doctor's shingle, reading "A. Brown, M.D.," above the door. A casual visitor entering the building would have no reason to suspect he was anywhere other than in the reception room of a physician's suite. However, farther inside, the medicine dispensed by "Dr. Brown" was actually a sampling of moonshine Capone could offer retailers.

Off to the side of this bogus "examination room" was a small office occupied by bookkeeper Jack Guzik, now a figure of considerable influence in the Torrio/Capone organization. A short, pudgy and pale man, Guzik had jowls that spilled over his collar and quivered when he spoke. He was never seen without his tortoiseshell glasses and broad-brimmed hat. One of 11 children born to an Orthodox Jewish family, he had worked in the vice trade for many years, mostly as a pimp, before Torrio recruited him as a financial advisor and bookkeeper.

Guzik became known as "Greasy Thumb," which may have been a reference to his culinary habits or his success in greasing the palms of police officers and politicians. It was a moniker that those who had dealings with him did not use, any more than Al Capone was known as "Scarface" to his cronies. Capone's more acceptable nickname was "Snorky," which in its Italian derivation means "elegant."

Torrio and Capone entrusted Guzik with all of their financial records. His accounting procedures were thorough and revealing, as federal investigators would gleefully discover. Separate binders neatly arranged in his office contained ledgers, indexes, memoranda accounts and day books involving more than 200 buyers of illicit beverages. Guzik's records also included truck and boat routes for transporting liquor from Canada and the Caribbean to Chicago. More important, they reflected which police officers, politicians and Prohibition officers were on the take.

In early 1924, Chicago police raided Dr. Brown's office and came away with boxloads of records. "We've got the goods now," beamed Mayor Dever. From these books, officials estimated the Torrio/Capone organization's annual gross income at $70 million, give or take a few million, making it one of the Midwest's most profitable business enterprises. Capone posted a huge reward for the return of the books. Days later, a municipal judge ordered the records impounded and returned to their rightful owners.

Capone survived another close call on May 8, 1924. Hearing that a low level gangster named Joe Howard had roughed up Jack Guzik during a barroom argument, Capone himself hunted down the assailant at a South Wabash Avenue saloon. According to eyewitnesses, as Capone swung through the door, Howard turned and called to him, "Hello, Al."

"What's the idea of pushing Guzik around?" Capone shouted.

"Listen, you dago pimp. Why don't you run along and take care of your broads?" Howard retorted.

Capone, deeply insulted by any reference to his involvement with prostitution, emptied a six-shooter into Howard's head and shoulders as three customers and a bartender looked on in shock. The witnesses told police what had happened, prompting a warrant to be issued for Capone's arrest, but he was nowhere to be found.

By the time Capone walked into a Chicago police station four weeks later to turn himself in, the witnesses had suffered memory lapses. No indictment was ever brought in the murder of Joe Howard.

Word soon reached federal investigators that Capone had established his official headquarters at the Hawthorne Inn in Cicero, next to all the numbers action at the Hawthorne Smoke Shop. Lawmen also learned that Capone now controlled the Hawthorne Kennel Club's dog tracks, where 400 greyhounds chased electric rabbits. The dogs were either overfed or starved to assure that they rewarded the preferred bettors.

Many Chicago and Cook County officials felt comfortable mingling with the gangsters at the Hawthorne Inn, since they were beyond the legal reach of Chicago's law enforcement authorities. Upstairs, Capone relaxed to his phonograph's sounds of opera music. A biographer, Laurence Bergreen, believes Capone was regularly using cocaine during this period of his life. Others contest his conclusion.

Back in Chicago, the uneasy alliance of the rival gangs was unraveling. Dion O'Banion brazenly started marketing his beer in Chicago and Cicero. The Genna brothers were cutting into whiskey sales previously controlled by O'Banion's forces on the North Side. Bloodshed was inevitable.

O'Banion was the first to fall, not long after he duped Johnny Torrio into visiting a North Side brewery and tipped-off police that this kingpin of the underworld would be on the premises. Arrested on the spot for bootlegging and conspiracy, Torrio produced a wad of bills from his pocket and peeled off over $12,000 to cover his bail.

On November 10, 1924, O'Banion was busily filling flower orders for another gangster's funeral when a dark blue Jewett sedan eased into a parking space on State Street, in front of the Gothic Holy Name Cathedral. Three men exited the car and strode to the flower shop.

"Hello, boys. Have you come for the flowers?" O'Banion inquired as he approached the trio, his right hand extended for a greeting. One of the assailants, Mike Genna, grabbed the outstretched hand and pulled O'Banion forward, off-balance, while the other men, John Scalise and Albert Anselmi, riddled the florist's body with six bullets. A final shot was fired into his left cheek as O'Banion lay sprawled among his flowers.

"Deany was all right and he was getting along better than he had a right to," Capone told one newspaper reporter. "But, like everybody else, his head got away from his hat... He decided to be the boss of the booze racket in Chicago. It was his funeral."

O'Banion's gang was swiftly reorganized under the leadership of Earl Wajciechowski, better known as Hymie Weiss. A devout Catholic who carried rosaries wherever he went, Weiss was somehow able to reconcile his savage instincts with his spiritual inclinations. He vowed swift and brutal revenge for O'Banion's murder.

Racketeers and bootleggers were growing far too disorganized and combative for Johnny Torrio. Shifting allegiances made him uneasy, so he and his wife embarked on a southern cruise, hoping that tensions would ease. Weiss's gunmen were only a day or two behind.

Capone was also a marked man. On January 12, 1925, he stepped out of his chauffeur-driven car and entered a restaurant at the corner of State and 55th streets. Seconds later, a limousine pulled up and three occupants raked Capone's vehicle from stem to stern with gunfire, injuring his driver. Capone soon learned that the assailants were Hymie Weiss and two accomplices, "Schemer" Drucci and Bugs Moran.

Drucci was a mid-level gangster who derived his nickname from his propensity for concocting farfetched hits and heists. George "Bugs" Moran was more violent, less stable, and insanely jealous of the Torrio/Capone organization's success.

Capone promptly ordered a custom-built Cadillac from General Motors, complete with a steel armor-plated body, double panes of bulletproof glass, a gun compartment and movable window. Bullets would splatter off this seven-ton portable fort as harmlessly as raindrops off a tin roof. It had a special combination lock designed to prevent Capone's enemies from jimmying a door to plant a bomb. The Cadillac and accompanying bodyguard, exceeding that of the President, became a familiar sight in Chicago.

Torrio eventually came back to face charges stemming from the brewery raid. On the evening of January 24, as he stepped out of his Lincoln sedan, Weiss and Moran emerged from a blue Cadillac and opened fire with a sawed-off shotgun and pistol. Two shots connected in Torrio's jaw and chest, sending him to the pavement, and two more bullets entered his arm and groin.

Weiss and Moran were shocked to read in the morning newspaper that Torrio was still clinging to life in a hospital bed. A grief-stricken Al Capone stood by as a sentinel. Within days, Torrio was interviewed by police. "Sure, I know who they are," he whispered from his bed. "But it's my business. I've got nothing to tell you." *Omerta.*

A few weeks later, a frail and bandaged Torrio limped into court and was sentenced to nine months in the Lake County Jail. His treaties broken and his profile much too high for his liking, Torrio transferred all of his holdings in breweries, brothels, gambling halls and speakeasies to the Capone family. With that, Al Capone had arrived at the top.

He established lavish new headquarters in a suite at the Hotel Metropole, 2300 South Michigan Avenue, just around the corner from the Four Deuces. The hotel lobby became a beehive of activity. Prominent criminal lawyers and high officials of the police department joined politicians and speakeasy owners waiting their turn to consult with Mr. Capone. Police officers in uniform streamed in and out. Upstairs, gambling went on openly and prostitutes visited at all hours of the day and night.

Capone showed himself to be as adaptable as he was invincible. When the police or Prohibition agents zeroed-in on breweries, Capone was forewarned and hastily converted the targeted facilities to production of near-beer. This legal brew would then be injected with a mixture of alcohol and ginger ale to become the "needle beer" that was a staple of speakeasies serviced by Capone.

Police continued to find corpses in alleys behind speakeasies, in trash heaps and in vacant lots. Business operators who resisted the extortionists found their stores blasted by "pineapples," the slang term for everything from high-powered dynamite to crude, homemade bombs.

Public tolerance of the gangland slayings began to run out on April 27, 1926, after William H. McSwiggin, a young Assistant State's Attorney of Cook County, was gunned down. The son of Sergeant Anthony McSwiggin, a highly-decorated detective of the Chicago Police Department, "Billy" had been friends with the O'Donnell gang ever since childhood. He and two of the O'Donnell brothers joined three cohorts for visits to several speakeasies. They settled in at the Pony Inn, one of the saloons that had switched from Capone to the O'Donnells for beer supplies.

Capone assembled five cars and about a dozen men to post themselves outside. When the group emerged, the motorcade moved into position and opened fire, mortally wounding McSwiggin and two of the gang members.

The police investigation of these slayings went nowhere. A grand jury blamed a conspiracy of silence in the underworld: "There is an element of fear involved, because anyone who does aid the public officials by giving facts is very likely to be 'taken for a ride.' Silence and sealed lips of gangsters make the solution of this crime, like many others, thus far impossible."

The consensus of police, private detectives and newspaper reporters was that McSwiggin was not an intended target of the assassins. Nevertheless, the public perception—"they only kill each other"—was changing. At long last, Chicago had been roused from its sodden lethargy.

Responding to public outcry and pressure from Sergeant McSwiggin and his influential friends, police swept through dozens of Capone-controlled speakeasies and gambling houses, destroying equipment and sending customers scurrying. They gathered evidence of Prohibition violations, and from the Hawthorne Smoke Shop came away with another batch of financial records documenting Capone's illegal business activities.

No one at the time realized the important role these ledgers would play in the government's case against several key figures in the Capone organization. Wrapped in plain brown paper, tied with a string and buried in an obscure cabinet at police headquarters, these documents contained breakdowns of gambling profits during an 18-month period. Every few pages, Guzik had taken and divided a balance between "A" for Al Capone, "R" for Ralph Capone, and "J" for Jack Guzik.

Capone fled to Lansing, Michigan, accompanied by two of his bodyguards, Machine Gun Jack McGurn and Frank Nitti. He considered turning over the rackets to Jack Guzik and Ralph Capone and finding a more secure way to make a living. With these thoughts in mind, as well as a desire to clear his name, Capone agreed to appear before a grand jury convened to probe the Cicero murders.

"I've been convicted without a hearing of all the crimes on the calendar, but I'm innocent and it won't take long to prove it," Capone declared as he re-emerged and spoke with newspaper reporters. "I trust my attorneys to see that I'm treated like a human being and not pushed around by a lot of coppers with axes to grind. Of course I didn't kill McSwiggin. Why should I? I liked the kid."

Capone then stunned all of Chicago by announcing that even the young prosecutor was on the mob's payroll. "I paid McSwiggin. I paid him plenty and I got what I was paying for." Independent investigations confirmed Capone's shocking revelation.

News of this payoff was plastered throughout the nation, dramatizing the cozy relationship between the Chicago underworld and those officials who were supposed to be enforcing the law. Even the Chicago Tribune, a "wet" newspaper, appealed to President Calvin Coolidge to "place the full weight of his administration and the vast power of the federal government behind the move to rid Chicago of the gangs of alien gunmen who are terrorizing the community."

Hymie Weiss and the other O'Banion forces, still out to avenge the florist's murder, orchestrated their own show of strength. On September 20, 1926, they dispatched eight touring cars to Cicero and riddled Capone's Hawthorne headquarters with gunfire. More than 1,000 shots were fired during the first of the high-profile "motorcade-style" attacks that would become commonplace in Chicago.

Three weeks later, Hymie Weiss and four of his associates parked in front of the Gothic Holy Name Cathedral, in the same space Dion O'Banion's killers had occupied. Bullets poured from the windows of a boarding house as the men reached the middle of the street. Weiss dropped to the pavement, his body fatally riddled with ten bullet holes. His bodyguard and beer-runner, Patrick "Paddy" Murray, lay dead beside him.

Capone was strongly suspected of being behind the killings, but steadfastly denied involvement "That was butchery. Hymie was a good kid. He could have got out a long time ago and taken his beer and been alive today. They began to get nasty. We sent 'em word to stay in their own back yard. But they had the swelled head and thought they were bigger than we were. Then O'Banion got killed. Right after Torrio was shot—and Johnny knew who shot him—I had a talk with Weiss. 'What do you want to do, get yourself killed before you're thirty? You better get some sense while a few of us are still alive.' He could still have got along with me, but he wouldn't listen to me. There's enough business for all of us without killing each other like animals in the street. I don't want to end up in the gutter, punctured by machine gun slugs."

Into this setting came a young, idealistic and untested Prohibition agent named Eliot Ness.

CHAPTER SIX

The Law Is The Law

Ness's first assignment provided him with a taste of the frustration he would face in his new job. Ted Kuhn, a veteran Chicago Prohibition agent who worked with Ness during his first week, recalled how excited his partner was to find a still.

"He couldn't wait to make an arrest," Kuhn said. "He thought it would have some kind of domino effect and scare away all of the other moonshiners. I said, 'You've got a lot to learn, kid. Did you tell anybody about what you found?' And he said, 'Just a couple of guys in the department.' I knew right then that we'd never be arresting anyone in that case, but I figured it would be a good lesson for Eliot.

"I told him, 'You better get an arrest warrant right away.' He nodded and filled out the paperwork. By the time we got to the home, the still was gone and the couple who lived there pleaded ignorance. Eliot vowed to act more swiftly and confidentially the next time. I'll say this for him, he was a fast learner."

Ness was soon teamed with another young officer, Dan Koken, and dispatched to Chicago Heights late in 1927 for an undercover operation devised to gather evidence of Sicilian bootlegging activity. Ness and Koken were sometimes joined by a third officer, a Greek known as A.M. "Nine-Toed" Nabors.

From Ness's original manuscript, which formed the foundation of the book, *The Untouchables*, co-written with Oscar Fraley, it is clear that Eliot Ness idolized Koken and was also impressed with Nabors. "Nabors was the handsomest man I have ever seen," Ness wrote, "built like a Greek god with natural, light wavy hair."

The three agents made one minor raid, seizing about $500 worth of liquor from a speakeasy, and were promptly approached by a Sicilian who suggested that, for $250 a week, Ness and his partners might be persuaded to look the other way. This was precisely the opportunity they had hoped for.

After they accepted the money, the three agents were welcomed at the Cozy Corners, a Chicago Heights saloon frequented by underworld figures. Soon, they were joined by a fourth officer, Burt Napoli, who spoke Italian and posed as the trio's chauffeur.

An excited Ness believed he was on a trail of criminal activity that would lead him directly to Al Capone. In reality, Capone's rivals controlled the Chicago Heights area where he was working.

Ness and his partners enjoyed rubbing shoulders with the bootleggers, drinking more alcohol than they should have, but gathering evidence all the while. "Rum-runners from Iowa, southern Illinois, St. Louis and as far away as Kansas City would come," Ness wrote of the Cozy Corners. "They would leave their cars, loaded with liquor, with the bartenders and the cars would be driven away by members of the Chicago Heights alcohol mob. The drivers from out of town would stay at the bar, drinking, or avail themselves of what the brothel on the second and third floors had to offer. That was one of their rewards for delivering the booze."

Some of the beverages peddled at the Chicago Heights speakeasies were produced much closer to home. Ness's team found one neighborhood where "alky-cooking" was so common that a foul-smelling odor enveloped the entire area. They cruised the area for two nights and discovered that two Cadillacs with three occupants each were tailing them. The next night, they changed cars and took a back route into Chicago Heights, escaping notice. The agents went house to house, compiling a list of those homes where they detected the telltale odor of fermenting mash.

Armed with the list of alky-cookers, Ness sought a meeting at the Cozy Corners with purported gang leader Joe Martino to demand additional money in return for the agents' silence. Martino, a short, smooth-faced, dark-complected man with wavy dark hair, was the lone survivor of a once-powerful Chicago Heights gang. His day had pretty much passed by this time, but Martino did serve occasional ceremonial functions.

Ness wrote in his original manuscript, "We had quite an argument about the amount to be paid. I was the main objector and the hungry one. We brought up questions about how much they paid other law enforcement officials and who, but they were careful not to bite too hard on these leads. At this meeting, in the same room, but sitting apart from the group, we noticed a swarthy, silk-shirted Italian who apparently did not understand a word of English nor did he speak any English. We agreed on a weekly sum, which I think was in the neighborhood of $500. As the meeting broke up, Burt Napoli turned white and, pulling me aside, said, 'The silk-shirted Italian has just asked whether or not he should let you have a knife in the back'."

As with many incidents recounted in Ness's original manuscript and the book that followed, it is difficult to determine where the truth leaves off and the sensationalizing begins. In the Ness/Fraley work, readers are informed that Nabors pulled a .45 from his coat and held the Sicilians at bay while Ness and the other agents left the Cozy Corners with $500 in cash and an assurance that the bribes would be doubled.

Following the meeting with Martino, Ness decided it was time to strike, even at the expense of blowing the agents' cover. They obtained eighteen warrants and swept through the alky-cooking neighborhood, arresting more than two dozen suspects, destroying equipment and seizing moonshine.

The Sicilians' response was as immediate as it was brutal. The lifeless body of Burt Napoli was found brutally beaten and shot, dumped in a Chicago Heights ditch.

"I had expected it, I suppose," Ness wrote. "You think that nothing can disturb you and that your nerves are impregnable. Yet, looking down at that familiar face, different somehow in its last repose, I realized that death is something to which we never become calloused if the person is someone close."

A suspect arrested for Napoli's murder hanged himself in his prison cell before investigators could get a statement. "The evidence on him was positive enough to make us feel that the person who had gotten Burt had been brought to justice," Ness wrote.

He and his partners went after the Chicago Heights villains with a vengeance. A longtime resident of Chicago Heights and acquaintance of Al Capone told author Laurence Bergreen, "One time two truckloads of merchandise were coming in. Ness and his men stopped the truck, grabbed the drivers, squeezed their balls and beat the shit out of them. Hit them with clubs. It looked as though the shipment would never be delivered, but then money changed hands and the truck got through." Unlike many officers in the Prohibition Bureau, Ness and his partners dutifully reported the bribes to their superiors.

They were joined by a new partner, Martin Lahart, a smiling Irishman and physical fitness buff who was not reluctant to use force when warranted. At Lahart's urging, the team stormed into the Cozy Corners and arrested everyone in sight, from bartenders to prostitutes.

Ness's memoirs detailed a telephone call to his parents' home, where he was still living, immediately after the raid. A rough voice on the other end of the phone warned: "I got a message for you. You've had your last chance to be smart. Just keep in mind that sometime soon you're going to be found layin' in a ditch with a hole in your head and your wang slashed off. We'll keep reminding you so you won't forget to remember."

Colleagues reported that Ness, although frightened, took the call as evidence he was making a difference. He immediately had his parents' home placed under 24-hour police guard and quietly moved into an apartment with two other agents. On many occasions, Ness slept over and ate his meals at his office in Chicago, afraid to be seen on the streets. Although his relationship with Edna Staley remained strong, he told her that because of the danger and secretive nature of his work it would be better if they stopped seeing each other for a while.

Chicago had not heard the last of Big Bill Thompson. Capitalizing on the unpopularity of Prohibition and using his own bombastic campaign style, Thompson announced, "I'm wetter than the middle of the Atlantic Ocean. We'll put police back traveling beats instead of sniffing around for a little home brew or frisking pantries for a hip flask."

His campaign coffers swelled with underworld contributions, Thompson rolled over Dever in the mayoral election and promptly filled many key positions with officials who were sympathetic to bootleggers. Police officers, politicians and magistrates were once again lining up for payoffs from Al Capone, who bragged that his organization was spending upwards of $30 million a year to buy cooperation.

Capone was seen in public more than ever, but remained an elusive target for his rivals. Joseph Aiello, head of an extended crime family that succeeded the Genna brothers as Little Italy's bootlegging kingpins, joined forces with Bugs Moran and other O'Banion disciples in an effort to unseat Capone. Four professional hitmen lured to Chicago by a $50,000 bounty his rivals placed on Capone's head left in caskets. Each was found with a nickel in his palm, the signature of Capone's top gun, Jack McGurn.

"I'm the boss," Capone declared to reporters in response to Aiello/Moran offensive. "I'm going to continue to run things. Don't let anybody kid you into thinking that I can be run out of town. I haven't run yet and I'm not going to. When we get through with Aiello, Moran and their guys, there won't be any opposition and I'll still be doing business."

Soon afterward, he was singing a different tune. The 1928 presidential election attracted the attention of the indomitable Bill Thompson, who knew he could never build a national constituency if he were allied with the man who was recently declared America's "Public Enemy Number One." Capone, a symbol of wealth and indulgence in a time of nationwide economic gloom, had grown too big for Thompson to explain away. The mayor proclaimed that the days of leniency and hand-holding were over. A series of well-publicized, albeit insignificant, raids on some of Capone's businesses created the desired illusion.

Capone played along, announcing that he was giving up the rackets and exiting Chicago. Leaning back in his huge chair, smoke curling from his fat Havana cigar, he told reporters:

"Let the worthy citizens of Chicago get their liquor the best way they can. I'm sick of the job. It's a thankless one and full of grief. I give the public what the public wants. I never had to send out high-pressure salesmen. I could never meet the demand! Sure, I violate the Prohibition law. Who doesn't? The only difference is I take more chances than the man who drinks a cocktail before dinner and a flock of highballs after it, but he is just as much a violator as I am. Ninety percent of the people of Cook County drink and gamble, and my offense has been to furnish them with those amusements. Whatever else they may say, my booze has been good and my games have been on the square. Well, tell the folks I'm going away now. I guess murder will stop. There won't be any more booze. You won't be able to find a craps game."

Chicagoans greeted Capone's news conference with everything from skepticism to celebration. Among those able to read between the lines was Eliot Ness. While his colleagues chuckled at the quotation from Capone in the morning papers, Ness did not crack a smile; Al Capone ran counter to all that he believed in.

Excitable and unsure of himself during his first few months with the bureau, the boyish-looking Ness, now 26, was beginning to exhibit more maturity. With dogged determination, he worked many hours beyond what was expected for his modest $2,500 annual salary. He complained openly to his superiors about the widespread corruption he observed within the Prohibition Bureau, and he didn't care whose toes he stepped on.

In May 1928, Ness was transferred from the Treasury Department to the Justice Department and was named a "special agent," at the same salary. Apparently, the new title did not represent any significant change in responsibilities or rank, but it did affiliate Ness with the Justice Department, an important step in his career aspirations.

Although he did not say so publicly, Ness was personally opposed to the Volstead Act and recognized the difficulty in enforcing it. In fact, he was a violator himself. Ness did agree with the emerging federal strategy of using Prohibition enforcement as one means of attacking Al Capone's financial foundation.

Thompson became the laughing stock of the 1928 presidential campaign and withdrew from the race, but he still launched a last-minute effort to influence local elections. Despite the usual terrorism and intimidation, the citizenry spoke with a voice that was loud and clear. Nearly every candidate connected with the Thompson administration was resoundingly defeated.

The Chicago Tribune called the election results "the work of an outraged citizenship resolved to end the corruption, the machine gunning, and pineappling, and the plundering which have made the state and the city a reproach throughout the civilized world."

The New York Times reported, "The political revolution in Chicago came as a surprise to most political observers. They had thought that the city was disgraced, but not ashamed."

"The election brought results that are gratifying to the entire country," wrote the Washington Post. "It was a mighty blow for the restoration of law and order in Chicago. The voters seem to have been aroused from their apathy."

To make matters worse for Capone, Herbert Hoover defeated Al Smith in the presidential election and announced plans for an all-out offensive against the organized crime networks symbolized by Capone. At the same time, the Supreme Court gave federal law enforcement officials a powerful, though sophisticated, weapon.

Manley Sullivan, a bootlegger, filed no tax return on the grounds that income from illegal sources was not taxable and to declare such income would be self-incriminatory. The high court ruled against Sullivan, finding no reason that a business that was unlawful should be exempt from paying taxes. As for the argument against self-incrimination, the ruling stated, "It would be an extreme if not extravagant application of the Fifth Amendment to say that it authorized a man to refuse to state the amount of his income because it had been made in crime."

Capone followed-up his announcement by moving with his wife and son to a lavish estate at Palm Island in Biscayne Bay, Florida, just outside of Miami. He also shifted his Chicago operations to the massive Lexington Hotel on 22nd Street and South Michigan Avenue. Scarface Al then set out to eliminate his competition.

The first to fall was Frankie Yale, who had hooked up with the Aiello gang to hijack trucks delivering liquor from New York to warehouses under Capone's control in Chicago. A half-dozen Capone soldiers tracked down Yale on 44th Street in New York, forcing his car into a curb, and pummeled his body with lead from sawed-off shotguns, revolvers and a tommy gun.

Undaunted, the Aiellos teamed with another familiar Capone nemesis, Bugs Moran, to establish hundreds of home alky-cooking stills in immigrant Italian neighborhoods. They marketed the synthetic liquor they produced to those speakeasy operators who were brave enough to buy it.

Moran even taunted Capone. "The beast uses his muscle men to peddle rot-gut alcohol and green beer," he told one reporter. "I'm a legitimate salesman of good beer and pure whiskey. He trusts nobody and suspects everybody. He always has his guards. I travel around with a couple of pals. The behemoth can't sleep nights. If you ask me, he's on dope. Me, I don't ever need an aspirin."

At least seven casualties—four on the Aiello side and three on Capone's—could be counted during a series of ambushes that followed Frankie Yale's murder. The event that came to symbolize the savagery and lawlessness of Chicago took place on February 14, 1929. The night before, Bugs Moran had received a phone call informing him that a truckload of prime whiskey, hijacked as it left Detroit bound for Capone's warehouse, was available at a cost of $57 per case. Moran told the caller to deliver the goods to a brick warehouse behind the offices of SMC Cartage Company, at 2122 North Clark Street.

A light snow was falling and the temperature was well below zero the next morning as a black Cadillac, looking very much like a police car, pulled in front of the warehouse. Two uniformed men and two others dressed in civilian clothes hurried into the building. Moments later, Moran and two associates turned the corner onto North Clark Street. Believing the sedan was a police car, the trio fled. Suddenly, gunfire erupted like a furious drumbeat and a dog barked in desperation. Two deeper blasts followed.

Neighbors looked on as the two plainclothesmen emerged from the warehouse, their arms raised in the air, while the uniformed men, holding pistols, ordered their captives to walk toward the car. They drove south and turned onto Ogden Avenue. Many of the neighbors went about their business, assuming that they had just witnessed the arrest of two North Siders caught in the act of bootlegging—a fairly routine occurrence except for the large amount of gunfire.

Troubled by the ceaseless barking of a dog from inside the building, one nearby resident went to investigate. He discovered a scene of carnage nearly beyond description.

Police would eventually reconstruct the "Saint Valentine's Day Massacre" as follows:

The seven men sent by Moran to unload the whiskey had been ordered to line up against the rear wall. Then the executioners opened fire with systematic efficiency, swinging their machine guns back and forth three times—at the victims' heads, chests and stomachs. Along the wall where the seven had stood, blood splashed down the yellowish bricks. Blood from their bodies continued to streak across the oily surface of the stone floor as police arrived. Two of the victims had survived the initial assault, as evidenced by the fact that their faces were blown away by shotgun blasts.

Despite being hit with fourteen bullets, one of Moran's men, Frank Gusenberg, was still breathing when police finally arrived. He regained consciousness long enough to tell a detective posted at his hospital bedside, "Nobody shot me... I ain't no copper." Then he died. *Omerta*.

"Only Capone kills like that," was Moran's angry reaction. He vowed to punish the assassins with "all the tortures of the Spanish Inquisition."

Capone had an alibi; he was in Florida when the massacre took place. However, phone records revealed several conversations in the days leading up to the killings between Capone, Jack Guzik and some of the syndicate's other Chicago operatives. Police also learned that Jack McGurn has visited Capone, then returned to Chicago just before Saint Valentine's Day.

Circumstantial evidence linked the killings to Capone's organization, but no arrests were ever made. When the warehouse was demolished in 1967, dozens of Chicago residents rushed to the scene to scoop up souvenir bricks.

CHAPTER SEVEN

Only A Matter Of Time

The Saint Valentine's Day Massacre was a wake-up alarm to the nation that things in Chicago had gotten out of hand. President Herbert Hoover, sworn into office on March 4, 1929, vowed to pick up where Coolidge left off in using federal resources to clean up the Windy City. Hoover honored his campaign promise by launching an all-out offensive to enforce Prohibition laws and collect evidence of income tax evasion by Capone and his colleagues.

No matter how much his associates urged him to keep a low profile, Al Capone flaunted his wealth. In the wake of the Supreme Court's decision in the Manley Sullivan case, that was a mistake. His purchase of the Florida property and expensive furnishings confirmed his bloated income.

The mission of verifying Capone's income fell to Elmer L. Irey, as head of the Internal Revenue Service's Intelligence Unit. Irey, 31, was a former post office stenographer who occupied a small Treasury Department office on the third floor of 1111 Constitution Avenue in Washington, D.C., directly across the street from that of his rival, J. Edgar Hoover, in the Justice Department building. Irey's Intelligence Unit operated almost anonymously in the shadow of Hoover's Federal Bureau of Investigation.

A prickly, self-effacing public servant, Irey initially argued that his agency did not have the resources to investigate Capone. Irey never had a chance against J. Edgar Hoover, who privately considered Capone too formidable a foe for the FBI to tackle. Hoover fell back on his political allies, of whom there were many, to successfully argue that the Manley Sullivan case shifted primary responsibility for the attack on Capone to the Treasury Department.

Under the scenario announced by Treasury Secretary Andrew Mellon, the Treasury Department would gather the evidence and the Justice Department would prosecute. Irey, in his book, *The Tax Dodgers*, wrote, "It all became clear. Justice was willing to prosecute (by law nobody else could) but in case of failure Treasury would have to take the blame, although Justice had its own investigative agents, the famous FBI. Sounds silly, but that's government. Anyway, Mellon was my boss. Ergo, 'Yes Mr. Mellon. We'll get right on it'."

For assistance, Irey recruited Frank J. Wilson, a former real estate salesman from Buffalo, N.Y., who had already established solid credentials by uncovering financial chicanery of lesser bootleggers as an investigator for the American Food Administration. Wilson, 40, looked to be in his mid-50s with his bald head and sunken eyes framed by wire-rimmed glasses, accented by a cigar that constantly dangled from his lips. He was a man of unquestionable integrity, known for his gritty determination and thoroughness.

On the Justice Department side, United States Attorney George Emmerson Q. Johnson joined the team. Johnson, 53, was a tall, wiry Swede with unruly hair parted in the middle and round wire-framed glasses. The "Q" in his name did not stand for anything; he only inserted it to differentiate himself from other George E. Johnsons.

Capone took solace in the fact that his gambling and bootlegging operations were cash-only. He did all of his business transactions through front men and third parties, avoiding any direct personal link to income sources.

Nevertheless, Capone underestimated his opponents. Elmer Irey and his forces were hot on his tail. At the same time, a new breed of Prohibition agent, symbolized by Eliot Ness, was arriving on the scene. With the death of Burt Napoli still fresh in his mind, Ness eagerly accepted an assignment to help with a massive raid in Chicago Heights. About 100 Chicago policemen joined Prohibition Bureau detectives and Treasury Department agents invading the haunts of every known gangster in the region. They broke into breweries, raided stills, seized gambling equipment, rounded up prostitutes, and gathered up ledgers that tied many of these criminal activities to Al Capone.

Ness and Lahart were given the honor of nabbing Joe Martino. "We read the warrant to him and he went to the closet to pick up a topcoat," Ness wrote. "At the same time, he threw a weapon on the floor. He became deathly sick and we had trouble getting him to the station."

Martino, at age 45, had survived the gang wars longer than most. No sooner was he freed on bail than the real heavyweights of the Chicago crime scene moved in. Capone's men, fearing that Martino would "sing," decided to remove him, even at the risk of angering the top brass of the Sicilian organization. As Martino stood quietly in front of his saloon on East 16th Street one afternoon, a large motor car containing four or five men drew up and paused long enough for gunmen to deliver twelve shots to Martino's body

"His hands were still clasped in the pockets of his working trousers," wrote a reporter for the Chicago Heights Star, who was among the first people to reach the scene. "The slaying was accomplished in the usual gangland manner."

Only after Martino's murder was Ness informed that the gangster was Capone's adversary, rather than a partner. He learned an important lesson from the Martino affair. After the initial shock and embarrassment faded, Ness became more cautious in his investigative work. Chicago newspapers made little mention of the young, aggressive crimefighter and when his name did appear in print it was invariably spelled "Elliott."

Trying to make a name for himself, Ness teamed with Marty Lahart once again to pull off an eye-opening sting operation right inside the Shakespeare Avenue police station. Lahart dressed as a skid row derelict and had himself arrested, under an assumed name, for vagrancy and public drunkenness. Taken to the station, he was approached by a uniformed officer carrying two pints of whiskey and invited to make an offer.

Lahart produced two dollar bills from his pocket and exchanged them for one bottle. "If you need any more, come back around here any night after midnight and ask for me," the officer told him. "But keep this to yourself. If you tell anyone, I'll have your ass back in here in a minute."

The agents' subsequent report on the experience prompted the firing of two policemen and the transfer of two others who knew about the private bootlegging operation and kept silent.

Even this bizarre episode drew little press attention. However, reporters did take note when a federal grand jury returned 81 indictments against members of the multimillion dollar bootlegging and gambling rackets in Chicago Heights. Capone ignored a subpoena to appear before the grand jury for questioning. When a Florida physician claimed Capone was too ill to make the trip to Chicago, a dozen federal agents were dispatched to Miami to gather evidence contradicting his claim.

Weeks later, Capone "recovered" from his ailments and slipped back into Chicago to address some more pressing challenges to his reign. The Chicago Heights raid had been troublesome, but of even greater concern to Capone were the Treasury Department agents who had begun shaking down his lieutenants, demanding information about financial transactions and income sources. And now, he learned from a Sicilian insider, the Aiello gang was acting up again and there was an even more concerted effort to kill Capone.

Acting through an intermediary, triggerman Frankie Rio, Capone invited a couple of Aiello's better-connected soldiers, John Scalise and Albert Anselmi, to a dinner at the Hawthorne Inn. Unknown to the duo, Capone and Rio had concocted a scheme to test their guests' loyalty. They staged an argument that culminated with Rio slapping Capone in the face and storming out. The following day, hoping to capitalize on the rift, Scalise and Anselmi approached Rio with a plot to kill Capone and seize control of his rackets.

On May 7, Capone summoned Scalise, Anselmi, and Joseph "Hop Toad" Guinta, new head of the Unione Sicilione, to a dinner. Feasting and toasting by dozens of Capone's closest allies lasted long into the night, finally interrupted when Capone pounded a spoon against his glass and called for silence.

"This is the way we deal with traitors!" he said angrily as he reached for a baseball bat and slowly approached the trio. Capone proceeded to batter each of them to within an inch of his life. Then several gunmen appeared to finish the job. The next morning, the bodies of Scalise, Anselmi and Guinta were found along a remote road near Wolf Lake, Indiana.

The brutal attack was stark evidence of Capone's rapidly deteriorating physical and mental condition. Now, not only was the federal government zeroing-in on Capone, many members of his own organization were questioning his judgment. They eagerly accepted an invitation to participate in a "peace conference" at Atlantic City, New Jersey. Little John Torrio, a free man again, was brought in to put his organizational skills to use.

About thirty delegates, cutting across all the old ethnic and national divisions, signed a pact that established geographic boundaries. Under the agreement, assassination of rival gang members would cease. Some of the smaller enclaves were given incentives to disband and affiliate themselves with the larger, more powerful organizations. Among the notable absentees was Bugs Moran, who continued to argue that Capone must be eliminated as revenge for the St. Valentine's Day Massacre.

Capone was a participant, but left the impression that he had no intention of adhering to the rules. Worried that his life was in danger, and seeking a safe haven, Capone arranged to have himself arrested in Philadelphia for carrying a concealed weapon. He entered a guilty plea, assuming that he would be sent to the Philadelphia County Jail for a few weeks. But Judge John E. Walsh imposed the maximum sentence: one year behind bars at Pennsylvania's Eastern Penitentiary.

If President Hoover needed any confirmation his approach was long overdue, the Atlantic City confab was it. This conference raised the ugly specter of a national crime organization that, if effectively operated, could render the federal law enforcement machinery impotent.

With Al Capone out of the picture, it was time to strike at Ralph Capone and the others tending to his criminal enterprises.

Financial assistance came from the Chicago Association of Commerce, which formed a group of underground saboteurs known as the "Citizens' Committee for the Prevention and Punishment of Crime." This organization consisted of six business leaders who, fearing retribution, insisted on anonymity. Among them were Chicago Tribune publisher Colonel Robert McCormick and Sears, Roebuck and Company President Julius Rosenwald. When the chairman, prominent businessman Colonel Robert Isham Randolph, refused to name the other members, the press dubbed them the "Secret Six."

"There is not a business, not an industry in Chicago that is not paying tribute, directly or indirectly, to racketeers and gangsters," Randolph declared. "The problem of corruption runs deeper than most people realize. The men who take money from bootleggers for overlooking violations of the Volstead Act are incapacitated for arresting them for any other crime."

Alexander Jamie, appalled and disillusioned by the corruption and inefficiency in the Prohibition Bureau, welcomed the opportunity to serve the Secret Six as chief investigator. Jamie, who retained his federal authority, coordinated the Secret Six's involvement with the Justice and Treasury departments. He was chosen to work with George Johnson and his new assistant, William Froelich, to establish a special squad of federal agents.

Each member would be carefully screened to ensure that the team consisted only of agents who were trustworthy, competent and incorruptible. When the conversation turned to leadership, Jamie enthusiastically recommended his young brother-in-law, whose personnel file reflected just those qualities.

These records, now available to the public under the Freedom of Information Act, showed that Ness served the Prohibition Bureau with "coolness, aggressiveness and fearlessness in raids"; that he had "far more than the average number of arrests"; and that he had "spoken out about the Prohibition Bureau's holding back in its fight against the mob, rather than cleaning house." On the other hand, these same files contained notes suggesting that Ness's superiors were concerned about his "tendency to want to make a name for himself."

Summoning Ness for an interview, Wilson and Johnson asked only a handful of questions before agreeing that he was well-suited to head the Justice Department's special "Capone Squad." Eliot eagerly accepted their offer.

Impressed with his heightened status, Ness telephoned Edna Staley, who had all but given up hope in their relationship, and asked her for a dinner date.

Ness's selection did not sit well with everyone, especially contemporaries who considered him too eager to strike and too inexperienced to be put in charge of a campaign against a target as sly and well-connected as Al Capone.

CHAPTER EIGHT

Sending A Message

The Capone Squad's mission was easily summarized: track down and destroy the mob's breweries and distilleries, thus drying up Capone's major source of income and collecting evidence of Prohibition and tax law violations.

"I want 'em clean, squeaky clean, and that's about the only thing I'm going to require," Johnson assured Eliot Ness. "We're going to give you free rein. You'll operate independently. If you have to bend a few rules, don't tell us about it. I think we all agree on that. We have to fight fire with fire."

Johnson authorized Ness to assemble a squad of up to a dozen men, using a list of candidates believed to be trustworthy, effective, and unlikely to shrink from dangerous assignments.

"This was like a dream come true," Ness wrote of his assignment. "It was something I had hoped for from the first day I became involved with the Prohibition Bureau. I knew that the only way to really go after Capone was to start fresh with officers who were not already corrupted. I couldn't wait to get started."

Ness settled into an office at the Transportation Building in Chicago and began to study Justice Department personnel files. He sought single men who were excellent marksmen with physical stamina and courage. The job would also require skills in surveillance, disguise, evasive driving and self-defense. Ness also considered factors such as ethnic background and drinking habits before finally deciding on five officers:

- Martin Lahart, who had already teamed with Ness for the Cozy Corners raid and the Shakespeare Avenue police station undercover work. Ness was well aware of Lahart's abilities and his commitment to the job.

- Thomas Friel, a wiry, medium-sized recruit who was tempered as hard as the anthracite in his native Scranton, Pennsylvania. A former state police trooper, Friel thirsted for undercover work.
- Samuel Seager, a former guard on death row at Sing-Sing. Seager's quiet, confident manner and hard, expressionless facial features, combined with his 6' 2", 200-pound frame, commanded instant respect.
- Barney Cloonan, a broad-shouldered Irishman with black hair and a ruddy complexion. Another of Ness's Prohibition Bureau acquaintances, the soft-spoken Cloonan longed for an opportunity to leave a desk job he found too confining.
- Lyle Chapman, a tall, lean, scholarly-looking former collegiate football player whose analytical mind had been focused on criminology since his early teens.

Ness also needed technical experts. Justice Department files yielded many possibilities from both inside and outside Chicago. Ness reviewed the credentials of about three dozen agents before he settled on:

- Paul Robsky, a wiretap specialist working out of the New Jersey division. The diminutive, easy-mannered Robsky served as an aerial photographer during World War I and spent a year rooting out moonshiners in South Carolina. He wore an old, oversized hat that came down over his forehead and nearly obscured his eyes.
- William Gardner, an expert at undercover work. Gardner, a solid, 240-pound Native American, had been a college football star. He was working out of the Prohibition Bureau's Los Angeles District when Ness summoned him to Chicago.
- Michael King, a drawling Virginian with an excellent memory and an innate ability to blend into a crowd and tail a suspect.
- Joseph Leeson, a 30-year-old agent from Detroit who possessed excellent driving skills. The oldest of nine men picked by Ness, Leeson stood 6' 2" and was as solid as a rock, with a jutting chin and granite hard eyes.

- Jim Seeley, a 27-year-old Chicago native who had worked as a private detective and cultivated many sources within the city's criminal gangs.

Another member of the group, who managed to keep his affiliation a secret for several years, was Al "Wallpaper" Wolff. Raised on Chicago's West Side, the tall, beefy Wolff had been closing down open-air stills in the Kentucky hills when he was transferred to Chicago shortly after the St. Valentine's Day Massacre.

William Froelich, Johnson's well-groomed and enthusiastic assistant, was chosen to address the group during an initial meeting. Froelich's direct tone of voice commanded instant attention.

"You'll have no hours and I'll back you up to the limit," he told the team. "The important thing is results. We want to dry up Chicago. I mean bone dry. I want every brewery and every still found and destroyed. Any records you get will be invaluable. I'll turn them over to Treasury for processing. They'll handle all the paperwork. What I want from you men is action."

"If anybody wants out, now is the time to say so," Ness interjected. "Some of us may not get out of this alive. Keep that in mind before you get into this too deeply. This is your last chance to walk away from it."

One by one, the nine recruits reaffirmed their commitment.

Ness's team was initially aided by contacts with leaders of rival gangs who had a particular interest in seeing Capone's influence diminished. Additional information came from Secret Six investigators who established a bogus speakeasy that accepted beer shipments from Capone. "Bartenders" on the payroll of the Secret Six fed numerous tips overheard from patrons and deliverers to government agents.

An unofficial inventory gave Ness an indication of the scope of Capone's bootlegging operations: at least twenty breweries, each producing more than 100 barrels of beer per day. In addition, investigators were aware that Capone's organization was buying huge quantities of whiskey, gin and other liquor from underworld sources.

Ness had serious reservations he did not share with his fellow agents. In the 1957 book, *The Untouchables*, he wrote, "Doubts raced through my mind as I considered the feasibility of enforcing a law which the majority of honest citizens didn't seem to want. I felt a chill foreboding for my men as I envisioned the violent reaction we would produce in the criminal octopus hovering over Chicago, its tentacles of terror reaching out all over the nation. We had undertaken what might be a suicidal mission."

Intelligence reports suggested that Capone had ordered the executions of as many as 300 people, most of them from rival organizations. Gangsters rarely assaulted federal officers, due to the harsh repercussions they would face if caught. They also observed an unwritten code protecting from harm all women, children and other family members not directly involved in the business enterprises. Ness wondered how long that policy would remain in effect once his group began to pound away at Capone's economic lifeblood.

Despite the laissez-faire approach of law enforcement officials, Capone had taken certain measures to conceal his production operations. Employees manned the breweries for only short periods of time. Because there was no overt activity during the daytime hours, and little at night, finding these facilities was not easy. Barrels of mothballs masked the usual brewery odors. Doors and windows were covered with black paint, cloth and other padding to prevent light leaks.

Ness began by breaking his team into pairs and directing these agents to trace the routes from the retailers back to warehouses or, better yet, to the breweries themselves. This involved posting his men at several speakeasies and surreptitiously following the trucks that drove off with empty barrels.

It did not take long for the Capone Squad to pick up a scent. Seager and Leeson positioned themselves outside Colosimo's Cafe at about two o'clock one morning just before a large truck drove up. Its two passengers loaded several empty barrels onto the back. The agents tailed the truck through the South Side, observing several more pickups, and then followed it to an abandoned factory at the corner of Shields and 38th streets, near Comiskey Park.

They rented a small apartment about a block away and summoned Ness, who arrived in less than an hour. Seager and Leeson agreed to take turns on a round-the-clock watch of the factory. Later that same day, King and Cloonan arrived early at the Transportation Building to report that they, too, had tailed a truck that collected empty barrels from several establishments and delivered them to the same factory.

After observing more than a dozen trucks pulling in and out of the building before sunrise, curiosity got the better of Seager. Donning some old clothes he found in a closet at the apartment house, he disguised himself as a vagrant and sneaked over to the plant. Climbing on the roof, Seager peered down through a skylight and spotted about a dozen men busily spraying and scrubbing beer barrels. Another six workers wiped the barrels dry and stocked them on wooden skids. This was no brewery; it was a barrel processing plant that gave the investigators a hint of how massive Capone's bootlegging operation had grown.

Ness called his team back to the Transportation Building to discuss how best to use the information without blowing their cover. He directed Leeson and Seager to follow some of the trucks coming out of the warehouse and pinpoint breweries where the clean barrels were being refilled. The group was interrupted by the late arrival of Robsky and Friel, who were out of breath and obviously excited by their discovery of an apparent brewery. The agents wanted to organize a raid for the same day, but Ness was against it until he had an opportunity to personally visit the site.

That afternoon, he joined Robsky and Friel for a trip to 2271 Lumber Street. The large, wooden-front building was amid a row of industrial warehouses. A sign reading "Singer Storage Company" was an obvious cover. Ness eased the big Cadillac into a parking lot about one-half block away and sat quietly, studying the warehouse and pondering how to attack it. Large double doors on both the front and the back of the building would allow the officers to mount their attack from opposite directions.

Ness laid out a plan by which Friel and Robsky would break through the rear door, their revolvers raised, at the same time Ness, Leeson and Gardner were crashing through the double doors in the front. Returning to headquarters, he summoned the others to go over the plans. That night, two cars loaded with shotguns, axes and crowbars pulled into the dark corner of a

parking lot near the brewery. After Ness and Robsky synchro-
nized their watches, Robsky and Friel drove off and parked on
an adjacent street, where they had a clear view of the rear doors.

A few minutes after ten o'clock, they observed a large truck
pulling into the driveway and up to the back doors. Three loud
honks of the horn caught the attention of somebody inside and
the doors opened just wide enough to allow the truck to pass
through. A second truck followed the same routine, using three
short horn blasts to gain entry. Ness loaded a pair of shells into
his sawed-off shotgun and motioned for the trio to move out.

Nervously, they moved into position. As the second hand on
Ness's watch passed the twelve mark at exactly 10:15, he raised
an axe behind his head and pounded it hard against the lock
securing the double doors. The wood cracked, allowing Gardner
to slip a crowbar under the lock, splitting it in an instant. However, rather than gaining immediate entrance to the warehouse,
the three came face-to-face with a solid steel door.

Ness's pulse quickened and sweat formed on his brow as he
made several feeble attempts to penetrate the door with his axe.
More than a minute had passed, and they were still on the outside,
making a lot of noise and jeopardizing the safety of their fellow
agents.

Now desperate, Ness pulled a .38 Colt from his shoulder har-
ness and fired a shot point-blank into the lock. The door still
would not budge. He took aim and fired again. This time, a large
section broke loose and fell to the pavement. Gardner jammed
his hulking shoulder into the double doors and one of them gave
way, allowing the three men to rush into the building. Weapons
raised, the agents were prepared for the worst, but there were no
workers to be seen. Robsky and Friel were also missing.

Lining one of the side walls in the large, well-lighted room
were numerous wooden vats, each standing eight feet tall. Two
shiny trucks, half-filled with beer barrels, occupied the center of
the concrete floor. A half-burned cigarette on a corner table sent
swirls of smoke into the air. The stench of sour mash was almost
overwhelming as Ness, Gardner and Leeson eased their way farther into the warehouse. A hard pounding from the back of the

building answered their questions about the whereabouts of Rob-sky and Friel. They had also been stalled by the heavier-than-expected security measures.

Ness was scoping the tightly-boarded windows, gripping the .38 in his right hand, when he spotted a flight of wooden stairs leading to a trap door in the ceiling. The mystery was solved. A fire escape on the side of the building had allowed the brewery workers to slip off into the darkness.

"Damn it!" roared Seager, grabbing an axe from Gardner's hand and savagely whacking a hole in the side of a vat. A stream of beer cascaded onto the floor and into a drain.

Although the raid netted no suspects, Ness and his partners did seize nineteen vats, each with a capacity of 1,500 gallons. They also confiscated 150 barrels of beer, sealed and ready for delivery to Chicago area speakeasies, and tons of mash.

If nothing else, the Capone Squad had sent a message, and the man at the top was sure to hear it from his Pennsylvania jail cell.

CHAPTER NINE

Inside Connections

During the early days the Ness team was together, there were several other raids of breweries and distilleries—unpublicized, poorly documented and producing few arrests. Often, the leads came from anonymous phone calls, some of them from rival gangsters. As the weather got colder, a visual inspection of a building's exterior was all Ness needed to confirm that it was a brewery or distillery. Yellow-stained icicles hung from the bricks like frozen urine, colored by the steam and fumes that seeped through the walls.

Capone's people responded by having stool pigeons feed Ness misinformation, recalled Al "Wallpaper" Wolff. "We'd go in blazing, like real gangbusters, and come up with dry holes," Wolff said. "This went on for several weeks. Finally, we learned to distinguish between the real leads and phony ones. Then we really went to town. The experience toughened Eliot. He still talked quietly, but with authority."

Occasionally, crooked cops would intercept the Capone Squad during surveillance missions or otherwise interfere with their effectiveness. Froelich solved this by obtaining deputy lieutenants' badges for each squad member.

By charting delivery stops and piecing together reports from federal investigators and a handful of reliable city policemen, Lyle Chapman produced a profile showing the breadth and diversity of Capone's empire—from its bootlegging operations to the brothels, gambling houses and hundreds of speakeasies scattered throughout an ever-growing circle around Chicago.

Using Chapman's charts, Ness posted a huge wall map and stuck colored pins in it to correspond with the location of speakeasies, breweries, barrel-cleaning plants, warehouses and delivery routes.

During his off-hours, Ness's romance with Edna Staley continued to blossom. When he was with her, Eliot was reluctant to
discuss his work, which was fine with Edna. As Alexander Jamie's
secretary, she recognized the complexities and confidential nature of the Prohibition Bureau's work, as well as its danger.

One summer night at a fashionable Chicago restaurant where
Eliot had taken Edna to celebrate her twenty-third birthday, he
proposed to her and she eagerly accepted. Within a month, they
were married in a quiet civil ceremony. The Nesses moved into a
small apartment above a clothing store in Kensington, not far
from Eliot's childhood home.

The government's attack soon took on a sense of urgency, as
news arrived that Capone would probably be released from jail
sooner than previously expected. For technical expertise, Ness
turned to Paul Robsky. One reason Ness recruited Robsky was
his advanced knowledge of electronics. He spent long hours discussing with Ness the possibility of running wiretaps on some of
the telephone lines being used by Capone's men. Not only could
this information help the Capone Squad locate breweries, it could
also bolster the government's case against Capone and his associates.

Federal investigators had already tapped the phones of the
Wabash Hotel, a South Side building where Jack Guzik tended to
administrative duties. Conversations loaded with specifics on
criminal activities and financial information were transcribed for
future use in tax evasion cases.

During Al Capone's absence, his brother Ralph had been far
too careless and open in the way he bought and sold illicit beverages. With George Johnson's blessings, Ness and Robsky
worked out an elaborate, albeit risky, plan to run a tap on Ralph
Capone's personal telephone at the Montmartre Cafe, a shabby
hotel and sandwich shop in Cicero where Ralph conducted much
of his business.

The plan presented logistical problems from the start. Every
room at the Montmartre had its own telephone, patched into a
single exchange located high on a pole next to the building. Suspicious activity at the junction box was sure to arouse the attention
of "the men in the pearl gray hats." Even if he could reach the

junction box, how would Robsky know which lines to tap? There was only one solution: create a cover for Robsky and get someone inside the building.

The first part was less challenging than the second. Ness contacted a childhood pal who was an executive with the telephone company and civic leader. The friend gladly supplied a fully-equipped telephone repair truck, complete with overalls and company hats.

Next, Ness had to decide which of his agents stood the best chance of infiltrating the mob as a member of the "in crowd" at the Montmartre. He finally settled on Marty Lahart, a natural extrovert who could easily make friends, and Tom Friel, the most experienced undercover man.

By that time, at least some members of the Capone Squad had noticed suspicious-looking vehicles following them whenever they cruised city streets. To counter this, Ness directed some of his reliable contacts in the Police Department to spread the word that Lahart and Friel had been reassigned to the Prohibition Bureau's New York District. Considering the cozy alliance between some police officers and the underworld, news of the two agents' "transfer" was sure to reach Capone's organization.

Lahart and Friel then dropped out of sight, holing up in a seedy Cicero hotel. They allowed rough beards to grow, acquired new wardrobes, and were welcomed into the Montmartre. A few days later, Lahart reported to Ness, tongue-in-cheek, that the duo had consumed more beer at government expense than the Capone Squad had seized during its raids.

Ralph Capone conducted most of his telephone conversations from an alcove behind the bar. He frequently let patrons use the same telephone for personal calls. The utility pole that contained the terminal box for all fifty of the Montmartre phones was in an area kept under round-the-clock guard. The only way Robsky would know which line to tap would be to hear a familiar voice.

"What are your chances of using Capone's phone?" Ness asked Friel the next time the agent checked in.

"I don't think my chances are too good, but Marty's got a good shot. He's gotten in pretty good with the big boys. And as long as we're spending money, these guys think we're great."

"That's good," Ness replied. "Tell him to find an excuse to use that phone and then see how they react. If they don't like the idea, tell him to back off. It's not worth getting killed over."

A week later, Lahart reported that he had used Capone's phone a half-dozen times. He had taken the plan one step further, supplying a Prohibition Bureau secretary with the phone number and receiving calls on the same telephone. His "friends" at the cafe were convinced that the calls were coming from a nagging wife.

The following afternoon, the team arranged for the secretary to place her call to the Montmartre at 4:00 p.m. By that time, Robsky was to be in place atop the pole, checking each junction until he located the one to Ralph Capone's telephone.

The guards posed a major obstacle. In the wake of the Lumber Street brewery raid and other recent activities, Capone's people were more suspicious than ever. There was no certainty they would fall for the phone company disguises.

Ness called in Leeson, Seager, Cloonan and Gardner to go over a plan to divert the guards' attention. "They've been tailing my car, so they should know it when they see it," he told the agents. "I want you to take my car and drive it past that hellhole a couple of times, real slow. You know, look like you're checkin' the place out. They'll start following. Just keep 'em busy while Paul does his work."

Time passed all too slowly for the squad that day. Ness, somber-eyed, studied the latest transcripts from Guzik's telephone conversations at the Wabash, trying to make sense of them. He stuck a pin on his wall map to identify another suspected brewery. The agents took turns reading the morning newspaper, where they learned that a judge, as expected, had granted Al Capone's petition for early release. He would be back in Chicago in a couple of weeks.

Much of the group's future activity hinged on whether the wiretap plan, a dangerous long shot, would succeed. Robsky had no way of knowing how many lines he would have to check before he found the right one, and there was always the chance that the truck would arouse suspicion, leading to a bloody confrontation. What if the telephone in Ralph Capone's office was unavailable? What if the guards came back before Robsky made the connections? What if Lahart and Friel were exposed, then tortured until they told all they knew?

Ness tried to erase those fears from his mind as he and Robsky drove to the telephone company warehouse, where the truck and two uniforms awaited them. About fifteen minutes before the secretary was supposed to place the call, Ness drove the service truck past two rough-looking men leaning on a railing in front of the Montmartre and pulled into an alley, just a few feet from the utility pole. The guards casually looked at the truck and then continued their conversation. Soon, a third man joined the others. After they spoke for a moment, the trio hurried over to a black Ford and drove off, tires squealing.

"I'll bet they saw my car," Ness said with a smile as Robsky adjusted the climbing spikes on the heels of his boots and strapped on an equipment belt. "I wonder how long their little joy ride is going to last."

"I hope it lasts long enough," Robsky said, testing the texture of the pole with one of his spikes. Ness looked at his watch. He tried to picture Lahart sitting nervously at the bar, waiting for a phone call he might have to prolong for twenty minutes or more, if Capone's people would let him.

The spikes rasped into the wood as Robsky made his ascent. Ness leaned against the pole, hiding his face from the Montmartre entranceway. Though usually cool in the most intense situations, the young lawman found himself jumping at every sound and straining his eyes to detect any movement.

Robsky made quick work of the box cover and his fingers were soon flying over the terminals. Ness instinctively patted his rib cage to be sure his revolver was ready. After about five minutes elapsed, Robsky leaned back against the strong leather of his security belt and shook his head negatively.

"Run over it again," Ness said in a loud whisper. Robsky nodded his approval. Suddenly, he stopped, then flashed an "OK" sign with his thumb and forefinger. Robsky fidgeted with an assortment of screwdrivers, wire cutters and pliers clipped to his belt. Within a matter of seconds, the tap was installed. He closed the metal box with a sharp click and hurried down the pole.

"You owe me a case of beer—some of Capone's finest," Robsky said, smiling.

"Hey, Paul, I'll give you your own god-damned brewery if this little stunt works," Ness replied, patting his partner on the back. He helped Robsky remove the equipment belt and the two climbed into the truck.

Back at headquarters, Leeson gleefully reported on the decoys' trip through the streets of Cicero. Capone's guards had tailed their every move before Leeson suddenly swerved Ness's Cadillac into a vacant lot and watched the pursuers cruise by.

"We kept the goons busy," said a beaming Leeson. "They're probably still scratchin' their heads, tryin' to figure out what we were doing and where we ended up. Maybe, someday, they'll figure it all out."

CHAPTER TEN

Nobody's Legit

As Al Capone anxiously awaited his release from Eastern Penitentiary, he was kept apprised of developments back in Chicago by his attorneys, who served as intermediaries between Capone and his top commanders. Capone was aware that his bootlegging empire was coming apart at the seams, but he felt powerless to rescue it.

The average person had less money to spend on alcohol, and those who did have the cash were complaining that the usually-reliable Capone was sometimes unable to meet their demands. This was one measure of progress in which Eliot Ness took great pride.

Capone had other problems, as well. The Treasury Department, once dismissed as a minor annoyance, was scrutinizing his financial dealings like never before. Any doubt about the seriousness of that probe was removed on October 29, 1929, when a grand jury returned seven indictments against Ralph Capone.

The charges stemmed from deposits Capone had made under several aliases with the Pinkert State Bank, located across from the Hawthorne Hotel in Cicero. In one of the bank's safety deposit boxes, government agents discovered Ralph Capone's $100,000 cache and records showing that, in 1927 and 1928, he deposited more than $974,000 in five different banks under as many names. Investigators also uncovered evidence that Al Capone had a financial interest in the highly-profitable Arsonia Stables, including ownership of seven thoroughbreds.

Ralph Capone's legal plight would have commanded huge headlines, but the public's attention was focused on another news development. On "Black Friday," October 29, 1929, sixteen million shares were tossed overboard on the New York Stock Exchange for whatever price could be obtained. The economic life of the nation was smothered in gloom.

No major city suffered more from the Great Depression than did Chicago. The city government ran millions of dollars in the red, prompting private groups to pass the hat in a desperate effort to keep schools open. A midwestern drought inflicted further hardship. Homeless families slept in alleyways, while clusters of shacks made of packing cases, tarpaper and cardboard formed "Hoovervilles" in the outlying parts of town.

The Depression altered Chicagoans' views of hoodlums. Unemployment and other economic factors lent a sense of urgency to the government's efforts to stop the underworld from skimming so much tax-free money off the top. Ironically, the federal government could not afford to continue bankrolling such a comprehensive law enforcement effort in Chicago. The Secret Six came to the rescue by helping to pay the salaries of the Capone Squad and several IRS undercover agents.

A badly-shaken Ralph Capone, still unaware of the Montmartre wiretap, freely discussed his defense strategy by telephone with lawyers, family members, partners in crime, and anyone else who would listen. The tone of the conversations suggested that Capone believed threats and bribery would cause the government's case to crumble.

Arriving at the Capone Squad's listening post in a rented hotel room one morning, Ness and Leeson found Chapman seated at a small table, reading a newspaper. A telephone headset rested next to his left elbow and a long, yellow legal pad along with several sharp pencils were spread out on his other side.

Ness and Leeson settled in to take the day shift. They heard scattered conversation during the afternoon hours, but nothing significant. Ness did take note of one call Ralph Capone received from a woman in New Orleans, informing him that the fix was in for a horse race that day. Capone told her to bet $15,000 on the prearranged winner and deposit the earnings in a bank account she was keeping for the syndicate in her own name. The remainder of the day's calls consisted of small-time beer orders and plans for social activities. Ness filled several pages with notes to use in adjusting the pins on his wall map back at headquarters.

In *The Last of the Untouchables,* a high-fictionalized book coauthored by Paul Robsky and Oscar Fraley several years after the Ness/Fraley collaboration was published, Robsky told of a "secret shakeup" on the Capone Squad at about this time. One agent, identified by Robsky as George Steelman, was alleged to have been acting as an informant for Capone's group. Absent any verification of Steelman's existence, and considering the glorification of the Ness team's experiences in both of the Fraley books, the validity of the story is in question.

Another agent, Jim Seeley, also left the team under circumstances never publicly explained.

While Ness and his men monitored the Montmartre wiretap and conducted additional raids in Chicago and Cicero, Frank Wilson sat for eighteen hours a day sifting through financial records seized from the Capone operations. "I know where Al gets his money, but it'll take a little proving," Wilson said during a meeting called to review the government's case against Al Capone. "Ralph is already going down. I can prove where Nitti gets his money, and how much. The same goes for Guzik. Nobody wants to say much about Al, so maybe if we put some heat on his buddies, these guys will be more inclined to talk, just to save their own hides."

On March 18, 1930, reporters, cameramen and curiosity seekers assembled outside Eastern Penitentiary at the announced time of Capone's release. Prison Warden Herbert B. Smith had told the press Capone would emerge from the prison gates and walk to a small private airplane.

In reality, Capone had already been smuggled out the previous night in the warden's car. He was taken to Graterford, about 20 miles northwest of Philadelphia, and held in the prison there until friends arrived the next day to pick him up. By the time Warden Smith emerged to greet the press, Capone was 200 miles away.

"We stuck one in your eye," Smith said smugly. "The big guy's gone."

Among those taking the greatest offense was Jake Lingle, a Chicago Tribune crime reporter who enjoyed a cozy relationship with the underworld. Furious that he was not informed of Warden Smith's ploy, Lingle phoned Ralph Capone. One of Ness's men was listening in.

"Where's Al?" asked an angry Lingle. "I've been looking all over for him, and nobody seems to know where he is."

"I don't know where he is, either, Jake," Ralph Capone insisted. "I haven't heard a word from him since he got out."

"Jesus, Ralph. This makes it very hard for me. I'm supposed to have my finger on these things. It makes it very embarrassing with my paper. Now get this: I want you to call me the minute you hear from him. Tell him I want to see him right away." Ralph promised he would.

Lingle called again later, infuriated that his plea had been ignored. "Listen, you guys ain't giving me the runaround, are you? Just remember, I wouldn't do that if I were you."

Ralph Capone knew full well where his brother was. Not twenty minutes before Lingle called, Ralph had received a phone call informing him that Al was celebrating his freedom with a night of drinking at the Western Hotel in Cicero. As the alcohol soaked into his brain, Capone flew into a violent rage.

"We're up in Room 718 at the Western and Al is really getting out of hand," a frantic caller told Ralph. "He's in terrible shape. Will you come up? You're the only one who can handle him when he gets like this. We've sent for a lot of towels." A follow-up call informed Ralph that his services would not be necessary; Al had passed out.

Sobering up the following morning, Capone slipped into his headquarters at the Hawthorne in Cicero to huddle with some of his lieutenants. Their immediate focus was Deputy Police Chief John Stege's bold declaration that he intended to "clap Capone in jail as soon as he sets foot in the city."

City police, including the two dozen staking out Capone's Prairie Avenue home, had orders to detain him upon sight. Stege had no legal authority to order Capone's arrest, but the law, in its frustration with the mob's control, sometimes treated underworld figures with little regard for their constitutional guarantees.

Capone's attorney, Thomas Nash, assured him the police were powerless to act unless they first secured an indictment listing specific charges. Accompanied by Nash, Capone marched into the Federal Building, a massive monument to civic dreariness at the corner of Dearborn and Adams, and demanded to see the indictment. He was met by Deputy Chief Stege and Assistant State's Attorney Harry Ditchburne.

"Al, what do you know about the Valentine Day massacre of the seven Moran brothers?" Ditchburne asked.

"I was in Florida then," Capone snapped back.

"Yes, you were in Florida, too, when Frank Yale was murdered?" Stege asked.

"I'm not as bad as I'm painted. If you sift through everything I was ever accused of, you'll find I didn't do it. I get blamed for everything that goes on here, but I had nothing to do with those things you're talking about."

"Personally, you don't commit the murders, but we're not far wrong, are we, in assuming that your gang is responsible?" said Stege.

"I'm not responsible for what others do," Capone insisted.

"You're not a very good citizen, Al," Stege continued. "If you were walking along the street with your brother and he was killed, wouldn't you come here and tell us who killed him?

"Well, put yourself in my place and see what you'd do."

"There used to be a time when the police department wouldn't have a hundred murders in ten years. But since you gangsters have been at war, we've had 300 murders in a year," said Stege, exaggerating the figures. "That's why we're driving you out of town."

"You, Mr. Ditchburne, as a lawyer, know the police can't do that," Nash interjected.

"I'm not here to tell the police what not to do," Ditchburne said. "I'm here to advise them what to do. I'm not interested in protecting Mr. Capone. If he feels he's being arrested wrongly, he has his remedy. He can sue for false arrest."

"I don't want to sue anybody," Capone said. "All I want is not to be arrested if I come downtown."

"You're out of luck," Stege told him. "Your day is done. How soon are you getting out of town?" Stege turned to Nash and said, "You'd better advise him to get out of Chicago."

"Lenin and Trotsky and others have rebelled against that kind of treatment," Nash retorted.

"I hope Capone goes to Russia," was Stege's parting shot as he rose from behind his desk and stormed out of the office. Ditchburne then conceded that police had no grounds to detain Capone, pending the filing of criminal charges for his failure to appear before the grand jury in its bootlegging probe many months earlier.

Reporters had learned of Capone's whereabouts and were waiting when he and Nash emerged from the Federal Building.

"It's kind of hard trying to figure out who wants me," Capone chuckled, loud enough for the reporters to hear, before he and Nash drove off.

Back at his big mahogany desk in the spacious offices at the Lexington Hotel, Capone did agree to be interviewed by Genevieve Forbes Herrick of the Chicago Tribune. Descending the hotel steps with his patent leather hair shining in the bright overhead lighting, he was vintage Capone:

"Why should I be indicted? All I ever did was sell beer and whiskey to our best people. All I ever did was supply a demand that was pretty popular. Why, the very guys that make my trade good are the ones that yell the loudest about me. Some of the leading judges use the stuff. They talk about me not being on the legitimate. Why, lady, nobody's on the legit. You know that and so do they. Your father or your brother gets in a jam. What do you do? Do you sit back and let him go over the road, without trying to help him? You'd be a yellow dog if you did. Nobody's really on the legit, when it comes down to cases. You know that."

Capone pressed a buzzer to summon his wife Mae and his sister Mafalda from an upstairs room. They came downstairs, nervously shared small talk with Herrick for a couple of minutes, and then returned to their suite.

"Did you notice my wife's hair?" Capone said. "Those streaks of gray— she's only 28 and she's got gray hair worrying over things here in Chicago." (Mae Capone was actually 31 at the time, two years her husband's senior.)

The exclusive interview was page one news in the Tribune. A sidebar told of Capone's generosity in donating money to a soup kitchen on the South Side, where thousands of people suffering through the effects of the Depression could get a warm meal. This was the same Capone who had purchased hundreds of turkeys for the poor people of the South Side the previous Thanksgiving.

Another story told of Capone's appearance at a horse racetrack in Charleston, Indiana, where thousands stood and cheered when he arrived with his bodyguards, waving his clasped hands above his head like a prizefighter entering the ring. George E.Q. Johnson, who was attending the races that day, bristled when the band broke into a rousing rendition of "It's A Lonesome Town When You're Not Around" while Capone, a sunburst in his yellow suit and yellow tie, took his seat.

Arriving at the Transportation Building to confer with Johnson, Eliot Ness picked up a copy of the Tribune and scanned the front page as he mounted the steps. "That bastard!" Ness exclaimed as he whisked through the doorway into Johnson's office, plopping the newspaper on his colleague's desk. "Have you seen this? Can you believe it? They turn this guy into a god-damned hero! How could that gal from the newspaper be so gullible?"

Johnson tried to calm him. "You know his days are numbered, Eliot. Everybody knows what he is, and he's no hero, that's for sure. It's just a matter of time 'til he's out of the picture. All of these guys are going down, eventually."

That assessment was reinforced by the treatment Capone received when he appeared at Dyche Stadium in Evanston, Illinois, to watch the college football game between Northwestern and Nebraska. He supplied dozens of Chicago area Boy Scouts with complimentary tickets, and the boys initiated a cheer of "Yea, Al!" which echoed around the stadium. However, before halftime, Capone and Jack McGurn were subjected to merciless heckling. When they finally decided they could take no more and rose to leave in the third quarter, they were followed by about 400 undergraduates who booed and hissed.

With Capone back in Chicago, Ness and some of his agents staked out the Lexington to watch the gangsters' every movement. Ness recognized that Capone was an elusive target. In a memo to his superiors, he wrote: "Acquiring the poise that comes with power, Capone has become even more dangerous. Together with his ruthlessness, he has the qualities of a great businessman. Under that patent leather hair he has sound judgment, diplomatic shrewdness and the diamond-hard nerves of a gambler, all balanced by cold common sense."

Ralph Capone came to trial on tax evasion charges in April 1930. Directing the prosecution was Frank J. Wilson, a rising star in the eyes of Elmer Irey and other federal officials carrying out President Hoover's directives.

"He fears nothing that walks," Irey wrote of Frank Wilson. "He will sit quietly looking at books seven days a week, forever, if he wants to find something in those books. He is soft-spoken and unemotional. Only the endless stream of nickel cigars he massacres keeps him from being a paragon of virtue."

The case went to the jury on April 26. Following deliberations that lasted just two and one-half hours, Wilson got what he was after. Ralph Capone was convicted on all counts and received a sentence of three years in prison, along with a $10,000 fine. The fine would be no problem for Capone, but the prison time was something he vowed to fight to the highest courts. He was allowed to remain free, pending his appeal.

"You got caught because you weren't smart," Al Capone told his brother in a telephone conversation recorded by Ness's team. "You talked too much and you put too many things in writing. You gotta be smart, Ralph."

The trial was a wake-up call to many Chicago area bootleggers. Recognizing that the 1927 Supreme Court decision in the Manley Sullivan case could just as easily apply to them, dozens of gangsters hurried to the Federal Building to pay whatever back taxes the Internal Revenue Service determined they owed.

Many saw the government's pursuit of Ralph Capone as merely a trial run for the case that would be brought against Scarface Al. Prosecutors were careful to focus only on the tax case, and not on Prohibition violations, since jurors would not be inclined to take Volstead Act enforcement as seriously.

The last thing Capone wanted was a long, messy trial that could expose so many aspects of his criminal empire. Seeing the four-foot-high stack of evidence against his brother, Capone retained the services of Lawrence P. Mattingly, a renowned Washington tax lawyer. Mattingly tried to cut a deal, but to no avail. He and Capone appeared before Frank Wilson and Ralph Herrick, the tax agent in charge of the Treasury Department's Chicago Enforcement Division, for a cat-and-mouse discussion of Capone's business activities and his tax obligations.

"What records have you of your income, Mr. Capone? Do you keep any records?" Herrick inquired.

"No, I never did," Capone replied in a low, respectful tone.

"Any checking accounts?"

"No, sir."

"How long, Mr. Capone, have you enjoyed such a large income?"

"I never had much of an income."

"I will state it differently— an income that might be taxable."

"I would rather let my lawyer answer that question."

Mattingly interjected that he had reviewed the issue with another of his clients, Johnny Torrio, and determined that Capone's salary as an employee of Torrio's was nowhere near the threshold above which federal income taxes had to be paid.

Wilson asked Capone if he had ever tried to conceal his own financial dealings by purchasing real estate and depositing money under the name of his wife or any other relative.

"I would rather not answer that," was Capone's reply, repeated several times as the questions grew more specific.

One potential witness who could have shed some light on Capone's finances was Chicago Tribune crime reporter Jake Lingle. As the wiretapped conversation suggested, Lingle was well aware of many financial enterprises in which Al Capone had a direct interest.

A Chicago West Side native, Lingle had prided himself on his ability to infiltrate the mob. He supplied facts to other Tribune staffers who fashioned articles based primarily on Lingle's information. For eighteen years, Lingle's work had given the Tribune countless exclusive stories from inside gangland. Although he enjoyed easy access to Capone, Lingle also was on good terms with the police.

But Jake Lingle was not all that he seemed. A heavy gambler, he often spent more money in one night of gambling than he made from his modest weekly salary. His clothing and his vehicles left no doubt that he enjoyed supplemental income.

Faced with the threat of being exposed as a Capone operative, Lingle told prosecutors he was willing to talk. Wilson arranged to meet him at the Tribune Tower the following day.

A nervous Lingle decided to visit one of his familiar haunts, the Washington Park racetrack, for some early afternoon action. He hurried down the stairs into the 85-foot-long pedestrian tunnel passing under Michigan Avenue, trying to catch the next train out of a nearby Illinois Central Railroad station.

A tall, blond man in his early twenties was seen elbowing people aside, trying to catch up to Lingle. As the man drew even, he took a gun out of his pocket, leveled it to the back of Jake Lingle's head and fired a bullet into the reporter's brain. Lingle fell forward, the day's horse racing form still in his hand and a burning cigar clenched between his teeth. The assassin dropped his gun and ran off.

CHAPTER ELEVEN

The Untouchables

Al Capone's celebrity status continued to eat away at Eliot Ness. He could not comprehend how the public tolerated a man who openly violated countless laws and was responsible for dozens of cold-blooded murders, all in the name of power and greed.

In his writings, Ness clearly saw his job as a mission, as if he had been chosen to defend all that was good about America against all that was evil. If order was not soon restored, Ness believed, the entire nation could crumble.

He began battering away at the bootlegging business with renewed vigor, more inclined than ever to ignore some of the formalities, including the need to obtain a warrant before entering suspected breweries.

"Eliot changed," Al Wolff noted. "The niceties of the law no longer meant all that much to him. He bent a few rules and even broke a few. We didn't always see eye-to-eye on that. Not that I'm criticizing him, but there were a couple of times when I refused to go. He understood."

Locating Capone's production facilities was sometimes easier than entering them. Besides falling for the occasional phony lead, too often Ness's team wasted precious time hacking through doorways with axes and battering them down with sledgehammers. This allowed those inside to destroy evidence or, as with the Lumber Street raid, to escape. A frustrated Ness summoned Lyle Chapman to help him draw up blueprints for a sturdy vehicle that would enable the Capone Squad to enter the breweries more efficiently.

This ten-ton flatbed truck was equipped with a giant steel ram specially built for smashing through heavily-reinforced doors. Handles were mounted in the cab so the raiders could hold on and avoid injury at the moment of impact. On either side of the truck were ladders, padded at the top to prevent noise when they were raised and positioned for access to roofs and fire escapes.

The truck was first used in a raid at 2108 South Wabash Avenue on June 13, 1930. Only scant details were recorded. Ness reportedly donned a leather football helmet and took his position in the passenger's seat as Chapman slipped behind the wheel. Four of the other agents spread out to cover the exits. As Chapman and Ness crashed through the front doors, five startled mob employees darted for the back exit, running into the waiting arms of Gardner and King. This was the biggest arrest yet by the Capone Squad. Agents collected a variety of evidence—from trucks and vats to beer barrels and distilling equipment. They dumped hundreds of gallons of beer.

Despite the admonitions of his bosses and the advice of his fellow agents, Ness insisted on sharing news of the raid with reporters. Some colleagues considered him a glory-seeker, but Eliot shrugged off his critics, insisting that extensive publicity of his team's activities would tell the underworld that a new era had arrived. How better to demonstrate that, Ness argued, than to prove that no one—not even Al Capone—was above the law?

One of the unfortunate consequences of notifying the press in advance was that journalists sometimes arrived at suspected breweries before the raiders. In one extreme case, mobsters spotted the reporters far enough in advance to move all of their equipment and beer supplies out. Ness and his crew ended up raiding a dry hole.

Privately, Ness recognized that publicity could make his team the target of retaliation. "We all realized we were sitting on a keg of dynamite with no means of determining the length of the fuse," Ness wrote in *The Untouchables*. This almost fatalistic approach to his work greatly disturbed both Eliot's parents and Edna.

That book also detailed a visit allegedly paid to Ness by a go-between called "The Kid." According to the story Ness told, this young visitor handed him an envelope containing twenty $100 bills and promised him weekly payments of the same amount would be delivered if Ness backed off.

"I could feel the anger rising in my chest," Ness wrote. "Fighting to get hold of myself, I walked around the desk and stood in front of him. Slowly, I reached down, pulled him out of the chair and, opening his jacket, stuffed the envelope back into his inner pocket. 'Listen, and listen carefully,' I told him. 'I may be only a poor baker's son, but I want you to take this envelope back to them and tell them that Eliot Ness can't be bought— not for two thousand a week, ten thousand, or a hundred thousand. Not for all the money they'll ever lay their scummy hands on.' With the boss back, the first step was bribery. What next?"

Apparently, Capone's people didn't give up easily. According to newspaper accounts, a pair of Capone's field men tried to buy cooperation by heaving a wad of $100 bills through the open window of a parked car occupied by Lahart and Seager. After a brief discussion with the hoodlums, Lahart tossed the money back at the men and drove away.

Whether these episodes actually occurred or not, they were the seeds from which the legend of Eliot Ness would grow. Ness called a press conference, inviting all of the influential Chicago area reporters. With flashbulbs popping and pencils scribbling all around him, he recounted the two bribery attempts in dramatic fashion. Ness boldly repeated his team's determination to destroy Capone's bootlegging operations and to bolster the government's mounting case against the most powerful criminal organization in America.

"Probably it wasn't too important for the world to know that we couldn't be bought, but I did want Al Capone and every gangster in the city to realize that there were still a few law enforcement agents who couldn't be swerved from their duty," Ness wrote.

A writer from the Chicago Tribune, in the next day's edition, coined the phrase, "The Untouchables," to describe this small band of gangbusters. This was the first prominent mention of "Elliott" Ness in the Chicago newspapers, and he savored the recognition.

"Ness is new on the scene," said a newspaper profile introducing Chicago to the head of the Untouchables. "He is six feet tall, with a lean 180-pound frame, and slim waistline offset by broad shoulders, a boyishly-handsome face and a wave of freckles across the bridge of his nose. He has a pleasant smile, wavy brown hair parted in the middle, sleepy blue-gray eyes that can suddenly turn icy and piercing. He immediately strikes one as 'all business,' then smiles and winks, as if the fact that he is merely acting in a role is just between you and him. He is, in short, an enigma—but an enigma with lots of promise."

Capone eventually resorted to one of Ness's tricks. By bribing telephone workers, he was able to install sophisticated taps on the phone lines of Ness and others at the Transportation Building. Through these devices, Capone learned the identity of each agent and made sure that mobsters were tailing the investigators. When the phone conversations suggested a raid was imminent, or when agents were spotted near an establishment, Capone ordered the brewery shut down for a "cooling-off period."

Capone's people also tried to discredit Ness in the eyes of his superiors and in the press by planting false information about his background and character. Then, perhaps just to irritate Ness, Capone's men stole his car, drove it into a ditch on the outskirts of the city, and left it there, a newspaper detailing the Untouchables' success draped over the steering wheel. Someone had drawn a target around Ness in the photograph that accompanied the story, and had scrawled, "You're Dead," inside the target. Still shaken by the murder of Jake Lingle, Ness took the threat seriously, and he eagerly shared the information with reporters.

The Chicago Tribune, joined by other newspapers and civic groups, offered a $55,000 reward for information leading to the conviction of Lingle's murderer. They also bankrolled a special investigative force whose activities smacked more of retribution than evidence-gathering. These agents raided and gutted countless brothels, speakeasies and gambling houses, arresting everyone they found on the premises.

They gained an important ally in Judge John Lyle, the self-appointed scourge of gangsters. Lyle set bail so high that most of the offenders were forced to remain behind bars for weeks or even months awaiting legal proceedings. They were always presented with another alternative: tell what they knew of Capone's illegal operations in return for leniency.

Lyle also shrewdly invoked a little-used section of the Illinois Vagrancy Law to have Al Capone arrested. Questioned about such an untraditional application, the judge caustically replied that Capone fit the description of "vagrant," because he had no admitted source of income.

"If he tried to pay the fine, he would have to explain where the money had come from," Lyle reasoned. "Were he to recite the sources of his income, he would be opening the door to criminal charges. And any claim to legitimate employment would launch an investigation that could conceivably result in perjury charges. There was also the possibility that a vagrancy hearing would assist Treasury agents in their efforts to develop an income tax case against Capone."

Lyle's strategy resulted in a series of arrests and convictions, all overruled by the Illinois Supreme Court. If nothing else, the vagrancy crackdown kept Capone and several of his advisors busy while Ness, Wilson, Irey and the others continued their work on the more serious charges.

Dark rumors continued to linger concerning Jake Lingle's affiliation with the mob. Evidence eventually surfaced to reveal that Lingle had served as a liaison between Capone's organization and City Hall, arranging for the protection of bootleggers and gamblers. In the process, he had cooperated with both Capone and his rival, Bugs Moran— a dangerous practice.

Ralph Capone and others could be heard on the Montmartre telephone wiretap discussing Lingle's killing, but government investigators could not piece together enough incriminating evidence to directly link Al Capone to the crime. Ness's conclusion was that Capone either ordered the shooting or laid the ground work by removing a protective shield he had previously maintained around Lingle.

Although dozens of witnesses got a good look at the assailant, no one would provide police with a useful description. Jurors eventually found that Leo Vincent Brothers, a labor union terrorist from St. Louis, had pulled the trigger.

Just three weeks after the trial, prosecutors received a letter from Mike de Pike Heitler, one of Capone's street enforcers, identifying eight Capone affiliates as conspirators in Lingle's killing.

This chilling communication arrived days after Heitler's charred remains were found in the ruins of a house that had burned in Barrington, northwest of Chicago. Heitler had sealed the letter and given to his daughter, with strict instructions that it be placed in the mail if he died an unnatural death. Many remain convinced that Bugs Moran ordered Lingle's death, anticipating that Capone would be blamed.

Revelations of Lingle's true role in the Chicago crime scene caused immeasurable damage to public confidence in the press's ability to expose and combat crime and corruption. Harry T. Brundige, an old-style reporter with the St. Louis Star, was granted an exclusive interview with Al Capone as part of his research for what would become a ten-part series exposing members of the Chicago press as blackmailers, bootleggers, bookmakers, influence peddlers, and close allies of the underworld.

"How many reporters do you have on the payroll?" Brundige asked.

"Plenty," Capone said. "You can't buck it, not even with the backing of your newspaper, because it's too big a proposition. No one will ever realize just how big it is."

The mounting evidence of crime and corruption only strengthened Ness's resolve as he visited Frank Wilson to deliver the latest pile of transcripts from wiretapped conversations at the Montmartre.

"We're gonna dry these bastards up pretty soon," Ness told him. "Here's some more ammunition for you guys. I've made a few notes in the border. It looks to me like Greasy Thumb Guzik is going to be running the show once Ralph is behind bars."

"Don't be so sure," Wilson replied, looking over the frames of his glasses. "We could take Guzik now if we wanted to, and probably Capone, too, for that matter. But I think we're better off letting them feed us more evidence. They're playing right into our hands."

"Well, my boys are getting impatient," Ness responded. "We've got ten times the evidence we need to nab these guys on Volstead, and we're about ready to take out two more breweries. My men can't understand what you're waiting for."

"We're getting close Eliot. I mean that. We've just got to make sure everything is in place. Hell, the whole country is watching this. We can't afford to make any mistakes."

Ness nodded his head and turned to leave. "Keep up the good work," Wilson encouraged him.

"We're not giving up," Ness promised. "We'll do our job, as long as I can tell my men that something is going to come out of all their hard work."

What Wilson didn't share with Ness was the fact that federal officials were placing diminished importance on all of the evidence the Untouchables were gathering. With the income tax evasion case coming together so rapidly, neither Wilson nor Johnson expected to prosecute Capone for Prohibition violations unless their other case collapsed.

Investigators in Florida had already gathered overwhelming evidence of Capone's lavish spending habits. These agents documented vehicle purchases, furniture and clothing orders, hotel bills, medical expenses, long-distance telephone charges and other verification of Capone's substantial income.

Back in Chicago, using cash payments and threats of incarceration, Wilson's men persuaded several prostitutes employed by Capone to sign affidavits incriminating their boss.

One of the Treasury Department agents, Michael F. Malone, was able to gain access to Capone's "fort" at the Lexington Hotel by posing as a Philadelphia gangster hiding out from the police. (Malone is referred to by the pseudonym "Patrick O'Rourke" in some accounts). His charade included false criminal records bearing the seal of the Philadelphia Police Department. Malone also mailed letters to friends in Philadelphia and received responses, all bogus correspondence designed to further establish his false identity. Not only did Capone's people steam open these letters and inspect the contents, they also searched Malone's room, including an inspection of his clothing, which—luckily for him—bore Philadelphia labels.

Wilson, in his memoirs, called Malone "the greatest natural undercover worker the IRS ever had." Malone systematically gathered volumes of evidence covering Capone's baseball bat assault of Scalise, Anselmi and Guinta; numerous murders on

Capone's behalf; and countless bootlegging, gambling, prostitution and racketeering operations.

Among the agent's most startling discoveries was a plot by the Capone gang to murder Wilson at the Sheridan Plaza, where he and his wife had been staying under assumed names. Wilson was immediately assigned a bodyguard and moved to another hotel suite.

Pressured as never before by President Hoover to move in on Capone, Wilson pleaded in a memo for more time: "All important witnesses are either hostile to the government and ready to give perjured testimony in order to protect the leaders of their organization, or they are so filled with fear of the Capone organization that they evade, lie, leave town and do all in their power to prevent the government from using them as witnesses."

The President's impatience was understandable. Al Capone was an all-too-visible symbol of lawlessness and an embarrassment to the troubled Hoover administration. Moviegoers were introduced to a caricature of Capone in First National's "Little Caesar," starring Edward G. Robinson, in early 1930. Warner Studios would follow with "Public Enemy," featuring James Cagney, in 1931. Theater companies were also getting in on the act, including Broadway's "On The Spot," which began in October 1930 and lasted for 167 performances. The Howard Hughes Studio also joined in, producing "Scarface," starring Paul Muni.

After a meeting with President Hoover, Wilson decided to play his ace in the hole: an obscure Capone operative named Fred Ries. As cashier for Capone's gambling houses and racing enterprises, Ries would pile the earnings in a gunny sack and deposit them under aliases at Pinkert State Bank, where he was legitimately employed as a cashier. He converted the money to cashier's checks and turned them over to Jack Guzik and Al Capone.

A tall, stooped figure, nearly bald, Ries fled in fear for his life after initially being questioned. He was tracked down in St. Louis and threatened with a long prison term if he continued to protect Capone. Ushered to Chicago to appear before a secretly-convened grand jury, Ries nervously detailed how Capone's gambling house was pulling in profits of more than $100,000 per night.

To lay further groundwork for the prosecution of Al Capone, the government moved forward against another of his key operatives, Frank "The Enforcer" Nitti. Mike Malone, who had become well-acquainted with Nitti during his stays at the Lexington, learned that Nitti was making regular deposits on Capone's behalf at the Schiff Trust and Savings Bank. Grand jurors secretly returned an indictment against Nitti for failing to pay taxes on income of nearly $750,000 over a three-year period. Evidently, it wasn't secret enough, because Nitti promptly disappeared from Chicago.

Less than two weeks later, he was apprehended in the Chicago suburb of Berwyn. "The Enforcer" admitted responsibility for bank deposits of more than $200,000, covering the profits of alcohol stills in Cicero, Little Italy and the West Side of Chicago, and from the Hawthorne Smoke Shop's gambling operations in Cicero. Nitti, good soldier that he was, insisted the money was his own, although the investigators knew better. His guilty plea to tax evasion charges brought a sentence of eighteen months at Leavenworth Penitentiary.

Combining evidence from a variety of sources, including the Untouchables' transcripts, prosecutors next persuaded a hastily-convened grand jury to indict Jack Guzik for avoiding federal income taxes on almost $1 million in earnings over a three-year period. Everyone knew whose money Guzik was managing, but he was not about to admit it.

At Guzik's public trial on November 19, 1930, Fred Ries appeared as a surprise witness to present damning evidence against not only Greasy Thumb Guzik, but Al Capone and others. Looking up at prosecutor Johnson through thick, horn-rimmed glasses that partially obscured his face, Ries detailed the accounting system used for ledgers showing the Pinkert State Bank deposits on behalf of the Capone brothers, Guzik and Nitti. Convicted of tax evasion and criminal conspiracy, the tight-lipped Guzik was sentenced to a five-year jail term.

Fred Ries, the greatest threat to Al Capone's freedom, was now a marked man. Chicago's Secret Six contributed $10,000 to help federal officials protect their star witness by sequestering him in

South America, under heavy security, while the crackdown continued.

From their cramped, windowless cubicle at the Federal Building, Wilson and two aides studied hundreds of thousands of papers, from bank records and faded old ledgers to handwritten notations and investigators' reports. Meanwhile, Al Capone returned to his retreat in Florida and sent back a settlement proposal to George Johnson and Frank Wilson. Capone promised to never again set foot in Chicago if the government would agree not to prosecute him for tax evasion or Prohibition violations.

Chief Judge John P. McGoorty was appalled: "Capone's most formidable competitors have been ruthlessly exterminated and his only obstacle towards undisputed sway is the law. Such a trade is unthinkable. The time has come when the public must choose between rule of the gangster and rule of the law."

Attorney Mattingly desperately wanted to avoid a full-scale trial, since a tax evasion conviction would mean almost certain jail time for his client. Perhaps in desperation, Mattingly committed a major tactical blunder, presenting the government with a document that would become the smoking gun prosecutors needed. It was a sworn affidavit from Al Capone estimating the crime boss's income at $66,000 for 1926-27, and $200,000 for 1928-29.

These were mere fractions of the true figures. Mattingly gambled that prosecutors would accept the guilty plea in return for Capone's agreement to pay a substantial fine and leave Chicago forever. What he had actually provided to the government was, in effect, a written admission of his client's guilt.

Capone was growing more irrational by the week. His bizarre behavior could probably be attributed to the effects that syphilis and substance abuse were having on his brain. The once-muscular Capone was a flabby 250 pounds and looked far beyond his years.

He suddenly rejected his lawyer's strategy and tried to resort to his old way of settling disputes. Capone hired five professional hitmen from New York and gave them orders to murder, Wilson, Johnson and Irey. Through information supplied by Mike Malone and at least one other undercover agent, the targets of this plot were forewarned of the plans. They summoned Mattingly and told him that they would hold both him and Capone personally responsible if there was any bloodshed.

Capone agreed to call off the assassination plot, only to fall back on another of his tried-and-true methods of persuasion. He offered Elmer Irey a $1,500,000 payoff if the IRS official could keep him out of jail. That proposition only strengthened Irey's resolve to put Capone behind bars for as long as the law would allow.

Chapter Twelve

Crumbling Empire

To divert attention from the tax evasion probe and gather additional evidence of Prohibition law violations against Capone, the Untouchables launched their most aggressive series of raids yet. The wall chart depicted delivery routes from the barrel-cleaning plant at Shields and 38th to breweries and speakeasies across the metropolitan area. The Montmartre wiretap also continued to provide a steady stream of information.

This stepped-up attack began at an abandoned factory on South Cicero Avenue. Ness took no chances that his force would be outmanned. All nine of the Untouchables were summoned to a strategy session. According to the plan, Chapman would blast the truck through the front door while Ness rode in the passenger's seat. Lahart was to ride on the back of the truck and step off just before impact so he could cover the hole in the door. They planned the attack for five o'clock the following morning.

At 4:47, Chapman turned the truck onto the cobbled surface of South Cicero Avenue. He stopped about forty yards from the double doors in the front so the men could quickly scan the area to determine if anyone had detected their presence. A squad car slipped behind the truck. Robsky, Friel and Gardner stepped out and unhooked an extension ladder from the side of the truck, sliding it up against the side of the building so they could climb to the roof.

Chapman gunned the engine while Ness tightened his grip on the revolver he extended out the window. "Hit it!" he commanded. The truck charged forward, slamming hard into the brewery with a ripping, rending crash and the shrill scream of tortured metal. The reinforced bumper scattered wood in every direction and the steel inner doors were no match for the truck.

CRUMBLING EMPIRE • 93

A separate wooden wall had been erected about 30 feet inside the warehouse.

"Hit it again!" Ness ordered, pointing to the wall. Chapman fired the gearshift into reverse, backed up, and plowed forward, collapsing the wall into a pile of splinters and dust. Ness counted five paralyzed, wide-eyed brewery workers as he leapt from the truck.

"Don't anybody move!" he shouted. "This is a federal raid."

King, Leeson and Cloonan arrived from the other end of the building, having chopped their way through the back doors. In his collaboration with Fraley, Ness reported that a mobster reached for his shoulder holster but thought better of it after Ness fired a warning shot over his head. Ness also wrote that one of the workers darted toward the back door and was tackled by Chapman before he could escape.

Interestingly, the Robsky/Fraley description of the same raid contradicted the account from *The Untouchables*. In his book, Robsky claimed he shot one hoodlum with a .38 and the victim plunged into a vat, his body landing face down in the beer. Newspaper reports telling of the raid did not mention these events.

Reporters' accounts did confirm that among the five men taken into custody was Steve Svoboda, reputed to be one of Capone's top brewmasters, and Frank Conta, a prominent member of Capone's hierarchy. The other three men were truck drivers.

The suspects were handcuffed and loaded into squad cars for booking, while Ness and Seager remained at the scene to inventory the equipment. They tore apart seven vats, each with a 320-gallon capacity, and seized three new trucks.

Less than two weeks passed before the Untouchables' next move, a poorly-documented raid on a smaller brewery and warehouse on Chicago's South Side. Four trucks were confiscated, along with alcohol supplies and equipment valued at approximately $200,000.

Next on the hit list was a brewery at 3136 South Wabash Avenue, operating under the guise of "The Old Reliable Trucking Company." Every day at dusk, a Cadillac occupied by two men pulled into the corner of an adjacent lot. The occupants, armed with what appeared to be tommy guns, never left their posts.

Trucks came and went at the brewery from seven o'clock in the evening to about three o'clock in the morning, after which a half-dozen men departed on foot.

Once Ness became familiar with the routine, he ordered a raid for the early morning hours of April 11, 1931. This time, as the truck's heavy bumper crashed through the double doors, it triggered an earsplitting clang of alarm bells. Ness whirled around in time to spot the black car with Capone's guards speeding past the brewery and out of sight. Anticipating that reinforcements were on the way, he knew his team had to move fast.

The truck barreled over the wreckage into a second set of doors, which fell with a loud thud. The brewery was in full operation. Three men scampered toward a dark hallway leading to the rear of the building, but Robsky and Friel were there to greet them at gunpoint. Two others who were tending to a huge vat raised their hands and surrendered without a struggle. As Ness stepped forward to handcuff the duo, he was shocked to discover that one of them was Steve Svoboda, the brewmaster, who had recently been freed on $5,000 bail.

"This is getting to be a habit," Ness laughed, pushing Svoboda hard up against a vat and frisking him. "Aren't you ever going to learn?"

"You bastards are gonna pay," Svoboda snarled. "You're out of your league, Ness. These guys will cut your nuts off, I guarantee it."

Among items seized or destroyed were fourteen brewing tanks, each with a 2,500-gallon capacity, along with five cooling tanks, modern electric pumps and a huge air compressor. Newspaper photographers captured Ness and Robsky thrusting axes into barrel after barrel of market-ready beer, pausing to watch the golden fluid cascade down the large drains in the middle of the floor. Ness filled several small vials with samples and then directed Robsky to open the valves on each fermenting tank. Thousands of gallons gushed out onto the floor, forming a pool that overwhelmed the drains with a thick foam.

Breweries were not the only targets of Ness's latest offensive. His Untouchables brazenly launched a series of raids on Capone's better-known speakeasies. Leading this attack was Al "Wallpaper" Wolff, who shared his experiences sixty years later during an interview on National Public Radio:

"I would go to a cabaret or a high-class tavern and carry a little tube. I'd put the whiskey in and have it analyzed by a chemist. Then we'd get a warrant, go in and arrest them, call the trucks and move 'em out. We'd move everything but the wallpaper. That's why they gave me the nickname Wallpaper Wolff. Capone himself came up with that one. He said I did a real clean job of takin' everything that wasn't attached."

Wolff was a master undercover agent who would sometimes knock off four or five speakeasies in a day. He spoke Yiddish, German and Polish. Blending into crowds as either a businessman or a truck driver, he would follow sugar trucks from the Jewish enclave of Maxwell Street to the brewing plants and stills Ness would later target for raids. Wolff's identity was kept confidential from most of the other members, who assumed he was a city detective.

"I always worked alone," Wolff said. "I seldom came into the office at the Transportation Building. I called Ness when it was time to go in and make a raid." Sometimes, Wolff said, the patrons were as upset as the owners of the speakeasies targeted for raids. "People were hissing us because, you know, the Germans didn't like to lose their beer. But we had orders to dry Capone out."

Wolff said the raids, wiretaps and threats had an obvious impact on Eliot Ness. "We were all tough guys and Eliot was young like me. He became a tough guy, too, but a tough guy with class. He was naive when he started, but he learned. He got a little rougher when it got more dangerous. I wasn't buddy-buddy with him, but I wasn't buddy-buddy with anybody. I was just doing my job."

One of the transcripts from the Montmartre wiretap revealed a conversation between Ralph Capone, who was still free pending his appeal, and a mobster identified only as "Fusco." They were plotting the reopening of the South Wabash Avenue brewery that Ness's team had raided just a few weeks earlier.

Ness waited only a week to move in. Details of the raid are sketchy, but newspaper accounts report that the agents blasted their truck through the reconstructed doors, taking six men into custody. Among the suspects was brewmaster Bert Delaney, who was out on bail after being nabbed in an earlier raid. Equipment and beer supplies worth an estimated $100,000 were destroyed or taken for evidence.

Al Capone's response to all of this sudden activity by Ness and his men was predictable. Through a middle man, Capone made a large cash payment up-front to Michael Picchi, a notorious hitman brought in from St. Louis for the sole purpose of killing Eliot Ness.

Picchi, a stringy, gaunt-cheeked veteran of the gang wars, was a stereotypical gangster, complete with cobra eyes and slicked-down hair. From a personal perspective, news of Picchi's imminent arrival was the most important information that came to Ness through the wiretap at the Montmartre Cafe. It probably saved his life. By the time Picchi pulled into town, Ness had already taken precautions to protect himself and Edna. He insisted that Edna move into a room at a large downtown hotel and assigned a round-the-clock guard detail outside his wife's room.

Ness also obtained a mugshot of the St. Louis hired gun and secretly distributed copies to those officers he knew to be reliable, asking them to be on the lookout. They were directed to arrest Michael Picchi on the spot, even if it meant fabricating a criminal charge.

"I was surprised that I didn't feel too perturbed about learning that I was marked for gangland execution," Ness wrote in *The Untouchables.* "Probably underneath I had been expecting just that for a long time."

He went on to present the following account of his one and only confrontation with Picchi. Ness was riding in the passenger's seat of a car being driven by Marty Lahart on Chicago's South Side when Lahart caught sight of a suspicious driver behind them.

"We're being tailed—I can tell," Lahart said, continuing to glance at the mirror. "That might be our boy. You better get down."

Ness slumped in his seat and slowly turned to his left to catch a glimpse of the driver. He could barely make out the silhouetted figure in a fedora, partially blocking the sunlight pouring through the car's back window. Lahart made a series of turns and the driver followed, closing the gap between the two cars. "You better get down and hold on," he cautioned Ness.

Lahart turned onto a side street in a residential section and followed it to an intersection, where he suddenly made a screeching U-turn. He steered the Cadillac straight in the direction of the other car and forced it up onto a sidewalk, then crashed into its rear bumper, jarring the driver forward.

The two agents jumped out, guns drawn. "Freeze, or you're a dead man!" Ness shouted. The instant he saw the driver's face, he knew it was Michael Picchi. Reaching under Picchi's overcoat, Ness removed a revolver from its holster. The weapon turned out to be a "killer's gun," complete with a scratched-off serial number and a chamber full of dumdum bullets. The agents loaded Picchi into their car and drove him to Kensington Police Station, where he was jailed on a charge of attempting to assault two federal officers.

Ness's next stop was his hotel room, where he found Edna pacing the floor, beside herself with worry. She tried to persuade Eliot to resign from the Prohibition Bureau and find a more secure career, but he was determined to complete the mission, as he saw it, of bringing Al Capone to justice.

Eliot did agree to move back into the couple's apartment, after he arranged to have a second officer added to the 24-hour guard detail. Edna still felt like a prisoner in her own home, keeping the shades pulled down day and night and never knowing when, or if, her husband would return.

CHAPTER THIRTEEN

Marked Man

Paul Robsky was all smiles as he burst into Eliot Ness's office, plopping a bulging stack of file folders on the desk. "Check this one out," he said, sliding a sheet across the desk to Ness. It detailed a conversation between a Cicero speakeasy owner and Jack Guzik, who was jail-bound following the denial of his appeal. The bar owner demanded a shipment of liquor and threatened to turn to other sources if Capone could not deliver. Guzik lamented the organization's depleted supply and pleaded for patience.

Another transcript covered the dialogue between Guzik and one of Capone's street thugs, who demanded more money for bribing a couple of police officers.

"Listen, Hymie," Guzik told him. "Tell the boys they'll have to take a pass this month."

"They ain't gonna like it."

"Too bad, but we just ain't makin' the dough. And if we ain't got it, we can't pay it." Guzik assured the caller these problems were temporary.

On February 24, 1931, Al Capone was ordered to appear before Federal Judge James J. Wilkerson on a charge of contempt of court, stemming from his failure to answer a federal grand jury subpoena two years earlier, shortly after the Saint Valentine's Day Massacre. Wilkerson, a handsome man in his early fifties, was openly appalled by the corruption that had swept through Chicago and was determined to teach Capone a lesson. Adding to the intrigue was the likelihood that Capone, if he were indicted for income tax evasion or Prohibition violations, would be tried in Judge Wilkerson's courtroom.

Spies who tracked Capone's activities in Florida contradicted the defendant's claim that he had been too ill to appear in court.

The judge found Capone guilty and sentenced him to a six-month term in the Cook County Jail. However, he was allowed to remain free on bail, pending an appeal.

George E. Q. Johnson was thrilled. He and the other prosecutors believed they had finally found a no-nonsense jurist who was capable of handling Capone without fear of retribution.

As aggressive as Eliot Ness and his Untouchables had grown in recent months, nothing could match the brazenness—some would say foolishness—of their next act. The idea was hatched when Ness learned that the trucks and other vehicles seized during raids of Capone's breweries and warehouses were headed for the auction block. Ness gleefully made plans for one of the most bizarre public displays downtown Chicago had ever seen.

He summoned the Capone Squad to a federal government warehouse to help wash and wax each of the vehicles. Early the next morning, he telephoned the Lexington Hotel, talked his way through a desk clerk, and spoke directly to Al Capone.

"Whad'ya want?" Capone grumbled.

"Well, Mr. Capone, I just wanted to tell you that, if you look out your front windows down on Michigan Avenue at exactly eleven o'clock, you'll see something that will interest you."

Ness hung up before Capone could respond. At the designated time, Ness and his team, joined by about three dozen recruits from the Prohibition Bureau, arrived at the garage and took their positions aboard the shiny trucks. They fell in behind a police escort and formed a line that covered three city blocks. With sirens wailing and lights flashing, the caravan lumbered forward on Michigan Avenue.

Forty-five vehicles seized in Prohibition Bureau raids paraded steadily toward the Lexington. Ness rode in the lead car, armed with a sawed-off shotgun, more for show than security.

Capone, appearing with bodyguards at an upstairs window, flew into a violent rage when he realized what was happening. An eyewitness reported that Capone lifted two chairs and smashed them over a table, screaming, "I'll kill 'im! I'll kill 'im with my own bare hands." Ness, in his memoirs, called the parade "a brilliant psychological counterstroke."

Two nights later, he and Edna were relaxing at their apartment, listening to opera on their phonograph, a cat sleeping on Eliot's lap, when the phone rang. The raspy voice at the other end warned Ness that his days were numbered. "You won't know when, and you won't know where," said the caller. "The next time I see you will be at your funeral."

In *The Untouchables*, Ness said he took several steps to tighten security. He spent most nights in hotels, rather than drive home and expose Edna to any danger. He also changed the routes he used to report to the Transportation Building, and he arranged to have a car with two agents follow him whenever he was on the road.

Ness claimed in his book that three attempts on his life followed in quick succession after the telephone warning. In the first, as Ness told it, he barely escaped a hail of bullets from a passing car:

"I hardly noticed the parked car facing in the opposite direction. But as I approached to within a few yards, there was a bright flash from the front window and I ducked instinctively as my windshield splintered in tune with the bark of the revolver. Without thinking, I jammed the accelerator to the floor. As my car leaped forward, there was another flash, and the window on my left rear door was smashed by another slug. Only the uncertain lighting and my sudden acceleration had saved me. I drove back into the city with my gun on my lap."

Next, Ness wrote, he was almost run down by a speeding automobile that veered toward him as he and Lahart crossed an intersection outside his office. Just days later, according to the Ness/Fraley account, he noticed something amiss with the hood of his car as he balanced his briefcase on the fender.

"Very cautiously, I raised the hood," he wrote. "Attached to the wiring system just under the thin panel separating the driver's seat from the motor was a dynamite bomb. I carefully lowered the hood and called the police. 'If you had touched that starter,' said the Police Department explosives expert as he gingerly removed the bomb from the car, 'you'd have been blown to kingdom come'. I was severely shaken, and sat for a long time in my car, trembling."

Historians and other researchers are split on whether any of these episodes actually occurred. However, there is at least a grain of truth in the reports. Mike Graham, a Chicago journalist who studied the "Roaring Twenties," found ample evidence that Capone really did want to have Ness executed. The assassination would have been carried out, if not for the better judgment of his associates.

"People with cooler heads—lieutenants in the organization—recognized that Capone was a marked man," Graham told a National Public Radio interviewer. "He really represented the old order of doing things. The garishness, the glamor and the violence were things that were going to have to be eliminated if the others were going to continue on when Capone went to jail."

Growing desperate, Capone moved to consolidate his criminal enterprises and prepare for the expected legalization of alcoholic beverages. He positioned his syndicate to gain a monopoly on the bottling of soda water and ginger ale as a source of post-Prohibition income.

As the summer of 1931 arrived, Eliot Ness turned his attention to paperwork. He and Chapman had filled three file cabinets with documents and were ordered by the prosecution team to reduce the material to the essentials for a grand jury. They relocated some of the more significant evidence to safety deposit boxes in a Chicago bank.

Finally, after more than two years of investigation, the Federal Government was prepared to move forward in its prosecution of Al Capone on two fronts. In early June, Frank Wilson and his Treasury Department colleagues presented only a small portion of their evidence and a grand jury quickly responded with a 22-count income tax evasion indictment of Capone.

"Capone's Days Are Numbered," heralded one Chicago newspaper.

A week later, Eliot Ness carried two briefcases with summaries of his evidence into the Federal Building. He took a seat in the corner of the building's impressive lobby and leaned back to collect his thoughts. Ness stared up at the high ceiling, which echoed with the dull roar of the business below, and tried to envision his appearance on the witness stand. Beads of perspiration formed on his brow and his heart began to pound in nervous anticipation. His mind was racing as he leafed through the documents in his briefcases and lit a cigarette. The minutes seemed to pass like hours. After only a few puffs, he snuffed out the cigarette, gathered his evidence, and proceeded upstairs to the courtroom.

For the first time in his life, Eliot Ness was center stage as he made his case against Al Capone. Ness read from lists of confiscated equipment and from transcripts prepared during the trials of Ralph Capone and Jack Guzik. Jurors also heard laboratory reports on the contents of beer and other illicit beverages seized during raids of Capone's facilities.

The sheer volume of evidence presented during Ness's three-hour stint on the witness stand was staggering, supporting more than 5,000 offenses by Capone and his allies. Based primarily on the Untouchables' work, the grand jury brought an indictment against Al Capone and sixty-eight members of his mob for conspiracy to violate the Volstead Act.

The New York Times, in its page one headlines, hailed Ness as a hero: "Faced Many Perils in Capone Roundup. Squad of Seven Young Dry Agents Credited With Successful Drive on Chicago Gangster. Leader Only 28 Years Old; Impervious to Threats of Death or Bribes. They Have Been Styled 'The Untouchables'."

"What of the offers of bribes and the threats of death that came the way of Eliot Ness and his youthful assistants?" the accompanying story read. "Ness is reluctant to talk about them. He calls them side incidents in the larger task of doing a job and doing it well."

Capone and his lawyers tried again to strike a deal with George E. Q. Johnson. He would plead guilty to a portion of the tax evasion and Prohibition charges, if Johnson would recommend a sentence of no more than two and one-half years.

Privately, the United States Attorney was thrilled with the offer. Not only would the plea represent a measure of success after many months of frustration, it would also immediately put the volatile Capone behind bars. Johnson also recognized that the longer Capone's lawyers postponed their client's trial, the greater chance that hired guns could remove some of the government's key witnesses. In addition, Johnson and others knew the United States Supreme Court was poised to revise its statute of limitations. If a new statute took effect, much of the government's tax evasion case against Capone would crumble.

As the prosecution team prepared to work out the details of the plea agreement, Eliot Ness and the Untouchables went back to work. With Capone about to fall, other criminal organizations were maneuvering to cash in on the multimillion dollar bootlegging business. These rivals were naturally eager to share with Ness any information they had on the location of Capone's production and distribution facilities, and Ness was pleased to oblige.

An anonymous telephone call to Ness told of a large brewery located in an abandoned garage at 1712 North Kilbourn Avenue on Chicago's North Side. Surveillance by two agents confirmed the report. Ness's team took the brewery without resistance, crashing through the front doors after posting agents at each exit. Less than a week later, based on information gathered by Leeson and Seager, the team blasted into another Capone brewery at 2024 South State Street. These two raids resulted in eleven arrests and the destruction or confiscation of equipment and supplies valued at close to $300,000.

Agent Marty Lahart orchestrated one of the most daring raids, which took place at a massive beer distribution center at 222 East 25th Street. Ness and Lahart donned dirty work suits and drove a beat-up Ford to the East Side. They positioned the car partly in the road and opened the hood. When Lahart spotted one of Capone's delivery trucks approaching, he bravely stepped out in the road, forcing the driver to stop.

"Can you give us a hand?" he yelled through the driver's side window.

"Go to hell!" the driver responded, stomping on the accelerator. As the truck started to pull away, Ness and Lahart slipped behind it, grabbed the tailgate and hoisted themselves up and over. They retrieved .45s from under their work suits and crouched down low to avoid detection. Ness pulled a tarp over the two agents to conceal them as they huddled between two rows of beer barrels.

A quick toot of the horn brought open the warehouse doors and the truck eased inside. As the workers milled around a makeshift lunchroom, Ness and Lahart quietly slipped over the tailgate, raised their guns and walked slowly toward the table. Not until the agents were about 20 feet away did anyone notice their presence.

"What the hell are you... ," one of them declared, stopping in mid-sentence as he realized what was happening.

"Federal raid, boys," Ness shot back. "Just stay where you are. You guys ought to be used to this by now."

Lahart walked backwards toward the double doors, his revolver still trained on the four mobsters, and released the latch. Robsky, Leeson, Cloonan and Friel charged through, guns in hand.

"Relax, fellas," Lahart assured them. "These guys are sitting ducks."

Inside the warehouse was a Prohibition agent's dream— a virtual treasure of moonshine, including dozens of cases of premium Canadian whiskey ready for shipment; 300 barrels of beer; 56 cases of bottled beer; and a wide assortment of notebooks and ledgers documenting delivery routes and payments. Soon, a half-dozen newspaper reporters and photographers were on the scene. Robsky lifted one of the whiskey bottles to pose for the photographers, the bright warehouse lights highlighting the deep amber liquid.

An anonymous phone call in the wake of that raid helped Ness put the final pieces in a puzzle he had been trying to solve for months. The Montmartre telephone conversations continually referred to liquor supplies coming from "Joyce." Ness assumed it was a code name for a Canadian whiskey runner, until the tipster directed agents to a six-story building on Chicago's Diversey Avenue. A legitimate business, the Joyce Company, occupied the first few floors. On the top two stories were the headquarters of a mysterious enterprise known as Sennett Paint Company.

Ness and Lahart visited the building one night, climbing a narrow, rusty fire escape that creaked and shook with every step. When they finally reached the fifth floor, they peered through the

Eliot Ness joins the Prohibition Bureau in Chicago, anxious to make a name for himself.

Eliot Ness's "get-tough" approach was evident from this expression on his official Prohibition Bureau badge.

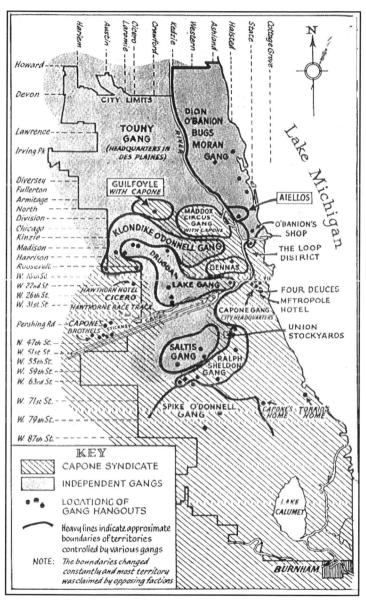

This map reflects the temporary balance of power in Chicago in the mid-1920s.

Alphonse Capone: "Public Enemy Number One."

Eliot Ness (right) didn't want to be deskbound.

William Hale "Big Bill" Thompson was Mayor of Chicago for nearly eight of the Prohibition years.

Some victims of the "Saint Valentine's Day Massacre."

One of the few photos of Eliot Ness (in driver's seat) and some of his "Untouchables." Seated behind Ness is Al "Wallpaper" Wolff.

(Chicago Historical Society)

(Wide World Photos)

Above: Albert Anselmi and John Scalise, Capone assassins who fell victim to his wrath.

Left: Jack "Greasy Thumb" Guzik kept detailed records as business manager of Al Capone's criminal organization.

Frank J. Wilson, known for his gritty determination and thoroughness, was brought in to help bolster the Treasury Department attack on Al Capone's organization.

Frankie Yale began as Capone's mentor, became his partner, but later fell victim to Chicago's most powerful crime boss.

(Chicago Historical Society)

Johnny Torrio, Al Capone's first and most important teacher

U.S. Federal Judge James H. Wilkerson had a secret plan to counter Al Capone's jury tamperimg efforts.

Above: Lawyers Michael Ahern (left) and Albert Fink (right) didn't have much chance to keep Capone out of jail after a plea bargain arrangement fell through.

Left: Elmer Irey labored in near anonymity as head of the Internal Revenue Service's Intelligence Unit. Irey, George E. Q. Johnson and Frank Wilson were the unsung heroes of the government's attack on Al Capone.

"Machine Gun Jack" McCurn was Capone's top triggerman for several years.

Eliot Ness grew more assertive and self-assured as his Prohibition Bureau service continued.

After Al Capone was convicted of tax evasion and Prohibition was repealed, Eliot Ness was dispatched to the "Moonshine Mountains" to enforce federal alcohol tax laws and confiscate homemade stills.

Ness (back seat, right) rides in a "touring car" on the grounds of the Great Lakes Exposition (1936).

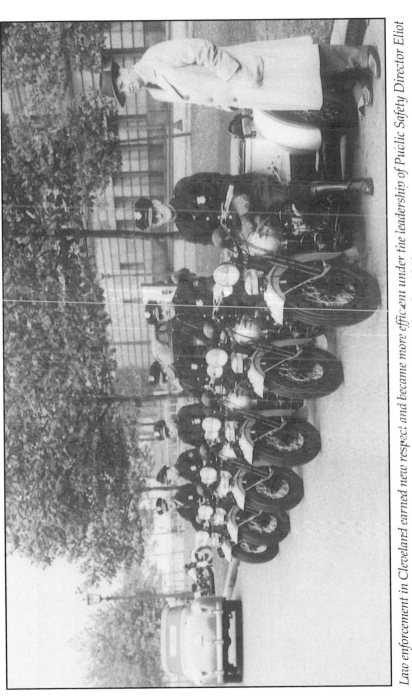

Law enforcement in Cleveland earned new respect and became more efficient under the leadership of Public Safety Director Eliot Ness, shown here with the Police Department's Motorcycle Unit in October 1940.

As a business major at University of Chicago, Ness never could have imagined that he would be called upon to investigate the serial killings of a Cleveland madman. Examples of the "death masks" Ness had produced in an attempt to identify victims of the Mad Butcher are shown in this display at the Cleveland Police Historical Museum.

(University of Chicago)

(Rebecca McFarland)

Eliot and Edna Ness's first home, located in Bay Village, offered solitude and a beautiful view.

Left: Elisabeth "Betty" Ness and her husband Eliot pause before casting their ballots in the 1947 Cleveland mayoral election. Democratic incumbent Thomas A. Burke defeated Eliot Ness, the Republican nominee, by a margin of almost two-to-one.

(Cleveland Plain Dealer)

(FBI Photo)

Federal Bureau of Investigation agents pose outside of Eliot Ness's former home in Lakewood, Ohio, on the shore of Lake Erie.

Evaline Ness drew this sketch of her husband in 1938 as he sipped a glass of scotch whiskey and read a newspaper. After her divorce from Eliot, Evaline became a prominent illustrator of children's books.

These posters appeared all over Cleveland in 1947, paid for by the Ness-for-Mayor Committee. Ness also sank much of his own money into the ill-fated mayoral campaign.

Eliot Ness's service revolver, a five-inch Smith and Wesson, was rarely-if ever-fired while he was on duty.

Dan Moore, one of Eliot Ness's closest friends and a former business partner, shown in his Cleveland Heights, Ohio, home in 1995.

Many investors anticipated big things with the Guaranty Paper Corporation, a subsidiary of North Ridge Industrial Corporation. Eliot Ness signed each stock certificate.

With great fanfare, Mrs. Anne Wells (left), wife of Judge Walter P. Wells, activated the press for production of checks at the North Ridge Industrial Corporation facility in Coudersport, Pennsylvania. Company founder G. Frank Shampanore is shown at far right (in foreground, wearing apron).

The products of Fidelity Check Corp. and its sister company, Guaranty Paper Company, held great promise. Many community leaders in Coudersport, Pennsylvania, eagerly supported the ventures as a business investment and an economic development project. However, production problems and mismanagement spelled the end of these businesses in 1957.

A talented sculptor, Elisabeth "Betty" Ness provided her husband with love, companionship and encouragement during several years of financial difficulties and personal setbacks.

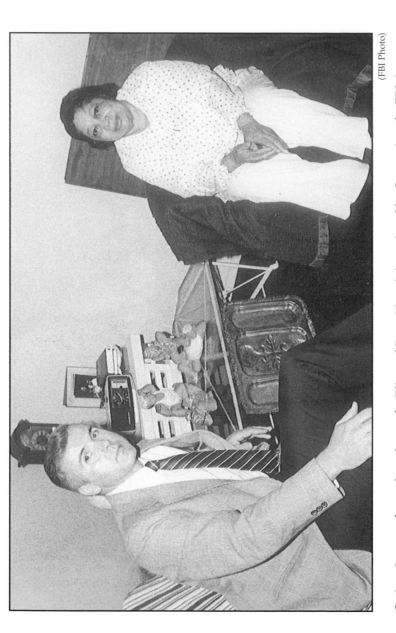

Corinne Lawson, former housekeeper for Eliot and Betty Ness, is interviewed by George Arruda, FBI Agent, at her home in Cleveland. The items on the table were given to Lawson by Betty Ness, who stayed at Lawson's home for several months after Eliot Ness died in 1957.

Above: Lewis Wilkinson is among dozens of people who hold onto stock certificates from North Ridge Industrial Corporation. Wilkinson said Eliot Ness admitted to him that certain sections of the book "The Untouchables" were dramatized to make it more commercially appealing.

Right: Fred Anderson was skeptical when Ness told stories of his days as a Prohibition agent in Chicago

The "Old Hickory Tavern" in Coundersport, Pennsylvania, where Eliot Ness spent many hours during the final 18 months of his life.

(B. Mark Schmerling)

William Ayers took what little was left of Guaranty Paper Company and formed T-C Specialties, which continues to thrive today.

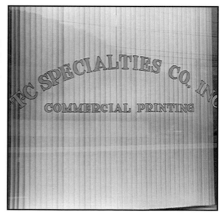

(B. Mark Schmerling)

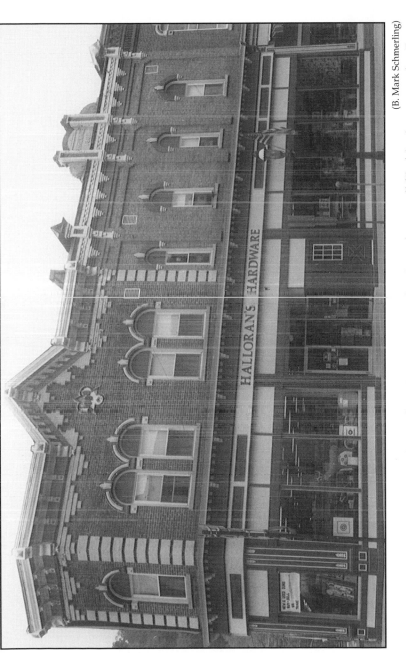

Eliot Ness enjoyed the small-town charm of Coudersport, Pennsylvania, and was well-liked in the community. For a time, his business office was located above what is now Halloran's Hardware.

Michael Husain (left), a producer for the Arts and Entertainment Television Network's "Biography" series, meets with Eliot Ness's physician, Dr. George C. Mosch (center), and Paul W. Heimel, author of <u>Eliot Ness: The real storey.</u>

Joe Phelps was described as "hale and hearty, extroverted, a natural salesman." Seated on their grandfather's lap are Wanda Bailey (left) and Julie Bailey.

Eliot, Betty and Bobby Ness lived on the first floor of this home in Coudersport, Pennsylvania, On May 16, 1957, Eliot was in distress as he entered the residence. He made his way to the kitchen, turned the water faucet, reached for a glass and collapsed. His death was attributed to a heart attack.

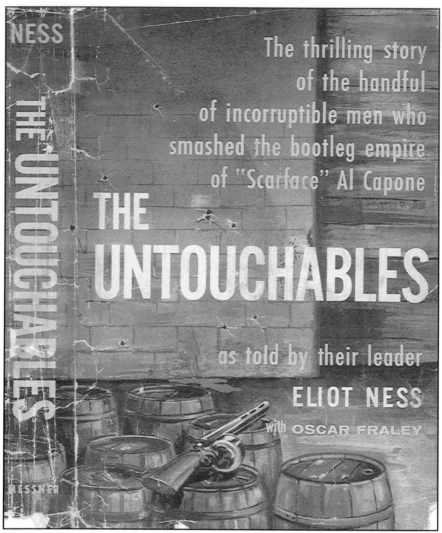

This book by Eliot Ness and Oscar Fraley was not a big seller, but it did help create the "myth" of Ness and the Untouchables.

Robert Stack portrayed Eliot Ness in the popular television series, "The Untouchables" as well as two made-for-TV movies based on the Ness character.

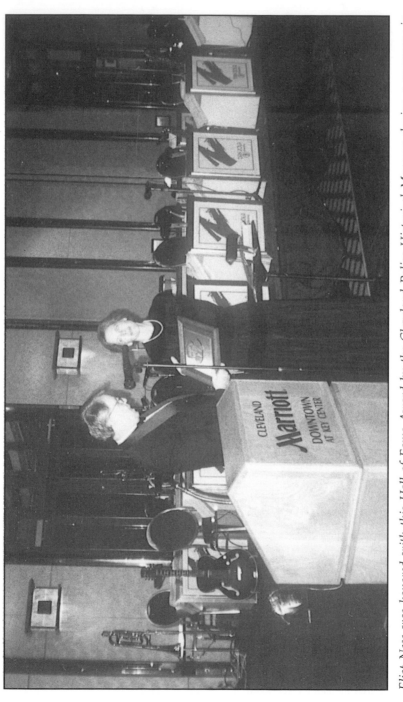

Eliot Ness was honored with this Hall of Fame Award by the Cleveland Police Historical Museum during a ceremony in November 1996. Rebecca McFarland, representing the Board Of Trustees, presented the award to Cleveland's current Public Safety Director, William Denihan.

window to discover a still so massive that a wide hole had been cut into the ceiling to accommodate it.

Ness returned to the Joyce Company the next day, posing as a real estate speculator interested in buying the building. The owners said they did not want to sell, especially now that the Sennett Paint Company had moved in and begun making generous rent payments, always early and always in cash.

Large freight elevators serviced each floor, but Ness feared the arrival of the elevator car would alert Capone's men that something was amiss. That night, just before midnight, Ness and Lahart crept up the fire escape to the fifth floor and smashed through a window. They aimed their guns at two startled workers who sat at a table in the corner of the huge room. One of them was Nick Juffra, alias Frankie Rose, one of Capone's leading henchmen.

The still was capable of producing 20,000 gallons of alcohol per day. Bottles and other supplies moved in and out under the cover of wooden crates marked with a Sennett Paint Company logo. A new machine seized as part of the raid was being used to imprint a diamond-shaped outline bearing a number on each crate. Speakeasy owners who were "obligated" to buy their stock from Capone used the numbering system to verify the source of each shipment.

The days of Capone's men boldly driving their big beer trucks down city streets in broad daylight were over, due in large part to the Untouchables' dogged efforts. Instead, the organization resorted to hauling its beer three or four barrels at a time in passenger cars. Larger shipments were made under the guise of ice delivery trucks.

Eliot Ness's star continued to rise. With Capone's bootlegging business in shambles, Ness saw his salary increase to $3,800. His job descriptions from that era are deceptive, incomplete and, in some cases, contradictory. One of the documents in federal archives recorded Ness's latest designation as "Assistant Special Agent in charge of Illinois, Iowa, Wisconsin, Minnesota, North Dakota and South Dakota," reporting to the United States Attorney General's Office. Ness saw the new title as a promotion—

another step in his life's goal of becoming a Federal Bureau of Investigation agent.

An increasing amount of moonshine was smuggled in from outside the city. Obsessed with drying up the Midwest, and anxious to demonstrate that he was equal to his new responsibilities, Ness sent his men out to intercept these shipments. They were also dispatched to remote areas beyond Cook County to track down Capone's suppliers.

Covering all bases, the Untouchables started watching rail stations and confiscating shipments of corn sugar. At times, they would allow the sugar to be loaded and then follow the trucks to their destinations—often isolated farmhouses where stills had been set up to produce corn whiskey.

On one occasion, agents arrested all three members of a small town police force for operating a still in a shed behind the police station. Perhaps it was a sign of the times that the community's outrage was directed not at the police chief, but at Eliot Ness and his Untouchables.

CHAPTER FOURTEEN

Federal Convict No. 40886

Skies were sunny in Chicago on June 16, 1931, as Al Capone, dressed in a bright yellow suit, appeared at the Federal Building. A fat cigar drooped from the corner of his mouth, dangling below the heavy makeup that covered his facial scar. Reporters shouted questions that Capone ignored as three bodyguards and a pair of uniformed officers cleared a path for him. The entourage headed toward an elevator, just as a judge tried to enter it. "You can't use this, Bud," the elevator operator told him. "It's reserved for Mr. Capone."

In a brief court session that was little more than a formality, Capone entered his guilty plea and Johnson recommended the two and one-half year sentence that had been agreed to. Judge Wilkerson adjourned the hearing to study the facts before pronouncing sentence.

"Smug" is the way one journalist described Al Capone during a discussion with reporters in his Lexington Hotel suite that afternoon. Dressed in white-bordered silk pajamas and pacing around his parlor, Capone decried the distortions that Hollywood was giving American movie fans.

"You know, these gang pictures, that's terrible kid stuff," Capone said. "Why, they ought to take them all and throw them into the lake. They're doing nothing but harm to the younger element in this country. You remember dime novels, maybe, when you were a kid? Well, you know how it made you want to get out and kill pirates and look for buried treasure? Well, these gang movies are making a lot of kids want to be tough guys and they don't serve any useful purpose."

Capone declared himself a scapegoat. "I've been made an issue, and I'm not complaining, but why don't they go after all these bankers who took the savings of thousands of poor people and lost them in bank failures? How about that? Isn't it lots worse to take the last few dollars some small family has saved, perhaps to live on while the head of a family is out of a job, than to sell a little beer, a little alky? Believe me, I can't see where the fellow who sells it is any worse than the fellow who buys and drinks it."

One reporter asked Capone what would become of his gang during his absence.

"It's really a shame to disabuse the public—to destroy one of their myths—but honestly there is not, nor has there ever been, what might be called a Capone gang," he replied. Capone said Johnny Torrio would assume responsibility for his "business enterprises" while he was serving his sentence. He speculated that good behavior would reduce the term to far less than the anticipated two and one-half years.

On July 30, Judge James Herbert Wilkerson dropped a bombshell that echoed all across America. "The parties to a criminal case may not stipulate as to the judgment to be entered," he announced. "The court may not now say to the defendant that it will enter the judgment suggested by the prosecution. It is time for somebody to impress upon the defendant that it is utterly impossible to bargain with a federal court."

Capone's jaw, which had been busily working on a thick wad of chewing gum, dropped as he looked at his lawyers in confusion. After huddling with their client, they announced that Capone would withdraw his guilty plea and proceed to trial.

"Very well," Judge Wilkerson said. "The court calendar will be cleared for two weeks in October."

After the gavel sounded, Johnson turned to Ness, seated on a first bench behind the prosecution table, and motioned for him to join them.

"This changes everything, Eliot," Johnson said. "You better go back through your files and make sure you're really ready to go to trial on Volstead. Frankly, I didn't think we'd need the Volstead material at all, but now it looks like we might have to hit him with both barrels."

Capone tried to polish his image by opening another highly-publicized soup kitchen on South State Street. He pooh-poohed his recent court battles. "Oh, they're only trying to scare me," Capone declared. "They know very well there'd be hell in this city if they put me away. Who else can keep the small-time racketeers from annoying decent folks? This is going to be a terrible winter. Us fellas has gotta open our pocketbooks and keep them open if we want any of us to survive. We can't wait for Congress or Mr. Hoover or anyone else. We must keep tummies filled and bodies warm."

Behind the scenes, Capone's men were taking great pains to insure a positive outcome from the trial. They obtained a list of potential jurors and set about winning their favor through threats of violence and offers of cash, jobs and prizefight tickets. Informed of this serious breach in security, Judge Wilkerson appeared unconcerned.

On the morning of October 6, a motorcade of Chicago City Police squad cars brought Al Capone to the Federal Building for jury selection. He was a bloated figure, too big for his blue suit. A white handkerchief was neatly stuffed in his breast pocket. Crowding around the prosecution table with George Johnson were four Assistant United States Attorneys. Among the witnesses seated directly behind them was Eliot Ness, complete with a bulging leather briefcase.

The sixth floor courtroom of Judge Wilkerson abounded in patriotic and legal imagery, from its massive walls finished with white marble to the gilded scrolls near the ceiling. Electric bulbs in chandeliers and sconces burned throughout the courtroom. Some walls were devoted to large murals depicting the Founding Fathers, darkened by age. Behind the judge's bench, Benjamin Franklin addressed the Continental Congress, his right hand outstretched to George Washington.

About twenty newspaper reporters filled several rows in the front of the courtroom. Judge Wilkerson emerged from his chambers, his deep-set eyes and oval face expressionless as he took his seat on the extreme edge of a swivel chair. Wilkerson glanced at the tainted jurors, then summoned a court attendant.

"Judge Edwards has another trial commencing today," he announced. "Go to Judge Edwards' courtroom and bring me the entire panel of jurors. Take my entire panel to Judge Edwards."

Capone remained rigid in his chair, bleakly studying the decor and avoiding eye contact with everyone as his facial features clouded with fury. Moments later, a group consisting of small-town tradesmen, mechanics, a real estate manager and an insurance salesman filled the twelve seats in the jury box. The judge made it clear to them that Capone was being tried on charges of violating the income tax laws, and nothing else.

Assistant Prosecutor Dwight Green and George Johnson soon embarked on an evidence spree that left Capone and his lawyers speechless. Three witnesses confirmed Capone's involvement with the Hawthorne Smoke Shop. They were followed to the stand by a surprise witness, Leslie Shumway. A pole-thin, nervous man known to all as "Lou," Shumway had been tracked down in Florida by Frank Wilson, secretly interviewed and protected until the trial.

He told the court that profits from the shop during the two years he kept the books exceeded $550,000. Shumway also detailed the entries he made in thirty-four looseleaf notebooks documenting gambling activities. These ledgers, seized during the raid that followed Billy McSwiggin's murder, had been uncovered and catalogued by Wilson several months before the trial.

The prosecution also entered into evidence tax attorney Lawrence Mattingly's letter conceding Capone's taxable income. Parker Henderson, a Florida hotel manager, told jurors how he befriended Capone and fronted for him in the purchase of his Palm Island estate. Henderson testified that he also signed numerous Western Union transfers of $1,000 to $5,000 and turned the money over to Capone. A series of witnesses told of selling goods and services to Al Capone— everything from real estate and jewelry to fancy clothes and prime cuts of meat.

Wilkerson insisted that the trial move rapidly. One of the few interruptions was the removal of Capone crony Philip D'Andrea from the courtroom. D'Andrea, whose menacing look may have intimidated some witnesses, was found to be carrying a .38-caliber revolver.

Wilson still had to buttress Lou Shumway's testimony tying the Hawthorne Smoke Shop profits to Capone. For that, he turned to Fred Ries, who had been returned to Chicago from his South

American hideout. Without fidgeting or shuddering, as Shumway had done, Ries implicated Capone and his associates in financial dealings involving hundreds of thousands of dollars.

Capone's defense team was comprised of Michael Ahern, noticeably tall and elegant in his gray suit and tan shoes, and Albert Fink, a round-bellied, fat-faced tax law specialist who came out of retirement to take the case. They first claimed Capone's income was more than offset by heavy losses in other business enterprises and at the horse racetrack. "The numbers just don't add up," insisted Fink, his gold-rimmed glasses riding the tip of his pointed nose.

Johnson poked holes in that argument with citations of previous cases specifying that gambling losses can only be deducted from gambling winnings for tax purposes, and Capone's attorneys had already insisted their client hardly ever won.

Waving his arms high, Fink urged jurors to consider Capone's intent. Clearly, he argued, his client had demonstrated a willing ness to pay income taxes by signing the affidavit drawn up by Mattingly. Fink also told jurors that, if they believed Capone was a man of considerable wealth, they must also question whether he would be foolish enough to risk a prison term by failing to pay taxes.

"Don't let yourselves be drawn away from the truth by the claim that Al Capone is a bad man," Fink cautioned. "He may be the worst man who ever lived, but there is not a scintilla of evidence that he willfully attempted to defraud the government out of income tax."

He continued, "In Rome during the Punic Wars, there lived a senator named Cato. Cato passed upon the morals of the people. He decided what they would wear, what they should drink, and what they should think. Carthage fell twice, but Carthage grew again and was once more powerful. Cato concluded every speech he made in the Senate by thundering, 'Carthage must be destroyed!' These censors of ours, these persecutors, the newspapers, all say, 'Capone must be destroyed!' Be careful of taking liberty from this defendant. You are the last barrier between the defendant and the encroachment and perversion of government and the law."

The prosecution team chose George Johnson to cement the issue of Capone's guilt in jurors' minds. His wing-like coiffure flapping with the vehemence of his emotions, Johnson stressed the importance of tax laws to the welfare of the nation.

"Gentlemen, the United States government has no more important laws to enforce than the revenue laws. Thousands upon thousands of persons go to work daily and all of them who earn more than $1,500 a year must pay income tax. If a time ever came when it has to go out and force the collection of taxes, the Army and the Navy will disband, courts will be swept aside, civilization will revert back to the jungle days when every man was for himself. Who is this man who has become such a glamorous figure? Is he the little boy from the Second Reader who has found the pot of gold at the end of the rainbow that he can spend money so lavishly? He has been called Robin Hood by his counsel. Robin Hood took from the strong to feed the weak. Did this Robin Hood buy $8,000 worth of belt buckles for the unemployed? Was his $6,000 meat bill in a few weeks for the hungry? No, it went to the Capone home on Palm Island to feed the guests at the nightly poker party."

Capone cast despairing eyes around him, as if appealing to the audience. His usual smile was missing as he squirmed from his slumped position while the jurors left for their deliberations.

Wilson, Johnson, Green and Ness retired to Johnson's office to wait. Wilson assured Ness that the government would come right back at Capone with the Volstead evidence if the jury returned with an acquittal.

Capone paced in the corridor, forcing a smile now and then for the people who stared at him from behind a cordon of guards. After several hours, he returned to the Lexington, where he smoked cigars and continued walking the floors, staying close to the telephone.

Newspaper reporters entertained themselves by holding their own mock deliberations. About half of them thought Capone would be convicted. Inside the jury room, the polling was not nearly as close. Only one juror expressed any doubt about Capone's guilt. For eight hours, the dissenter held his ground before bowing to the majority.

Court officials summoned all of the important players just before midnight. Reporters scurried for their seats in the front rows. Johnson, Ness and the others hurried downstairs and pushed through the crowd to reach the courtroom. Ness took his customary seat in the first row behind the prosecution table. A soft murmur echoed around the courtroom.

At the Lexington, Al Capone never removed the cigar from his mouth as he answered the phone on the first ring. "Yeah?" he grunted, followed by a brief silence. "All right. How's it look?" More silence. "Let's get it over with."

Capone hung up the phone and snuffed out his cigar. Donning his overcoat and fedora, he led the entourage out to the limousine that would take him the three miles to the Federal Building. By the time Capone settled into his seat at the defense table, he was perspiring profusely. He cleared his throat and leaned forward, resting his elbows on the table, before Judge Wilkerson ordered him to stand. The clerk read the verdict:

- guilty on three counts of income tax evasion from 1925, 1926 and 1927;
- guilty of failing to file a tax return for 1928 and 1929.
- not guilty on assorted other charges.

The crowd erupted in spontaneous applause and reporters hurried for the nearest telephones. Capone looked at his lawyers, then at the floor, before he returned to his seat. His supporters sat motionless amid the revelry.

Attorney Fink sprang from his seat to announce that he would appeal. "You are certainly within your rights to do so," Judge Wilkerson responded. "In the meantime, I plan to spend the next five to seven days studying the record of these proceedings and reviewing case law before I render my sentence. Until that time, Mr. Capone, I will allow you to remain free on bond which has been posted, but I would also advise you not to leave the area." Capone nodded.

Outside the courtroom, Capone told friends he was not surprised by the verdict. He rationalized that it would be good to live in an environment where rival gangsters could not reach him, then emerge as a man who had "paid his debt to society."

Capone, dressed in a dark purple suit, accented by a white handkerchief, returned to the courtroom on October 24. Judge Wilkerson entered looking grimmer than usual. Capone approached the bench, locking his hands behind his back as he heard his fate:

"On Count One, the defendant shall go to the penitentiary for five years, pay a fine of $10,000, and pay all costs of prosecution."

Capone looked calmly at his lawyers, his fingers twisting and turning behind his back. The defense had expected the five-year sentence for one tax evasion count, with the other sentences to run concurrently. But Judge Wilkerson followed a different script. To the horror of Capone and his attorneys, the judge imposed a separate five-year sentence for the 1926 and 1927 violations, then tacked on another year for Capone's failure to file a tax return in 1929. The total sentence was eleven years in prison, plus a fine of $80,000.

All eyes in the courtroom fell on Capone. His tongue moved in his cheeks and his fingers, still locked behind his back, twitched and twisted. He looked helplessly at the defense table.

Fink stared incredulously at the judge. "Your honor," he said, "we request that our client remain free until such time as a timely appeal can be filed."

"Motion denied!" Judge Wilkerson snapped back. He ordered a United States Marshal to remove Capone to the Cook County Jail, where he would be held during the appeal process.

On his way out of the courtroom, Capone was approached by an Internal Revenue Service agent, who nervously announced that a tax lien had been placed on all property of Alphonse and Mae Capone. "Please do not attempt to transfer your assets, Mr. Capone, until we settle this tax matter first," the agent said in a near monotone. Capone muttered an obscenity and drew back his foot to kick the IRS man before he regained his composure. He slung his coat across his left arm and clamped his fedora down on his head.

"Get enough, boys," Capone said angrily, as newspaper photographers surrounded him on his way out of the Federal Building to a waiting police car. "You won't see me again for a long time."

Johnson, Wilson and Ness remained in the courtroom long after the crowd dispersed. They recognized that Capone had the money and political connections to fight the conviction and sentence on every imaginable front.

"You better hold onto everything you have, and keep it in a safe place," Johnson instructed Ness. "The more weapons we have against this guy, the better. Who knows if the conviction or the sentence will hold up? We're in uncharted waters, really."

"I'll guard it with my life," Ness assured him.

Reporters peppered Johnson with questions as the prosecutors filed out of the courtroom. He stopped long enough to express his faith in the criminal justice system and to express his appreciation to Judge Wilkerson and the jurors. Johnson said the battle against Capone could never have been won without the combined efforts of public crimefighters and private financiers. "It was a victory of an aroused public that demanded justice. I believe this is the beginning of the end of gangs as Chicago has known them for the last ten years."

Public reaction to the downfall of Capone was mixed. For every citizen who applauded the government for finally subduing Scarface there was another who thought that limiting the charges to tax evasion was a miscarriage of justice. Eliot Ness may have shared that sentiment, but he never said so publicly.

Of the verdict and sentence, the New York Times editorialized: "Chicago has been terrorized by its gangsters or rather that part of the population of the city which came closest to them has been. They seemed invincible. It has probably made the career of the gangster somewhat less alluring. In that fact, and in the realization that gang rule cannot exist without the connivance or tolerance of great numbers of people who consider themselves law-abiding, may lie Chicago's hopes."

Even as a convicted felon, Capone exerted his influence at the Cook County Jail. He was placed in a private cell, from which he could place telephone calls and send telegraphs to lawyers, bookies, organizational contacts, and well-placed city officials. One of Capone's closest friends from outside the world of organized crime, Doc Kearns, paid him a call.

"What are you going to do?" Kearns asked, eying a photo of 13-year-old Sonny Capone on a bedside dresser.

"I got no idea," Capone said with a frown. "I guess it ain't too stiff of a rap. The organization should sort of hold together until I get back. 'Course, you never know what a difference a few years can make and there's no tellin' how things might be, one way or another, when I finally get out. Hell, the booze racket's about shot to hell right now."

In a popular newsreel making the rounds of U.S. theaters, the gruff-voiced announcer reported, "His white hat will probably be out of style when he gets to wear it again," as moviegoers viewed black and white footage of Capone's exit from the Federal Building.

Eliot Ness and his colleagues made one final sweep of the bootlegging rackets. They rounded up over a dozen other Chicago mobsters, at least some of whom were affiliated with Capone. Among them was George Howlett, known in gangland as Capone's "society lieutenant," who had been wanted by the government for failing to pay more than $50,000 in income taxes.

The United States District Court of Appeals denied Capone's bid for a new trial on February 27, 1932. Two months later, the Supreme Court refused to review the decision. Out of options, Capone was ordered to begin serving his sentence in the federal penitentiary at Atlanta.

Largely as a symbolic gesture to lessen the sting of Prohibition violations never coming to trial, Johnson designated Eliot Ness and his Untouchables to escort Capone to Dearborn Station. There, he was to be handed over the federal marshals manning the Dixie Flyer for the long ride to Atlanta.

At the Cook County Jail, Capone bade farewell to Mae and Sonny and other family members. He and another prisoner, a car thief named Vito Morici, were led out into the jail's courtyard, where photographers were waiting.

At the end of the sidewalk leading through the courtyard to the prison gates, Capone for the first time came face-to-face with the man who helped reduce his once-lucrative bootlegging business to shambles. He paused as he looked up at Ness, finally able to connect a real, live face with the image he had formed from press clippings and discussions with other gangsters. Capone fumbled to find something to say as Ness made full eye contact with him.

"Geez," he muttered in a sarcastic tone, looking away from Ness and out into the early evening sunset. "You'd think Mussolini was passin' through, with all the fuss you guys are makin'."

Ness, gratified to be placed in charge of this official sendoff, painted this picture in *The Untouchables*: "I was determined to see there would be no rescue or that no assassin's bullet would cheat the law. We arranged a five-car caravan to escort Snorky from the jail to Dearborn. Lahart, Seager and I were to ride in the first car. Behind it was to be another car with Capone, followed by Robsky, Cloonan and King in another, followed by two automobiles carrying Chicago policemen. All of us were heavily-armed; my crew was ready with sawed-off shotguns, revolvers and automatics loose in shoulder holsters."

"It was every driver for himself," wrote a Chicago journalist covering the event. "Fenders and bumpers clashed and pedestrians were trampled in the stampede to avoid being hit by the fast-moving officials' motors. Police officials described the ride to Dearborn Station as the wildest and noisiest in their experience."

With their sirens wailing, the police cars moved along Ogden Avenue to Clark Street. Capone looked out at the old warehouse where the St. Valentine's Day Massacre had occurred, and at the Federal Building, where his freedom had slipped away.

Alphonse Capone—Snorky, Scarface, Big Al, The Boss—left the city with yet another name: Federal Convict No. 40886.

A Wasserman blood test administered at the federal prison in Atlanta conclusively showed that Capone suffered from "central nervous system syphilis." After years of latency, the disease had finally erupted into the tertiary stage. His battles now would be private ones. Capone had given the rival gangs, the cops and the politicians all they could handle. Now, he was fighting for his sanity, and for his very life.

CHAPTER FIFTEEN

Making A Difference

Organized crime continued to flourish in Chicago, as rival gangs began to flex their muscles. However, most of the rules had changed. Gangland murders, which numbered almost 700 between 1920 and 1931, were becoming rare.

The most notable slaying occurred on February 15, 1933, in Biscayne Bay, Florida. That afternoon, Chicago Mayor Anton "Tony" Cermak, a well-connected Democrat who had upset Big Bill Thompson in the 1931 election, was attending a reception for President-elect Franklin D. Roosevelt. Walking toward Roosevelt's car in a crowded amphitheater, Cermak was struck in the right armpit by a .32 caliber bullet. The gunman was Guiseppe Zangara, a former infantryman in the army of his native Italy.

The presumption was that Zangara had meant to assassinate Roosevelt, but observers of the Chicago mob have long contended that he got his man. Cermak died nineteen days later. Following a guilty plea to homicide charges, the man described by doctors as a psychopath was silenced forever by the electric chair.

Back in Chicago, Eliot Ness packed away the piles of evidence he had amassed to document Volstead Act violations by Al Capone and his gang. Ness never had his day in the sun as a witness against Capone, but publicity about his activities apparently resulted in one lasting memorial, although Ness's connection remains unknown to most people.

An innovative comic strip by Chester Gould, entitled "Dick Tracy," began to appear in the Chicago Tribune and other newspapers. Unlike many cartoonists of his day, whose strips relied on fantasy heroes such as Buck Rogers or Tarzan, Gould drew his from the news of the day.

Writer Max Allen Collins quotes Gould as saying that the inspiration for his detective came from Eliot Ness, whom Gould envisioned as a latter-day Sherlock Holmes—fearless, technologically adept, and committed to direct action. Al Capone also appeared in the strip after his tax evasion trial made him front page news across the country. Capone was the basis for a character labeled "Big Boy" by Gould.

The next logical career step for Eliot Ness was the Federal Bureau of Investigation. His reputation as a Prohibition agent and special investigator for the Treasury and Justice departments was unquestionably solid. However, Ness's dream of becoming an agent in the Justice Department's Investigations Bureau, as it was called at the time, remain unfulfilled. In all likelihood, this can be traced to the paranoia, jealousy and pettiness of FBI Director J. Edgar Hoover.

Hoover, who had backed away from the Capone investigation when he had his chance, believed that Johnson, Ness and the others had stolen the bureau's thunder. He was particularly troubled by Ness's self-promotion and his "play by the rules" attitude, an approach that did not fit with Hoover's operation of the FBI.

The director went so far as to establish a confidential file on Ness, charting his activities with the same degree of thoroughness as the FBI employed with suspected criminals. This file, made public only recently under the Freedom of Information Act, contains numerous handwritten notes by Hoover ordering FBI personnel to have nothing to do with Eliot Ness. The records reveal that Hoover considered Ness a dangerous, reckless vigilante. He was, largely, the victim of his own success.

The vast majority of Americans saw Prohibition for what it was—a failed social experiment. It was costing the nation more than $1 billion from lost taxes and import duties. Clandestine drinking had become a very symbol of personal liberty. In February 1933, Congress voted to submit the 21st Amendment, repealing Prohibition, to the states. By the end of the year, President Roosevelt proclaimed that the necessary thirty-six states had ratified the amendment, putting an end to the dry law.

As the Prohibition Bureau was dismantled, many of the Untouchables moved into other roles with the federal government.

Leeson and Robsky remained in Chicago to help Ness with the "mop-up duty." Eventually, Leeson was transferred to Kansas City. Robsky went on to chase smugglers off the coast of Florida and Georgia, intercepting their shipments of whiskey from the Bahamas. He later entered private detective work, a virtual unknown despite his affiliation with the Untouchables and his efforts, with Oscar Fraley, to capitalize on the success of the Ness/Fraley collaboration.

Some of the Prohibition Bureau's responsibilities were turned over to a new Alcohol Tax Unit within the Bureau of Internal Revenue (Treasury Department). The same United States government that had, in one role, stalked the producers of alcohol as criminals now sought to share in their gains through taxation. The government also began to focus on regulating the quality of alcoholic beverages. Of greatest concern was the sudden growth of moonshining by those who found the cost of liquor prohibitive, due to federal taxes and new market dynamics. Often, dangerous and potentially lethal concoctions were made available on the black market.

Nowhere in America was this problem worse than in the "Moonshine Mountains" of southwestern Ohio, Kentucky and Tennessee. Chicago mobsters may not have been inclined to shoot federal agents, but the same rules did not apply to these mountain moonshiners. They saw any intrusion by the government into their affairs as an affront to their lifestyle.

The Bureau of Internal Revenue needed a leader with experience, integrity and courage to enforce federal liquor laws in that volatile region. Eliot Ness, now 30, eagerly accepted the offer. He was dispatched to the Cincinnati District in early 1934, with instructions to assemble a team of investigators.

Ness hated his new assignment from the start. It offered all of the danger, but none of the glory, of his Chicago work. He was given little direction and not nearly enough agents. Thousands of stills were in operation in a vast, hostile territory that had its own code of silence. During less than a year as a "revenooer," Ness narrowly missed being shot from ambush several times during raids on hillbilly stills. "Those mountain men and their squirrel rifles gave me almost as many chills as the Capone mob," Ness told one interviewer.

Ness's nephew and childhood friend, Wallace Jamie, who was Assistant Safety Director in St. Paul, Minnesota, offered him an administrative job with the police department in that city. Ness considered the invitation, but opted to remain a federal employee, believing it would enhance his chances of becoming an FBI agent.

He finally did escape the Moonshine Mountains on August 16, 1934, when he accepted an appointment as Investigator-in-Charge of the Alcohol Tax Unit for Northern Ohio. Ness settled into his own office at the Standard Building in Cleveland, a block from City Hall, and was provided with a large, black Ford coupe. His salary remained at $3,800.

Edna, who had remained behind in Chicago, joined him at a modern gray cottage on the lakefront in Bay Village, an hour away from downtown Cleveland. There, they were able to put the pressures of Chicago and the dangers of the mountain moonshiners behind them and enjoy a more traditional lifestyle.

The modest, one-story home came with a garden, a small reflecting pond, and plenty of room for their six cats to roam. In their cozy living room, they could build a fire, sit back and read or talk. However, Ness often stayed on the job until as late as 10:00 p.m.

For just over a year, Ness routinely coordinated reports from approximately three dozen field investigators who uncovered hundreds of moonshining operations throughout Ohio's Cuyahoga and Lake counties. The largest of these raids was a massive distillery operating behind a legitimate business at East 30th Street in Cleveland. Agents seized and demolished equipment capable of producing 1,000 gallons of bootleg liquor a day, which cheated the government out of approximately $30,000 each week in taxes.

Another time, Ness was tipped off that a suspicious substance was flowing into the Cuyahoga River from a warehouse beneath High-Level Bridge. One whiff of the discharge was all he needed to identify the source as a large distillery hidden behind the brick facade of an abandoned garage.

Ness plotted the attack with all the thoroughness of a Chicago-style brewery raid. At the sound of a hand-held whistle, four Alcohol Tax Unit agents climbed through a skylight and descended a rope into the warehouse. Four others, Ness among them, barged through the front doors. They discovered a huge boiler unit being manned by a lone employee. He was arrested on the spot, as were six other workers caught by surprise as they reported for night shift duties.

Next, a group of investigators under Ness's command took over the offices of a bootlegging business on Cleveland's East Side. For the next four hours, they answered telephone calls complaining about late deliveries. This gave investigators a list of more than a dozen establishments marketing the illegal brew.

For Ness, who was never comfortable with desk work, these raids were too infrequent. He was also disturbed that the press took little interest. Reporters considered the flow of illegal liquor trivial when compared with Cleveland's problems with organized crime, official corruption, gambling, youth gang violence and prostitution.

The city had many other woes. Its economy was depressed, its traffic control chaotic, and its air so polluted that a dark cloud hung over the city, sometimes obscuring any view of the massive Terminal Tower that protruded from the landscape like a lone candle. On the sidewalks, panhandlers, pimps and prostitutes prowled among the passing pedestrians.

Ness, raised in a city where the lakefront was sacred, now had to look down upon an oily, yellow Cuyahoga River that flowed out to Lake Erie. Cuyahoga, an Indian word meaning crooked, was also adopted as the name of the county surrounding Cleveland. The river snaked crazily through the industrial valley known to Cleveland residents as "The Flats." Steel mills, oil refineries, huge factories and warehouses sprawled through this bottomland section, where a railroad line passed decaying docks and scattered industrial debris. At night, The Flats was a world of darkness cut only by an occasional streetlamp or the muted glow of a rundown waterfront bar.

Cleveland's political climate was similar to Chicago's. The public had long ago lost faith in its city institutions. Cleveland did not have a public enemy as identifiable as Al Capone, but its police department was an embarrassment. Corruption ran rampant, from the beat cop all the way to the judge's chambers.

Due in large part to the police department's lethargy, the underworld had rapidly expanded its domain with little interference, and often with complicity, from the people who were supposed to be enforcing the law. Prohibition had helped many mobsters acquire enormous wealth and power. In addition, union racketeering had spread through blue collar Cleveland.

Voters elected a reform ticket in November 1935, headed by Harold Hitz Burton, a former Republican State Representative who ran for mayor as an Independent. Burton vowed to clean up corruption, wage war on crime and make city streets safe again. To do so, he knew he would need a clean and competent Director of Public Safety.

The Public Safety Director had supreme authority over municipal law enforcement and ancillary services. The incumbent, Martin J. Lavelle, had made a mockery of the position and outraged many citizens in the process. Burton sought an individual of integrity and skill to command the entire system of crime prevention, firefighting and traffic control. Among the names on his short list was Eliot Ness.

Burton had never heard of Ness, but local newspaper reporters, businessmen and reliable city officials spoke highly of this recent arrival from Chicago. United States Attorney Dwight W. Green, one of the federal prosecutors in the Capone case and a future Governor of Illinois, gave Ness a ringing endorsement. Echoing Green's opinion was Wes Lawrence, a respected reporter with the Cleveland Plain Dealer.

Ness was also enthusiastically supported by William Clegg, a politically-connected Chicago stock broker who was foreman of the federal grand jury that indicted Al Capone on Prohibition violations as a result of Ness's testimony.

The fact that Ness was an outsider appealed to Burton. When he learned that Ness had turned down bribes and made a point of exposing those who accepted payoffs, Burton knew he had his man.

Ness first heard that he was under consideration from a couple of Cleveland newspaper reporters. His excitement was tempered by Edna's lack of enthusiasm. Nevertheless, when the call came from Mayor Burton on December 11, 1935, Ness eagerly accepted the position, which came with a $7,500 salary.

On his first day of work, he arrived at City Hall in a tan camel-hair topcoat and snap-brim fedora. His first appointment was with the new mayor.

"What I really wanted to know was how far I could go," Ness wrote of the meeting. "Were these men serious about cleaning house, or was I just hired for window dressing? I had no intention of remaining in Cleveland if the people around me weren't as serious about my mission as I intended to be."

A Harvard graduate, Burton had enjoyed a successful legal career in Cleveland, but he yearned to leave a mark on the city. According to Ness's description of their first meeting, Mayor Burton began to pace the floor before stopping in front of the tall, wide window that allowed him to look out over the smoky landscape. He struck a match and lit a long Havana cigar. Blowing a cloud of smoke into the air, he turned to face Ness.

"We checked up on you. Did you know that?"

"I'm not surprised," Ness replied. "I'd do the same thing if I were you."

"You seem to get high marks all the way around. Maybe a little too aggressive from time to time. That's something you're going to have to watch around here."

"Agreed. I'm aware of it."

"I don't really know too much about you, other than the fact that you helped out on the Capone matter and kept your nose clean."

"I guess that about sums it up," Ness said, loosening his tie and reaching for the coffee Burton's secretary had just delivered.

The mayor went on to detail Ness's duties. He said the new director's inexperience might work in his favor, since he had no ties to Cleveland's political machinery. However, Burton cautioned Ness that he would have to step on some big toes to perform his duties effectively. While he was expected to attack the problems of corruption and inefficiency in the Police Department,

Ness also had to avoid alienating members of City Council, who controlled the purse strings of city government.

"I think I can handle it, under one condition," Ness said. "I don't want to be deskbound. I want to be out on the beat. That's where I function the best."

"I don't have a problem with that," the mayor responded. "If you're visible, you'll get attention, and the publicity could really do us some good at budget time, if it's the right kind of publicity."

The idea of commanding the police force and Fire Department at first seemed overwhelming to Ness.

"Here I was, one of the youngest men employed in city government, and suddenly I was put in charge of more than 2,500 men," he wrote. "Perhaps I had gotten more than I bargained for."

After his meeting with Burton, Ness drove his Ford to Central Police Station, a four-story sandstone fortress at 21st and Payne on Cleveland's East Side. There he spent an hour with George J. Matowitz, Cleveland's Chief of Police. A 31-year veteran of the department, Matowitz was immediately defensive, though Ness took great pains to put him at ease.

The chief, a stocky six-footer, struck Ness as lazy, a common perception around Cleveland. No one had accused Matowitz of tolerating police corruption, but there were suspicions that he was so uninvolved that he had no idea how far the cancer had spread. Ness left the meeting believing that, as long as Matowitz knew people were watching, the chief would be an important ally.

Cleveland news reporters caught up with Ness as he left Central Station. Having heard of his activities in Chicago, they expected to see a stern, nondescript lawman. Many were surprised to find that the new Public Safety Director was a well-dressed, handsome young man with a pleasant smile and a soft voice.

"I'm not going to be a remote director," Ness promised them. "I plan to be right in the front lines combating crime, but only after I become a little more familiar with the police force and the local crime scene."

Dropping a heavy load of books, pamphlets and file folders on the passenger's seat of his car, Ness walked around to the driver's side and opened the door. "This is my homework," he said, pointing to the stack. "I'll know a lot more tomorrow and a lot more than that the next day. I'm going to do plenty of studying."

CHAPTER SIXTEEN

Cleveland: One Tough Town

Eliot Ness demonstrated his commitment to the new job the very first night he spent as Director of Public Safety. He and Edna joined another couple for dinner and drinks at a downtown Cleveland restaurant. Hearing a police siren down the street, Ness bolted from his seat to investigate. He stepped out into a fierce wind that blew in from Lake Erie, then spotted the flashing red light of a police car two blocks away and ran to the scene. Ness was greeted by a uniformed officer who was keeping the gathering crowd away from a two-story brick apartment building that was the focus of attention.

Police had been summoned by a tenant who returned home to discover two young men burglarizing his apartment. Officers originally believed the thieves were trapped on the roof, but discovered that they had jumped down onto the top of an adjacent building and escaped into the night.

As the policemen regrouped at their squad cars, Ness accepted an invitation to join two of them on patrols in the crime-ridden Third Precinct, the so-called "Roaring Third." The Public Safety Director received an eye-opening driveby tour of the brothels and gambling houses that operated unimpeded on virtually every street. Asked by Ness why they ignored the obvious criminal activity, the officers said they were under orders not to make arrests in vice cases without the approval of their precinct captain.

Later, the patrolmen saw flashing red lights several blocks away and proceeded over to a fire at an office building. Ness would later write of his disgust with the inefficiency he witnessed among the firefighters. He was equally appalled by the outdated, unreliable equipment firemen were forced to use.

As the clock neared 2:00 a.m., the officers were summoned to assist with a raid at a small brothel on Orange Avenue. By the time police broke through the door, the prostitutes and their customers had vacated the building and no arrests could be made. One of the officers conceded to Ness that the targets of the raid had, in all likelihood, been forewarned by a contact in the police department, business-as-usual in Cleveland.

A crime reporter with one of the city's newspapers heard of Ness's activities on his first night and alerted colleagues. The next morning, the new Public Safety Director was greeted outside City Hall by four reporters eager to hear his reaction.

"That was a quick getaway," Ness said with a grin, acknowledging the fact that the prostitutes had been tipped-off. Reporters wanted Ness to talk about his experiences in Chicago, but he downplayed his role and reminded them that tax evasion, not bootlegging, put Al Capone behind bars. Ness said he preferred to focus on his current assignment.

"I'm still just finding my way around this place," he told the reporters. "I'd rather talk about what we can do after we do it."

That brief encounter was the beginning of what would blossom into a cozy and mutually beneficial relationship between Eliot Ness and the Cleveland press. Not only did Ness seek to polish his own image, he also recognized the importance of building public support for his plans. He was page one news the next day.

"Six feet and 172 pounds of fight and vigor, an expert criminologist who looks like a collegian but can battle crime with the best of them, Eliot Ness is beginning his job of upholding law and order in Cleveland," read one story, headlined "Act First, Then Talk, Says Ness." Mayor Burton was given high marks in the story for "hiring a Safety Director without political ties or aspirations who has a spotless record of battling corruption in a major American city."

Less than a week later, in a maneuver that almost cost him his job, Ness sent an even louder message to all of Cleveland. He investigated a tip that two veteran patrolmen, Michael Corrigan and Joseph Dunne, were drinking while on duty. Not only did Ness determine that the report was accurate, he also learned that

Dunne was a habitual offender. When the men arrived for work the next morning, Eliot Ness demanded their badges.

"I will not stand for this," Ness vowed to a Cleveland Plain Dealer reporter who heard of the dismissals. (It is unclear whether Ness spread the news himself, or merely acknowledged his actions when confronted by the reporter). "It is this simple," he continued. "Either we have a decent, law-abiding community, or we don't. These men don't fit."

Some of the top brass in the police department, stunned by Ness's abrupt action, demanded that Dunne and Corrigan be reinstated. At least two newspaper editorialists joined the chorus, charging the Safety Director with overstepping his authority. One of them called on city officials to replace the gung-ho Ness with a director who was more in tune with Cleveland's way of life.

"Boy Scout" and "College Cop" were among the derisive terms used by police department veterans to describe him. But Ness would not yield an inch, especially after Cleveland's most influential newspaper, the Plain Dealer, called on its readers to support his efforts to mold the police force in his own image.

Next, Ness met with Traffic Commissioner Edward Donahue and urged him to insist that traffic police practice salesmanship and courtesy, instead of carrying "the big stick." With Cleveland scheduled to host a series of major conventions in 1936, the time was right for a friendlier demeanor.

Just before Christmas, Ness announced a major shakeup of the Police Department. With concurrence from Chief Matowitz, he replaced the head of the Detective Bureau, transferred captains and lieutenants to new precincts, and reassigned nearly 100 officers to new beats. His aim was to sever the cozy alliances that many officers had developed with the city's criminals.

One by one, he summoned precinct captains to his office and warned them that they would be held personally responsible for any misconduct by the men who were under their command. More serious offenses would be punishable by immediate suspension of both the officer involved and his precinct captain.

Veteran police officers huddled to discuss ways to force him out, but Ness took his case to the court of public opinion. At thirty-three, he was the youngest Public Safety Director in the city's history. With his Scandinavian good looks, wearing the latest double-breasted suits and living with an attractive wife in Bay Village, Ness was seen by many as the dynamic symbol Depression-weary Clevelanders needed at the time.

Ness spelled out his mission during a speech to the Cleveland Advertising Club in early January 1936, and he made sure the press was there to hear him. "In any city where corruption continues, it follows that some officials are playing ball with the underworld... The dishonest public servant hiding behind a badge or political office is more detestable than any street criminal or mob boss. If town officials are committed to a program of protection of the lawmakers, police work becomes exceedingly difficult, and the officer on the beat, being discouraged from his duty, decides it is best to see as little crime as possible."

Ness said many Cleveland police officers were regularly accepting bribes, tipping off criminals about impending raids and even serving as enforcers for the mob. Other policemen were apathetic and lazy, and many were drinking while on duty, he pointed out. "And the worst part is that we have officers who match all three descriptions— crooked, lazy and drunk!"

Playing to his audience, Ness pointed out that the police department's shortcomings were allowing the mob to flourish, exacerbating the city's economic woes. Skyrocketing profits from gambling and bootlegging had led to unabated growth of organizations such as the Cleveland Syndicate and the Mayfield Road Mob, a vicious gang of Jewish and Italian criminals working in profitable harmony. The most lucrative of their enterprises, even with the demise of Prohibition, was bootlegging. The mob produced its own whiskey and smuggled truckloads of Canadian liquor across Lake Erie.

This was, in large part, testimony to the effectiveness of Morris "Moe" Dalitz. A diminutive figure with a prominent nose and affable smile, Dalitz landed in the Mayfield Road Mob after cutting his teeth with Detroit's notorious "Purple Gang."

Other underworld figures were being attracted to Cleveland because of the vast opportunities that abounded. Ness estimated that organized crime was robbing Cleveland's economy of more than $1 million monthly from illegal gambling alone. He surprised many businessmen present when he said he supported legalized gambling—a position that ran counter to Mayor Burton's pronouncements. His rationale was that such a move would cut deeply into the mob's profits. However, Ness also acknowledged that any attempt to make gambling legal would be politically suicidal.

Eventually, he would change his position and speak out against the legalization of gambling, citing case studies demonstrating that criminal activity inevitably follows.

Clevelanders' affinity for gambling fueled the widespread popularity of the Harvard Club, a notorious night spot on the outskirts of Newburgh Heights, just past the jurisdiction of city police. Ness was shocked to discover that this full-scale casino had, for more than five years, operated openly and unmolested by local law officers. Its chief operator was James "Shimmy" Patton, one of three co-owners who directed the majority of gambling profits to the Cleveland Syndicate. At the same time, the Mayfield Road Mob controlled the lucrative alcohol business at the Harvard Club.

Not far from there was the Thomas Club in Mayfield Heights, run by another of the Mayfield Road Mob, "Gameboy" Miller. Moe Dalitz also had his own place, the Mounds Club, in Lake County, just outside Cleveland.

Ness found a natural ally in Cuyahoga County Prosecutor Frank T. Cullitan, who shared his disgust that these gambling houses operated with apparent immunity. Cullitan, fifty-five, was a respected tactician whose strong courtroom oratory had helped him send seven murderers to the electric chair.

On January 10, 1936, Cullitan shocked the underworld by deputizing almost two dozen private detectives and sending them out to shut down the gambling dens. Their stiffest resistance came at the Harvard Club, where Shimmy Patton's bouncers greeted them with submachine guns.

Several dramatic and contradictory accounts of this encounter have been published over the years. Apparently, Patton himself eventually appeared at the door and threatened Cullitan and his deputies. The prosecutor then tracked down Eliot Ness at a Cleveland City Council meeting. Ness, as expected, was eager to help, but Mayor Burton did not share his enthusiasm. The mayor finally agreed to let city police officers serve as special deputies of the Cuyahoga County Prosecutor's Office, with the understanding that they were acting independent of any affiliation with the city.

Ness rounded up twenty-seven willing volunteers and led a caravan that rolled into Newburgh Heights at about 11:00 p.m. Only moments behind them were three cars carrying newspaper reporters and photographers, responding to vague reports that the Public Safety Director was about to generate some interesting news.

This army of volunteers, armed with an assortment of revolvers, high-powered rifles, sawed-off shotguns and tear gas guns, caught Cullitan off-guard. He emphasized that under no circumstances were shots to be fired.

The Harvard Club was a barnlike building that had once served as a warehouse. A fancy New Orleans-style facade erected in the front could not obscure the building's actual purpose. Ness directed each driver to maneuver his vehicle into place in the parking area, leaving the headlights on to fully illuminate the club. Many of the customers who rushed out at the first sign of trouble hours earlier returned to watch the raid from a safe distance. Ness and Cullitan did not know it at the time, but among those who had left in all the commotion was one of the FBI's most wanted criminals, Alvin "Creepy" Karpis, suspected in several murders and two kidnappings. About fifty gamblers remained on the premises, seemingly unconcerned.

A half-dozen officers hurried to the back of the building to cover that exit. Without a word, Ness, unarmed, broke from the pack. He boldly walked up the porch steps to the heavy steel door at the front, took a deep breath, and knocked loudly. The tiny speakeasy slot flew open and slammed shut just as quickly.

Ness returned to the parking lot, where he and Cullitan stood quietly, their heavy breathing creating clouds of steam in the cold night air. The Harvard Club standoff continued for another five minutes before the front door slowly opened and a husky character in a tuxedo invited the group to enter. Most of the gambling apparatus had been dismantled and carried out. Shimmy Patton was nowhere to be found.

Despite some of the more sensationalized accounts that would be published, the raid was fairly uneventful, except for its symbolic value. Ness drew quiet satisfaction out of shuttering a notable gambling den and letting the Cleveland Syndicate and the Mayfield Road Mob know that he meant business. He was especially pleased to see city police officers taking an interest in the raid on a voluntary basis.

News reporters, unaccustomed to such access to a city law enforcement official, applauded Ness for his get-tough approach. Less supportive were many members of the Police Department. Some officers, including those who were clean, clammed up when Ness summoned them individually and grilled them about their knowledge of corruption among the ranks. Newspaper reports telling of the Safety Director's ire over this lack of cooperation only strengthened the conspiracy of silence within the department.

If the police wouldn't talk, Ness reasoned, maybe the criminals would. A series of meetings with Prosecutor Cullitan resulted in a new policy that encouraged offenders to tell what they knew about police corruption. Among the inducements were reduced sentences, immunity from prosecution, protection against retaliation, and financial reward.

Nobody could fault Eliot Ness's thoroughness, nor his commitment to this purge of the police department. Considering the poor credibility of many informants, he knew it was imperative to verify every accusation and to give each officer a fair hearing. Ness did much of the field work himself. At night, he could be found talking to prostitutes, pimps and other criminals in bars and back alleys.

Gradually, veterans of the police force grew less inclined to scoff at Ness or mock his Ivy League appearance and quiet manner. The honest officers who had nothing to hide were beginning to respect him for his tenacity.

A small news item buried behind the headlines of the January 27 newspapers drew little attention from Clevelanders. It told of a neatly dismembered female body discovered jammed into two burlap sacks in an alley near East 20th Street in the Roaring Third. Through fingerprints, police identified the victim as Flo Polillo, a 41-year-old prostitute who lived a few blocks from the spot where her remains were found.

CHAPTER SEVENTEEN

Crooked Cops Pay The Price

Eliot Ness was riding high, his popularity probably exceeding that of Mayor Burton. He was a featured speaker at business luncheons and was hired to deliver law enforcement lectures at Cleveland College. As long as Ness expressed no political ambitions, the mayor welcomed all of the positive publicity that his young Public Safety Director could garner.

Ness fit the mold of an all-American hero, with his glimmering eyes and modest voice. Among those enamored by Ness was Clayton Fritchey, a prominent reporter and nationally-syndicated columnist with the Cleveland Press. Fritchey, recognizable to most Clevelanders by his round glasses and polka dot bow tie, was widely respected for his courage and thoroughness in covering the city government beat.

Fritchey had been anxious to ally himself with Ness and capitalize on the Safety Director's fast-growing popularity. So when he stumbled onto evidence linking a prominent police official with the Cleveland mob, Fritchey knew just where to turn.

It all began with a series of investigative news stories on the sale of nonexistent cemetery plots to the immigrant population of the greater Cleveland area. Frank T. Cullitan used much of Fritchey's information to bring charges against a handful of police officers with known underworld connections.

Fritchey continued to be bothered by the repeated appearance of one name, John L. Dacek, on ledgers, memos and canceled checks seized during Cullitan's probe. There was no mention of Dacek in any official records. Eventually, it dawned on Fritchey that, by switching a couple of letters, the name very much resembled that of Sixteenth Precinct Police Captain Louis J. Cadek.

Long suspected of having mob connections, Cadek had hidden behind a wall of protection and political power he had built throughout the Police Department, particularly within his own precinct. "Nobody went to the bathroom without Cadek's permission," recalled one of his police colleagues. "He called the shots. There wasn't a cop on the force who carried more clout."

Convinced that he had solved the riddle, Fritchey met with Eliot Ness to share his evidence. Thus began a relationship that would be mutually beneficial for the remainder of Ness's days in Cleveland. Fritchey, in effect, became an extra investigator for the city. In return, he obtained exclusive material that improved the Cleveland Press's stature in the highly-competitive newspaper business.

Ness and Fritchey determined that Cadek's involvement with bribery and conspiracy dated back at least fifteen years. He had earned more than $80,000 from the fraudulent cemetery lot sales scheme alone. Bank records subpoenaed by Ness revealed large, unexplained investments since 1921. Cadek's savings account showed a balance of $150,000, despite an annual salary that had only recently been increased to $3,500. He had received two fancy Cadillacs as gifts from men with known underworld connections.

The investigation spread out into the Sixteenth Precinct, where Ness and Fritchey found the incriminating evidence they needed. In return for immunity from prosecution, operators of speakeasies and gambling houses agreed to testify that Cadek had extorted tens of thousands of dollars from them during Prohibition, promising police protection in return.

Cadek's conviction sent shock waves through the Police Department, particularly after the captain bargained for a reduced sentence by pointing the finger at some of his colleagues. Clevelanders now realized how widespread the corruption in their police force had become.

While Ness continued to focus on police corruption, investigators were called to the Kingsbury Run area. Two boys had set out for a day of fishing near the Kinsman Road bridge when they came across a man's severed head resting near the riverbank. The next day, a couple of railroad workers found the matching body about one-quarter mile away. Although police were not telling the public as much, they were convinced that this victim and three others, including Flo Polillo, were murdered and dismembered by the same savage killer.

From the start, Ness wanted nothing to do with that case, nor with any other assignment that would sidetrack him from his probe of police corruption and organized crime. Nevertheless, Mayor Burton insisted that Ness oversee security for the 1936 Republican National Convention in Cleveland. Burton saw the event as an opportunity for the city to improve its poor public image. The convention went off without a hitch, with delegates choosing Kansas Governor Alf Landon to "win back the presidency" from Franklin D. Roosevelt.

An even greater distraction was the Great Lakes Exposition of August 1936, which brought an estimated four million visitors to Cleveland. Ness spent a great deal of time organizing security for the event and preparing an award-winning booth designed to boost Cleveland's image and rally public support for law enforcement. Despite all of the attention that was showered upon him during the Expo, Ness welcomed the opportunity to return to the business at hand.

Anton Vehovec, an outspoken, politically-connected Cleveland City Council member, had been patiently waiting to meet with Ness to discuss serious allegations against another high-ranking police officer, Captain Michael J. Harwood of the Fourteenth Precinct. He alleged that Harwood had been accepting bribes for many years to protect racketeers in his precinct. Pressed for specifics, Vehovec pointed to the popularity and apparent immunity of the Blackhawk Inn, a gambling house on Ivanhoe Road.

After a raid of the Blackhawk confirmed the councilman's allegations, Ness suspended Harwood indefinitely, pending the outcome of a full-scale investigation.

Cleveland police officers recognized that Eliot Ness meant business. However, severing their ties with the underworld was not without its own risks. Many of them opted for early retirement, which allowed Ness to begin filling the ranks with a new breed of officer. At the same time, honest policemen who had resisted the bribes welcomed the support that had been denied them for so long and came forward with incriminating evidence against their corrupt colleagues. There was also an increase in tips from citizens and greater willingness—in some cases, eagerness—by witnesses to testify.

While the tide was turning in favor of honest, effective law enforcement, Ness was putting together plans for an Untouchables-style raid on a West Side gambling house. For over a decade, the casino on West 25th Street in the aptly-named Rowdy Run area had operated under the cover of "McGinty's."

A handpicked team of proven officers infiltrated McGinty's, posing as gamblers, and gathered descriptions of the organizational structure, games in operation, a layout of the building, and evidence of complicity by city police officers. A week later, Ness made his move.

Seventy-seven gamblers were issued summonses on the spot and nine employees were taken into custody. The raiders seized stacks of financial records, including evidence tying McGinty's to Arthur Hebebrand, a co-owner of the Harvard Club. Another veteran police captain, Adolph Lenahan, whose Eighth Precinct officers were so tolerant of McGinty's, was suspended.

Ten more gambling raids followed in downtown Cleveland during July, all under Ness's orders and a few with the Public Safety Director's personal involvement. Press reports praised Ness for his aggressive attitude. The July 26, 1936 Cleveland Plain Dealer reported:

"Eliot Ness, with his boyish face and enigmatic manner, is well aware of what is going on in the department, and attending to one matter at a time. The cops were at first inclined to scoff at him, but by now are aware he knows his business. It is fairly obvious that he considers his business the rebuilding of a police force which has gone badly to seed. His greatest handicap is that he must investigate by himself, and can trust so few others."

That situation was about to change with the appointment of Robert Chamberlin to the new position of Administrative Assistant in the Public Safety Director's office. Chamberlin, a young attorney and Ohio National Guard officer, was well-known throughout the Cleveland area as a high school football star. He and his wife had befriended Eliot and Edna Ness soon after they rented their cottage from the Chamberlins, who owned a large home next door.

Just after he began work, Chamberlin was among city officials summoned to the Kingsbury Run area, where a mutilated body was found in a sewer between The Flats and Jackass Hill. A white male, approximately twenty-five years old, the unidentified victim had been dead for about forty-eight hours. For the first time, the newspapers were reporting that police considered as many as six Cleveland area murders to be the work of the same man, now called the "Mad Butcher" or "Torso Killer."

Pressured by politicians to calm public fears, Mayor Burton announced that Eliot Ness would be working with Cuyahoga County Coroner Arthur J. Pearse to solve the crimes. Reluctantly, Ness visited the city morgue to view the remains and confer with the investigators. He then traveled to the ditch where the victim was found.

Ness summoned a Fire Department search and rescue crew to dredge a nearby pool of stagnant water. As hundreds of people looked on in shock, the missing body parts were pulled to the surface. The following day's newspapers were crammed with sensationalized reports, biting editorials, reckless speculation and revealing photographs. All of Cleveland now knew a monster was on the loose.

Ness immediately assigned twenty-five detectives to fan out over all of Cleveland and track down every lead, no matter how remote. He also organized a brutal roundup of all the vagrants and hobos inhabiting Kingsbury Run. Officers paraded their hapless captives into police headquarters, where detectives grilled them extensively. Only a handful reported seeing anything that might be connected with the murders, and those clues were either inconsequential or discredited by further investigation.

Exhausted and frustrated by the five hours of interrogations, Ness had no sooner stepped out the door of Central Station when he was surrounded by newspaper reporters and photographers.

"You're the big G-man who's supposed to be solving this," one of the reporters shouted. "What are you doing?"

"Like everyone else, I want to see this psychopath caught," Ness responded angrily. "I'm going to do all I can to assist in the investigation, but I'm not going to be much help to you folks."

Ness pushed his way through the crowd and toward his car, ignoring further questions. This was the first time the Public Safety Director had been anything but accommodating to the press, and his brusqueness was duly noted in the next day's editions.

Seeing that Ness needed some positive publicity, Clayton Fritchey provided it. "Thousand Young Dick Tracys Thrill & Cheer As Ness Tells How G-Men Got Capone Gang," read a banner headline in the Cleveland Press, over Fritchey's story on Eliot's appearance before a group of Boy Scouts.

An editorial in the same edition cited a recent crime statistics summary. "There is one interesting—very interesting—paragraph in the report of Cleveland's Safety Director: 'Cases of vandalism totaled 89 this year, as against 300 for the same period last year.' For that single sentence, Mr. Ness, you are entitled to take a bow."

Ness made no secret of his relief when Detective Sergeant James T. Hogan, the newly-appointed Director of Homicide, took charge of the Mad Butcher case. Hogan summoned thirty-five Cleveland area law enforcement officials for a brainstorming session at the Central Station Police Laboratory.

They concluded that the killer probably lived in or near the Third Precinct, close to Kingsbury Run. His lifestyle or profession brought him into contact with vagrants and alcoholics on a regular basis. Considering the precision of the dismemberments, officials concluded that the murderer had probably received some type of medical and/or surgical training.

Based on the condition of the bodies and the likelihood that they had been carried or dragged a long distance, Ness told the group the killer was undoubtedly "a big man with the strength of an ox." He suggested investigators look for some type of "bloody laboratory" where the Mad Butcher performed his operations, even if that meant a house-to-house search of the region.

As a result of the lengthy meeting, two of the Detective Bureau's top men, Peter Merylo and Martin Zalewski, were assigned primary responsibility for the investigation. Ness agreed to establish a special telephone exchange at City Hall, where the public could report evidence that might help police.

A study of homicide records within a 300-mile radius of Cleveland produced two reports of dismemberments. One victim was a white male whose headless, decomposed body was found along railroad tracks in Haverstraw, N.Y., about twenty miles from New York City. Investigators could find no other similarities between that slaying and the Mad Butcher's work.

The other gruesome killing was more intriguing. The nude, headless corpse of a male was discovered in the rail yards just outside the western Pennsylvania community of New Castle. Based on the way the victim had been decapitated and the rail link between New Castle and Cleveland, Merylo and Zalewski concluded that the Cleveland maniac had struck again.

Ness was able to deflect the public's attention away from the serial killings by releasing results of his exhaustive investigation of police corruption. His 86-page report identified twenty high- or mid-level officers who were on the take. The names of dozens of witnesses willing to testify against the offenders were turned over to County Prosecutor Frank Cullitan.

"Any action now is up to the prosecutor," Ness told reporters at a press conference. "I'm going on vacation."

Cullitan, facing a tough challenge in the upcoming election, gleefully prepared arrest warrants, while Eliot and Edna Ness spent the next two weeks enjoying each other's company. They took cruises on Lake Erie, dined in the finest restaurants and slept late into the morning hours.

Cullitan was re-elected by a huge margin, but County Coroner Arthur J. Pearse was not so fortunate. He was upset by a Democratic challenger, Samuel R. Gerber, who had seized on the Mad Butcher case to suggest Pearse was inept.

Gerber, small and charismatic with his thin mustache and wavy, graying hair, was intelligent and industrious. He let it be known from the outset that he was unimpressed by the Safety Director's handling of the investigation. But Ness would not engage in verbal sparring.

To reporters who asked him to comment on Gerber's declarations, he replied, "As I've said before, we are investigating these homicides and doing everything within our power to bring the killer or killers to justice. Just because a homicide investigation is underway doesn't mean we should drop all of our other work."

Late in 1936, a grand jury empaneled by Cullitan returned indictments against eight suspended police officers, including Captain Michael Harwood. Arriving at his trial proud and confident, Harwood kept his composure as a parade of witnesses verified the captain's financial interest in night clubs, gambling houses and taverns.

Bootleggers told how Harwood ordered them to pay cash in exchange for the privilege of running their supplies into his precinct. Cullitan closed his case by presenting shocking evidence of last-minute attempts to bribe and intimidate jurors. Harwood was convicted and sentenced to a minimum term of two years in a state penitentiary.

In a scene straight from Hollywood, the captain's daughter shuffled past Ness on her way out of the courtroom and spat on his shoulder. "Nobody is above the law," he responded, reaching for his handkerchief.

Two lieutenants and four other officers either entered guilty pleas or were convicted by jurors. Ness used evidence presented during the trial to suspend five more officers. Dozens of others faced less drastic disciplinary measures for misconduct or negligence that did not rise to the level of official corruption. In some instances, to avoid a messy trial, Ness merely confronted the offender and asked for his resignation.

Cleveland's crackdown on police corruption was trumpeted in newspapers across the country. The Cleveland Press earned an award for civic achievement, while Eliot Ness received a citation from Carl V. Weygandt, Chief Justice of the Ohio Supreme Court, for "outstanding completeness and care with which he assembled evidence against police officers." The Veterans of Foreign Wars honored Ness as their Outstanding Citizen of Cuyahoga County.

CHAPTER EIGHTEEN

A Better Cleveland

The only way to ensure a respectable law enforcement agency, Eliot Ness believed, was to set that tone early in each officer's career. Using that argument, he persuaded City Council to provide the money for a new training program that would create a cleaner, more professional police force.

Recruits had to meet rigid eligibility standards. Once inside, they were required to demonstrate their proficiency in crime detection, marksmanship, self-defense, approach psychology, arrest procedure and other aspects of modern law enforcement. Then, they had to pass a Civil Service qualifying examination, which over three-quarters of them failed. The training school Ness established eventually become the highly-respected Cleveland Police Academy.

Ness swore-in one class of rookie officers with this advice: "If people have been accustomed to giving you things for nothing prior to your becoming a policeman, I suppose it's all right for you to continue to accept those things. However, if people who never gave you anything for free before now want to give you something without charge, you can conclude they are buying your badge and your uniform."

That same week, Ness appeared before a gathering of the League of Women Voters to promote his reforms. He urged the public not to expect miracles, reminding his audience that, to be effective, an officer has to be "a diplomat, a marksman, a memory expert, a boxer, a wrestler, a sprinter and an authority on a wide variety of subjects."

A handful of the more outstanding graduates were enrolled in follow-up training supervised by Ness. Under a cloak of secrecy, they learned the fine points of undercover work— from wiretapping and infiltration of known criminal outposts, to cultivating informants and tailing suspects. Among the early students was James M. Timber, who would become one of Cleveland's most famous law enforcement figures. Also in the original group was Richard Wagner, who later served as Cleveland's Chief of Police.

"Ness laid down the law," Wagner recalled. "He said, 'Here's my private phone number. If anyone asks you to take any money at any time, call me immediately. If you do get asked and don't call me, don't plan on being a police officer for very long.' He meant it, and it worked."

To nudge his recruits up in the ranks, Ness revamped the promotion system so marksmanship and other skills helped compensate for points historically awarded for mere seniority.

In a scenario similar to the "Secret Six" arrangement in Chicago, he secured donations from the Chamber of Commerce and the American Legion to launch an undercover fund. Many of the donors were Cleveland area businessmen suffering from the mob's widening infiltration of commercial enterprises, both legal and illegal.

Using officers who distinguished themselves during training, Ness formed two units to combat corruption and inefficiency. The "Minute Men," so named by reporters who followed the Public Safety Director's activities, were a visible presence on the street. They reminded gamblers, bootleggers, prostitutes, extortionists and even some police officers that times had changed. The presence of the Minute Men was also a cover for a second group, "The Unknowns," consisting of "untouchable" police officers and detectives who collected information on patrolmen or commanders suspected of being corrupt.

The identity of the Unknowns was a closely-guarded secret. Among the group were Sam Sagalyn, a recent Police Academy graduate; Tom Clothey, who came in fresh from an investigation of police corruption in St. Paul, Minnesota; and Keith Wilson, a former Alcohol Tax Unit agent who had worked for Ness earlier in his career and would eventually become a judge in Chicago.

Bob Chamberlin, who was probably Ness's best friend at the time, was named Assistant Safety Director. Chamberlin was one of the few people who could persuade Ness to take time off. They took long walks together and sometimes attended football games or other sports events. Even during these off-hours, Chamberlin recalled, Ness had a hard time keeping his mind off his work.

Because of his strong local ties, Chamberlin assumed a major role in the investigation of union racketeering in the city. Through their strong-arm tactics, union thugs were scaring out-of-town developers at a time when Cleveland could least afford to lose them.

Ness and Chamberlin, working with the Unknowns, set up a sting operation at the massive Northern Ohio Food Terminal, where extortionists affiliated with local labor unions and the underworld had long been preying on farmers who sold their goods there. Officers posing as farmers' representatives gathered evidence that resulted in criminal charges against two of the city's most powerful union bosses: Harry Barrington, business agent of the Carpenters' Union, and Harry Wayne, an officer of the Kosher Butchers' Union. As soon as Barrington was released on bail, he fled.

While this undercover work continued, the Mad Butcher struck again. Partial remains of a seventh victim washed ashore at Euclid Beach and were discovered by a beachcomber on February 23, 1937. Ness called upon his friends in the press to downplay the discovery, to no avail, particularly after County Coroner Gerber released detailed information.

Ness then pulled both the Minute Men and the Unknowns off their assignments so they could search the streets, mental hospitals, taverns and slums for evidence. He also drew the Nickel Plate Railroad Police into the case, pressuring them to interrogate the hobos and vagabonds who hopped the trains at Kingsbury Run.

Public unrest was growing, and much of the criticism was being directed at Mayor Burton and Safety Director Ness. Many wondered why Cleveland's chief law enforcement officers devoted so much attention to wrongdoing by police officers and union operatives while the Mad Butcher continued his killing spree.

Trouble was also brewing for the administration from organized labor. Union leaders labeled Burton and Ness as too sympathetic to wealthy industrialists bent on destroying the city's labor organizations. The situation came to a head after the Congress of Industrial Organizers ordered thousands of workers to walk off their jobs in the Flats, prompting companies to bring in scab laborers. Brawls and vandalism ensued, and the industrial leaders turned to the mayor's office for help.

Ness sent out the police, armed with clubs and tear gas, and ordered them to take whatever measures were necessary to disperse the picketers. Barricades were erected outside the factories and police were ordered to arrest anyone who trespassed on company property.

After sympathetic union members arrived to swell the picketers' ranks, the mob crashed through the barricades and blocked the replacement workers from entering the factories. Mayor Burton panicked, calling in the National Guard. After hundreds of guardsmen descended on the Flats, equipped with riot gear, rifles and bayonets, union members finally backed off.

During ongoing patrols that followed the confrontation, one of the National Guard members was peering into the waters of the Cuyahoga River off the Third Street Bridge when he spotted the lower half of a man's body floating just offshore. Searchers soon found the other body parts, including much of the upper torso wrapped in newspapers and crammed in a burlap bag. The Mad Butcher's body count, as best as investigators could determine, now stood at nine.

Criticism of the city's Police Department had never been harsher. Ness took steps to deflect the negative publicity by calling a press conference to announce the latest crime statistics. They showed that serious crime had plummeted twenty-five percent during his first eighteen months as Public Safety Director. Arrests and convictions were twenty percent higher than the previous year.

"Most important," Ness told the reporters, "organized crime is moving out of Cleveland and our police officers are more honest, more professional. We have made an excellent start and, with the public's support, we can make a lot more progress."

Harry Barrington could run, but he could not hide. Federal agents found the Carpenters' Union head in California and placed him behind bars until extradition papers could be prepared. Once Barrington was back in Cleveland, Ness and Chamberlin visited him in his prison cell, hoping to strike a deal. The feisty union boss wouldn't hear of it, but when he was faced with a 15-year sentence on extortion charges, he had a change of heart.

Barrington's information was a bonanza for investigators who had been trying for years to get the goods on two particularly powerful labor leaders: Donald A. Campbell, president of the Painters' District Council and Glaziers' Union, and John M. McGee, who headed the Laborers' District Council and Window Washers Union.

The duo had built a brutal and highly-efficient army of hitmen and professional bombers who terrorized hundreds of Cleveland area business owners. Any builder or merchant who bought glass from suppliers other than those under Campbell's control paid a stiff price. Unions also exacted a "hiring fee" from business owners for any new worker added to the payroll. Construction projects were halted when union officials demanded additional payoffs. The stubborn few who resisted found their windows smashed, or worse. Dynamite and acid bombs were also used by the union tacticians to get their point across.

A permanent police tail was placed on Campbell and McGee, more to harass the pair than to gather evidence. They delighted in taunting their followers with long rides in the country and wild tours of Cleveland's back alleys.

Politicians intent on unseating Harold Burton made Eliot Ness's union-busting a major campaign issue. The Democratic forces said that what Cleveland needed as "not a G-man from Chicago," but rather a local Safety Director who understood and could effectively deal with the city's problems. As effective as these tactics were, Burton survived the 1937 election by a narrow margin and promptly reaffirmed his support for Ness.

On November 7, Ness received a telephone call from his brother Charles, a successful businessman in Indianapolis, informing him that their mother had died in her sleep the previous night. The 73-year-old Emma Ness was laid to rest beside her husband Peter, who had died in 1932. Eliot and Edna drove to Illinois for a small funeral service attended by family members and a few close friends. Ness would never again set foot in Chicago.

One by one, almost forty business operators took the witness stand during a series of trials in February 1938 to tell how Campbell, McGee and their operatives bashed, bombed and bullied them. Cleveland newspapers, though often sympathetic to union interests, heaped praise on Eliot Ness, as did the national news media. Newsweek praised him for successfully combating police corruption, vice and union racketeering in Cleveland. The magazine compared him with another Republican reformist, Thomas Dewey of New York.

Ness still had his enemies. The American Federation of Labor dispatched investigators to Washington to pore through Prohibition Bureau records in search of blemishes in the Safety Director's past. Except for an affinity for alcohol and suggestions of brutality early in his career, they found no ammunition.

He also came under fire from Dr. Samuel Gerber, the Cuyahoga County Coroner. The two locked horns in April 1938, after the lower half of a woman's leg was discovered lodged against a tree limb overhanging the flood-swollen waters of the Cuyahoga River. Gerber concluded that the Mad Butcher had struck again, but Ness considered the declaration premature and chided the coroner for what he perceived as an effort to discredit the Police Department.

Following a heated exchange between the two, Ness called in a respected pathologist from Western Reserve University to review the evidence. Gerber was so outraged that he blocked the entrance of the medical examiner's office and refused to allow the pathologist to see the limb. Unfortunately for Ness, further evidence that surfaced two weeks after the initial discovery confirmed Dr. Gerber's suspicions. Two burlap bags were pulled from a section of the Cuyahoga near West Third Street Bridge. Inside them, police found more severed body parts matching the leg of a woman now officially referred to as "Victim Number Ten."

The outcome of this scrap with Gerber prompted some within his own department to question Ness's effectiveness and his commitment to the Mad Butcher case. He confided to friends that he knew of no effective way to locate the serial killer. Desperate to silence his critics, Ness called in Chamberlin and detectives Merylo and Zalewski to arrange for a massive evidence-gathering sweep through the Kingsbury Run area. Police rummaged through tents, homemade shelters, junk piles, campfires and abandoned railroad cars, looking for bones, blood stains, saws, or any other evidence of the Mad Butcher's presence, but came up empty.

"This killer has great cunning," Ness told the Cleveland Plain Dealer. "He certainly doesn't leave many, if any, clues. About all we have to go on is that one of the victims we've been able to identify was a pervert and another was a prostitute. This man seems to specialize in the sort of people nobody is likely to miss."

In contrast to Ness's low-key approach, Gerber ignored the pleas of law enforcement authorities not to fuel public hysteria. In great anatomical detail, he shared with the public all of the evidence he had collected. When he was publicly criticized, Gerber reminded his detractors that he was an elected official and did not have to answer to anyone except the voters of Cuyahoga County. Reporters hung on the coroner's every word and Gerber's popularity continued to grow.

Eliot Ness was thankful that another public official was attracting the news media's attention. It gave him the opportunity he needed to focus attention on a serious problem ignored by each of his predecessors: traffic control.

Cleveland had more traffic-related deaths and injuries than almost every other American city. When police officials wanted to ease a veteran officer toward retirement, it was common practice to assign him to "Siberia," a derisive term for the poorly-administered traffic division.

Ness took the opposite approach, designating some of his most energetic and innovative officers for a new Accident Prevention Bureau. He also sent word throughout "Siberia" that officers who were caught drinking on the job, taking bribes to ignore violations, or failing to take their work seriously could lose their jobs and their retirement benefits.

He worked with community leaders and city officials to restrict traffic flow to areas with high accident rates, to tighten motor vehicle inspection standards, and to crack down on speeders and drunken drivers. One of the most obvious, and most effective, solutions was the establishment of one-way streets in narrow or congested sections.

Posters and flyers appeared everywhere, thanks to the support Ness received from business groups, schools, churches and civic organizations. An incentive plan rewarded police officers in those precincts that had the fewest traffic accidents and the most arrests. For the first time, drivers who failed to pay their fines or appear for hearings lost their privileges and motorists who committed multiple violations were tracked down and jailed.

Money flowing into the city's coffers from stiffer fines and increased arrests was used to finance the purchase of new police cars and communications equipment. Cleveland Police unveiled a fleet of thirty-two new red, white and light cream Ford squad cars, as well as thirty Harley-Davidson motorcycles to replace the old "foot beat, call box and jump on a street car" system.

The "Cleveland Police Emergency Mobile Patrol" was established, consisting of twelve trucks operated by teams of police officers trained in first aid. These vehicles, forerunners of today's ambulances, were equipped with modern lifesaving apparatus.

Police cars and other emergency vehicles carried RCA two-way radios, patched into a communications center Ness established at Central Station. Anyone in Cleveland who needed to contact the police or Emergency Mobile Patrol could do so with a single telephone call. A new teletype system ordered by Ness helped criminal investigators exchange information with other cities.

To promote these reforms, precinct captains held neighborhood meetings, while Ness worked the luncheon circuit. Often, he brought a two-way radio to his public speaking engagements. As a test, he would summon police to the gathering and measure how long it took for an officer to respond. For a time, Ness arranged to have a policeman hide under the speakers' table. As soon as the Safety Director placed the call, the officer would pop up and exclaim, "At your service, sir!," much to the audience's delight.

Ness's study of the Fire Department's deficiencies also began to bear fruit. After taking an inventory of leaky hoses, poor-fitting hydrant connectors and dilapidated trucks, Ness persuaded City Council to approve a reorganization plan that called for stricter fire safety codes, new equipment and advanced training for firefighters.

He next turned his attention to a problem that had been festering in the city for generations.

CHAPTER NINETEEN

Troubled Times

Some of Ness's most impressive, least publicized, and most lasting accomplishments took place on the streets of Cleveland, where violent youth gangs had staked out their territorial claims. Vandalism, fights and burglaries had risen to alarming numbers in some sections, particularly the Roaring Third. Ness, dressed in sweat shirt and casual slacks, walked right into the riot-torn Tremont section and met with gang leaders on their own turf. With his quiet sincerity, he coaxed the restless youths to air their concerns and discuss their interests.

A language wall had developed between foreign-born parents who spoke little English and their American-born children, to whom English was a first language. Many of the youths had rarely held a meaningful conversation with an adult. Once they got over their suspicions of him, they opened up to Ness.

He promised the youths that the city would provide recreational opportunities, including basketball courts, baseball fields, gymnasiums and playgrounds, if they would police their own ranks in curbing illegal activities. Ness then went to work to keep his side of the bargain. He established Boy Scout troops and recruited young police officers and firemen to serve as leaders. Local merchants signed up as sponsors and city officials agreed to let the scout troops use municipal buildings as meeting halls. Ness himself was named to the Executive Council of the Boy Scouts of America.

Ness also worked out partnerships with schools and churches that would allow youths to use their recreational facilities. He spent many nights and weekend hours building rapport with the troubled youths, and persuaded many of them to enter the Civilian Conservation Corps.

"Keep them off the streets and keep them busy," was the Public Safety Director's advice to civic leaders and city officials. "It's much better to spend time and money starting and keeping them straight than it is to spend even more time and money catching them in the wrong, then trying to set them straight."

Ness established a separate Juvenile Unit in the Police Department, designating some of his younger officers for a new beat that focused exclusively on youth problems, often in conjunction with family service agencies. One of the social workers who worked with this Juvenile Unit, Katharine Dorfeld, marveled at the young Safety Director's accomplishments.

"I knew some of the families of these salvaged kids," Mrs. Dorfeld said. "They were very appreciative of Eliot Ness and his common-sense approach. He was certainly persistent, the kind of man who was able to command respect. Eliot never got the credit he deserved for helping the inner-city kids, but it was something he was proud of and something people should remember him for."

After initially coming under fire by some opponents for "coddling punks," Ness silenced critics by showing early statistics confirming a dramatic decrease in juvenile crime.

The Mad Butcher case continued to haunt Ness, particularly after two more bodies were uncovered in the lakefront area along Lakeside Avenue, near East 9th Street. The same pattern had been used to dismember the victims, leaving little hope that either would ever be identified. The next morning, Ness had to push himself through the mass of reporters who jammed City Hall, demanding answers.

Mayor Burton and Ness conferred for over an hour. Ness then left City Hall, ignoring the reporters, and traveled to Central Station to join Police Chief Matowitz, Assistant Safety Director Chamberlin, and detectives Merylo and Zalewski. That session, which lasted for three hours, produced one of the most controversial acts in the history of Cleveland law enforcement.

Police officers from all over the city converged at Central Station on the night of August 17, 1938. At around midnight, the group emerged to form a caravan of eleven squad cars, six police vans and three fire trucks. With news reporters and photographers falling in behind, the vehicles progressed to the Flats. They stopped at Canal Street, near the Eagle Street ramp, and huddled for a brief strategy session. In the distance, down over a weed-covered knoll, several small campfires were burning, silhouetting a series of flimsy shacks and shelters.

About ten officers spread out around the perimeter of this makeshift village. Ness and twenty-five others, armed with guns, axes and torches, then moved out in the direction of the vagrants' quarters. Reporters who tried to follow them were ordered away. Ness, who walked several steps ahead of the others, carried a bright flashlight in one hand and an axe in the other. Once everyone was in position, Ness turned around and flashed a signal up the hill.

The area suddenly became illuminated by bright floodlights as the fire trucks rumbled forward. Ahead of them, Ness and the others charged through the heavy brush and rubbish, reaching the shanties in less than a minute. An assortment of hobos and derelicts began to emerge, shielding their eyes from the bright lights in bewilderment. A few of them panicked and tried to flee, only to be chased down and handcuffed by officers. Within a matter of minutes, forty people were loaded into police vehicles and taken to Central Station, where they were jammed into holding cells for later questioning.

The convoy progressed farther down into the Flats and launched a similar raid on another enclave under the Lorain-Carnegie Bridge, then progressed to Kingsbury Run to clear out a third Shantytown beneath the East 37th Street Bridge. These two raids netted another twenty-five homeless people.

At daybreak, while police were still grilling the detainees, Ness and some of the other officers combed through the debris, hoping to find some evidence of the Mad Butcher's presence. Then, as reporters looked on in disbelief, Ness ordered firemen to set the shacks ablaze. Within minutes, thick, black clouds of smoke curled into the air and a heavy stench enveloped the Flats.

Nine of the men and two of the women who had been rounded up were wanted on criminal charges. Another twenty-five people convinced police they were employed or had family members who would care for them. The rest were temporarily jailed on vagrancy charges and eventually directed to social services agencies.

As well-intentioned as the act may have been, it produced no evidence that helped in the investigation. Ness declared that, if nothing else, officials had cleaned up part of Cleveland and perhaps removed some of the Mad Butcher's potential victims. Furthermore, he pointed out almost ghoulishly, fingerprints taken from some of those who were detained might later help in the identification of murder victims.

Ness expected public praise for his aggressive action. Instead, he got mixed reviews. Some Clevelanders applauded him for eliminating an all-too-visible sign of the city's economic and social problems while removing potential victims of the Mad Butcher. At the same time, Ness was criticized for insensitivity to the city's less-fortunate.

"To most of us, the arrest of the Mad Butcher would seem more important than the completing of arrangements for the identification of a possible corpse," scolded the Cleveland Press in a prominently-placed editorial entitled 'Misguided Zeal'. "That such Shantytowns exist is a sorrowful reflection upon the state of society. The throwing into jail of men broken by experience and the burning of their wretched places of habitation will not solve the economic problem. Nor is it likely to lead to the solution of the most macabre mystery in Cleveland's history."

Ness weathered the storm of public criticism without complaint. Only a few close friends, Bob Chamberlin among them, realized that the Public Safety Director was preoccupied. His private life was rapidly deteriorating, draining Ness of the enthusiasm and energy he had brought to the job.

Ness was not inclined to attend social functions at night, perhaps because he was enjoying them so frequently during the day. He and some of his cronies regularly joined the noontime gaiety at downtown Cleveland spots such as the Golden Pheasant and Lotus Gardens, where big-name bands would entertain with midday sets. This was not an unusual phenomenon in the 1930s; executives, government leaders and others who could afford it saw the lunch break as an opportunity to mix business with pleasure.

Earlier in their relationship, Edna had enjoyed dressing up, meeting important people and appearing at her husband's side. But, as time elapsed, she felt imprisoned. Eliot wasn't home enough, and when he was, she felt a certain distance. When she was younger and more impressionable, Edna was blind to Eliot's shortcomings. Now, she believed, his career meant more to him than their relationship, and she was less tolerant.

The Nesses concluded that their relationship was irrevocably broken. Eliot agreed to move into the small apartment he was already renting in the Hampton House complex, at the corner of West Boulevard and Clifton Street in Cleveland. Originally, Ness had secured this apartment at the request of Mayor Burton, who faced flak because his Safety Director who was not a bona fide resident of Cleveland. Ness had stayed at the apartment on occasion when he worked late into the night, but he still used the Bay Village cottage as his primary residence until the separation.

Eliot did express concern that the divorce would damage his reputation in Cleveland, and even entertained thoughts of resigning as Public Safety Director, but Edna talked him out of it. She assured him that, despite their problems, she would attend social functions with him to preserve his public image.

Any chance of reconciliation ended when Edna returned to Chicago to live with relatives. She and Eliot never spoke again. Ness's reaction was to bury himself even deeper in his work, spending sixteen or more hours on the job each day.

When local industries thumbed their noses at the city's new Anti-Smoke Code, designed to curb air pollution, Ness chartered an airplane to carry him and two assistants over the city, looking for violators. Some of those he discovered to be ignoring the ordinance were federal government defense contractors who used political connections to avoid prosecution.

Ness became a regular guest on a popular radio show, "Masterminds: Attention," which aired on Cleveland's WGAR. Ness was among the celebrity panelists grilling witnesses who could answer "yes" or "no" to questions about a mystery. Ness was often so quick to solve the case that the show's producers had to scramble to fill the remaining air time.

While Gerber attracted most of the public attention, Ness quietly consulted with respected criminologists from across the country for advice on the Mad Butcher case. Still believing that the best way to identify the killer was to locate the building where he dismembered his victims, Ness formed six search teams, each consisting of three police officers and a fireman. They inspected every home, hotel, boarding house and commercial establishment in the Third Precinct, purportedly for enforcement of the Fire Safety Code. The raiders discovered poverty and squalor beyond their worst expectations, but not a shred of evidence to suggest that the murders had been committed there.

Editorial writers were chiding Eliot Ness not only for his inability to find the Mad Butcher, but also for his visits to some of Cleveland's trendy night spots with frequent and varied female companions. The city's conservative, Catholic population was critical of Ness when he calmly confirmed reports that his divorce had been finalized. "It was a mutual decision," he told reporters. "We both realized a mistake was made, and we set out to correct it."

Colleagues urged Ness to curb his social activities, but he insisted that he had matters under control. He became such a regular visitor at the Bronze Room in the Hotel Cleveland and the Vogue Room of the Hollenden Hotel that the owners reserved a table near the exit for the exclusive use of Ness and his guests.

Some bizarre, and at times embarrassing, behavior prompted his friends' concern. Once, he invited Ohio Governor Martin L. Davey and State Securities Commissioner Dan T. Moore Jr. to join him for a drink at a commoners' pub. While the three men chatted, a man at the bar created commotion by threatening a waitress. A brief scuffle ensued and police were summoned. The governor, concerned about the publicity that would result, slipped down a fire escape. In reality, Ness had hired an actor to play the assailant as a practical joke.

"I was in on it," recalled Moore during a 1995 interview. "Eliot had pulled that stunt on a couple of other people, but doing it to the governor was going a little overboard. That's just the way

Eliot was at that stage of his life—a fun-loving guy who wasn't beyond an occasional practical joke."

Despite his outward composure and a seemingly constant need to draw attention to himself, Ness could also be shy and nervous. He developed a habit of biting his fingernails to the quick and picking at his thumb with an index finger until the skin was shaved away. He smoked cigarettes, but often extinguished them after taking only a few puffs. Sometimes, he would unwrap a cigar and chew on the end of it until it was a mushy mess, never lighting it.

Ness had plenty of reasons to be nervous—the demise of his marriage, the negative publicity, the frustrations of the Mad Butcher case, and the pressures he was facing as prosecutors prepared to bring some of Cleveland's most powerful underworld figures to justice.

Ness's Minute Men played a major role in the raid of a large home on East 36th Street, where a dozen men working for crime boss Angelo Lonardo were arrested for running a multimillion dollar numbers racket. Among those taken into custody was Moe Dalitz, who had risen to leadership of the Mayfield Road Mob and had threatened Ness in the past.

Word leaked out that Dalitz had offered substantial rewards in return for the identity of jurors and witnesses in the pending trials. Ness responded by placing jury members, witnesses and some members of the prosecution team—himself included—under round-the-clock protection.

"We will not be bullied around by those forces who believe that they are above the law," he declared during a press conference. "Anyone who attempts to tamper with jurors or witnesses will be prosecuted to the full extent of the law."

On April 26, 1939, grand jurors returned indictments against almost twenty-five gangland figures. Among the notables were longtime numbers boss "Big Angelo" Lonardo, "Little Angelo" Scirrca, Charles Pollizi, John Angersola and his brother George. Several Mayfield Road Mob members, Moe Dalitz among them, fled Cleveland, further evidence that the organization's stranglehold had been loosened.

While some of Cleveland's most notorious criminals were being brought to justice, Ness was also back in the news in Chicago, as reporters looked back on the work of the Untouchables following Johnny Torrio's guilty plea to tax evasion charges. Torrio was sentenced to a prison term of two and one-half years. During that same week, Al Capone was transferred from Alcatraz to the new Federal Correctional Institute at Terminal Island near Los Angeles, where he was treated for advanced syphilis.

Chicago reporters asked Jack Guzik if his old friend might someday return to Chicago and pick up the pieces of his criminal organization.

"Naw," said Guzik. "Al's as nutty as a fruitcake."

CHAPTER TWENTY

Social Protection

Ness drew attention wherever he went. Women were attracted by his good looks, his considerate manner and his celebrity status. At Cleveland's night spots, he was often accompanied by Evaline McAndrews, an attractive former model with light brown hair and a ready smile. Evaline, at 27, was nine years younger than Eliot. She had studied at the Art Institute of Chicago before becoming a fashion designer. The two had met casually on a train bound from Cleveland to Minneapolis.

Eliot also became friends with the Stouffer family, which operated a restaurant business in Cleveland and appreciated the Safety Director's attack on extortionists and union arm-twisters. The Stouffers, who would later make their fortune in a frozen foods business that continues to thrive today, allowed Ness to host gatherings at their small boathouse at the mouth of Rocky River on Clifton Lagoon.

With Evaline at his side, Ness was the life of the party. Newspaper reporters and politicians joined in on midnight swims and pre-dawn motorboat rides, causing tongues to wag. They would drink long into the night, yet Ness would arrive fresh at the office the next day.

Evaline set up an art studio in the boathouse, taking advantage of the natural light provided by large windows on all four sides.

On July 7, 1939, with great fanfare, officials from the Cuyahoga County Sheriff's Department announced that they had solved the case of the Mad Butcher. They arrested Frank Dolezal, a despondent Cleveland drifter who had worked as a bricklayer and a slaughterhouse laborer. Although Dolezal had no criminal record, he had once been seen with Flo Polillo, the Mad Butcher's first known victim. One witness told police Dolezal liked to display the knives he carried wherever he went.

Under questionable circumstances, Dolezal signed a confession to one of the early murders. It was not much to go on, but Cleveland's law enforcement agencies were desperate. Ness was skeptical from the start. Publicly, he expressed hope that police had found their man. Privately, he didn't believe Dolezal had murdered anyone.

The more Dolezal talked, the more the case against him crumbled. He had a variety of stories to tell, many of them inconsistent or contradictory. A week after his arrest, he withdrew his confession. Dolezal then told a tale of being blindfolded and beaten by sheriff's deputies until he told them what they wanted to hear.

On August 24, the lifeless body of Frank Dolezal was found dangling against the bars of his cell door at the Cuyahoga County Jail. He hanged himself with a rope made of cleaning rags. An autopsy revealed that six of his ribs had been broken, possible corroboration of his claim that he had been beaten.

Eliot Ness and Evaline McAndrews drove to Greenup, Kentucky on October 13 and exchanged wedding vows before a justice of the peace. Two days later, Ness was back at his desk, where he found a file folder marked, "Eliot: Urgent!" Inside he found a stack of newspaper clippings and memos from Detective Merylo containing the latest news of the Mad Butcher.

A group of boys looking for walnuts discovered the nude, headless corpse of a male in a weed patch about 150 yards from a railroad track near New Castle, Pa. The killer had apparently taken the body to the woods and attempted to burn it by igniting a pile of newspapers, one of which was a three-week-old edition of the Youngstown (Ohio) Vindicator. That ruled out Frank Dolezal as a suspect and all but eliminated any possibility that he was the Mad Butcher. The victim's head was found almost a week later in a railroad car.

Merylo and Zalewski traveled to New Castle to inspect the remains. Based on the way the victim had been decapitated and other factors, Merylo told a New Castle News reporter that the killer was probably "a train-riding pervert who possibly holds forth in box cars or hobo jungles, where he finds his victims and then uses a box car for an operating room."

The victim was never identified. Investigators concluded he was probably a Cleveland area vagabond who rode into Pennsylvania as a stowaway on the same train that carried his killer.

Evaline Ness resumed her career as an advertising designer at Higbee's Department Store. Her first few months as Mrs. Eliot Ness exceeded all of her expectations. The two mixed business and pleasure in the proper doses, attending to their professional responsibilities by day and socializing with some of Cleveland's wealthiest and most influential couples at night.

"That may have been the best part of Eliot's life," Evaline said. "He was a happy man who enjoyed what he was doing. He never really talked about his work much. We'd go out at night and have a good time, but there wouldn't be talk about his job. He always kept his emotions controlled. In fact, Eliot was probably the most controlled man I ever knew."

Ness resumed playing tennis whenever his schedule allowed and prided himself on remaining trim. He faithfully exercised each morning and frequented a health club for sessions of jujitsu or handball. His fitness was remarkable, considering his drinking and eating habits. Ness rarely ate salads, vegetables and spiced food; even the smell of a strong spice could make him ill. His diet was usually meat and potatoes. And he rarely had time for those who complained of minor illness or injury. Ness hardly ever missed a day of work himself and was not very sympathetic to those who did.

Ness sometimes walked the street beat with police officers, trying to keep in touch with the common citizens, particularly teenagers. Ted Kuhn, the former Chicago Prohibition agent who became an Alcohol Tax Unit officer in Cleveland, told of the time he and Ness stopped at an East Side tavern. Suddenly, a patron excitedly approached the bar and demanded a payoff for hitting the jackpot on the "Paces Races" pinball machine. Ness stopped the transaction, walked over to a pay phone, and summoned police to confiscate the machine.

"Who are you?" the bartender asked.

"I'm Eliot Ness, Public Safety Director."

"No, you're not," said a wag at the end of the bar. "I know Ness personally, and you sure as hell aren't him."

Ness rose to button his overcoat and motioned for Kuhn to join him as he stepped away from the bar to leave. "If you don't believe me," he shouted back to the bartender, "just ask the cop who's been hiding in the corner since we came in. His drink is still on the bar."

The Mad Butcher case moved back to the front page on May 3, 1940, after the rotting remains of another victim were found stuffed into a burlap bag discovered on a train boxcar after it arrived in McKees Rocks, Pennsylvania, from Ohio. Inside another car, police found a second body sprawled on the floor, stripped naked and decapitated. A third butchered victim was discovered in another car. Evidence compiled over the next few days traced the murders to Youngstown, Ohio, sometime around Christmas 1939.

"I think it's safe to say that the Mad Butcher's victims now number twenty-three," Detective Peter Merylo told a stunned Cleveland public.

A conclusive body count was impossible to make; Merylo's figure was probably high. No other murders would be attributed to the Mad Butcher, which somewhat vindicated Ness for his decision to destroy the vagrants' quarters. Although Merylo continued to investigate, both as a city employee and as a private detective, the case was never solved. It became the subject of a well-researched book, entitled *Torso*, by Steven Nickel (1989, John F. Blair, Publisher). Merylo's six-year mission resulted in over 1,000 arrests for sex offenses, an unrelated murder, abortion, immigration law violations, drug trafficking, burglary and white slavery operations.

One by one, Ness saw his colleagues move away. With World War II escalating, Bob Chamberlin left to join the Army. Tom Clothey, who had worked for Ness as one of the Unknowns, became Assistant Safety Director before leaving to join U.S. Naval Intelligence. Ness lost another important ally when Mayor Harold Burton was elected to the U.S. Senate. He was succeeded by his Assistant Law Director, Edward Blythin.

Eliot Ness's final attack on crime took place in mid-1940. Armed with incriminating evidence against one of Cleveland's remaining union power brokers, Albert Ruddy, Ness paid a call on Harry Barrington at the State Prison Farm in Mount Vernon. In return for his freedom, Barrington promised to detail for the court how he carried out direct orders from Ruddy to pry shake-down money from dozens of Cleveland area business owners. He was also able to point the finger at Ruddy for the 1936 murder of Albert Whitelock, a rival union leader, and the 1933 bombing of a downtown Cleveland laundry.

Despite elaborate security precautions, Cleveland's union lead-ers learned of the meeting and sent word to Mount Vernon that Barrington would be executed if he talked. Ness knew he had to move quickly, so he rented an apartment in the Cleveland suburbs and held Barrington there under armed guard.

A grand jury indicted Ruddy and his enforcer, Vincent Dylin-ski, in June. Defense lawyers focused their attention on the cred-ibility of Eliot Ness and his star witness, Harry Barrington. They argued that Ness was a self-promoting union-buster who would stop at nothing, including the fabrication of evidence, to advance his personal career. The attorneys also contended that Barrington, whose record included blackmail and extortion convictions, was merely trying to reduce his own jail time by presenting false testimony.

Jurors lacked sufficient evidence to support a murder convic-tion, but did find Ruddy guilty of racketeering. He was sentenced to a four-year prison term. The ever-fickle Cleveland newspapers praised Ness for his unwavering fight against Cleveland's most elusive criminals. "Ness was never content to put Al Capone behind bars," the Cleveland News editorialized. "Apparently, he will not rest until every enemy of the people has been brought to justice."

By then, Capone was a free man, obese, partly bald, and diso-riented as he roamed the grounds of his Palm Island estate. Ca-pone regularly expressed regret for his misdeeds and told visitors that he had accepted Jesus Christ as his savior during prison revival services.

Back in Cleveland, there was much speculation that the low-key mayor, Edwin Blythin, would step down in 1941 to pave the way for Eliot Ness to run for the position. Republican friends tried to persuade Ness to throw his hat into the ring, but he declined. Ness, in fact, was looking for new career opportunities outside of Cleveland, either in business or police administration.

As the war effort escalated, the government sought a high-profile spokesperson with skills in public safety education to warn military recruits about the dangers of venereal disease. Ness accepted the part-time position as a consultant to the new "Federal Social Protection Program," even as he remained in office as Public Safety Director. Critics chided Ness for his long absences as he traveled to government offices in New York and Washington, as well as military bases across the country, promoting abstinence and safe sex. Ness responded by citing the public service example set by New York Mayor Fiorello LaGuardia, who also served as the nation's Civil Defense Chief.

Ness also found time to author a series of articles for American City magazine, providing suggestions for urban leaders to combat crime and improve traffic safety.

The frequent separations took a toll on Eliot's relationship with Evaline. Like Edna, she understood his dedication to duty and the importance of his work, but Evaline was lonely and restless, much too vibrant a woman to stay at home every night. When he was on the road, Ness spent a lot of his time in taverns and night clubs, failing to check in with Evaline for days at a time.

"Evaline liked being Eliot's wife when he was a famous and influential public official, and when he was home," said one of the Nesses' friends. "She liked his prominence and power and fame. And he loved her, no question about it. He always called her 'Doll'. But Eliot started drifting back to his carefree lifestyle. Something had to give."

Ness's connections with Cleveland's political establishment were also loosening. Frank Lausche, the Democrat who was an easy winner in the November mayoral election, owed much of his success to Democratic County Chairman Ray T. Miller, who was no fan of Eliot Ness. Miller had lined up solid union support for Lausche by promising, among other things, that Ness would be fired if Lausche were elected. Miller had even contacted another Ness opponent, J. Edgar Hoover, to line up a "qualified" replacement.

But Lausche admired and respected Ness, dating back to the 1936 raid at the Harvard Club when, as judge, Lausche had issued the warrant to County Prosecutor Frank Cullitan. Upon taking office in January 1942, he steadfastly refused to fire Eliot Ness. This show of independence would come to characterize Lausche's later career as Governor of Ohio and a United States Senator.

Other problems were brewing for Ness. He was unable to track down the principles of the dreaded National Death Incorporated insurance racket actively operating in Cleveland. Investors took out numerous life insurance policies on chronic alcoholics, then kept the insured parties supplied with copious quantities of alcohol until they either died from overconsumption or were hit by a car, sometimes intentionally.

His reputation slipping, Ness trotted out statistics showing that traffic fatalities in Cleveland had been reduced by forty percent, resulting in a corresponding drop in auto insurance rates. Newspaper reports heralded the findings and gave much of the credit to Ness, but the public was more interested in the Safety Director's shortcomings.

Ness was also being pressured to disband his undercover unit, the Unknowns, who had been hidden on the city's payroll as laborers. The Cleveland business community was not nearly as generous with donations to the special investigative fund, now that organized crime had lost so much of its clout.

While the controversy over his future in Cleveland swirled, Eliot Ness on March 5, 1942 provided political opponents with the ammunition they needed.

CHAPTER TWENTY-ONE

'I'm Sure Having Fun'

On a cold, rainy night, Eliot and Evaline Ness joined friends for several hours of dining, drinking and dancing at the Vogue Room of the Hollenden Hotel. This 14-story red brick Victorian structure near Public Square was considered the hub of Cleveland's downtown social life, and it drew the elite among its patrons.

The Nesses and another couple stayed to close the lounge, then retired to a private room to continue their socializing. Finally, at about 4:30 a.m., they made their way to the parking lot and Eliot started to drive home.

A frigid north wind had transformed an earlier rain into a frozen glare on the highways. Ness eased the couple's Cadillac onto Buckley Avenue, near what is now the West Memorial Shoreway, when he spotted two tiny headlights approaching in the opposite lane.

As the lights grew brighter, they flashed annoying reflections on the icy roadway. Suddenly, as Ness turned the steering wheel to negotiate a slight curve to the left, his car started to slide sideways. The lights of the oncoming car filled most of Eliot's field of vision and the vehicles collided.

Evaline Ness was hurled, shoulder first, against the dashboard. Squinting her eyes and rubbing her head, she tried to get her bearings. Eliot hurried over to check on the other driver. He was Robert Sims, a 21-year-old East Cleveland resident who was still seated behind the wheel, his driver's side door open and his feet resting on the car's running board.

Sims had struck his head on the steering wheel and jammed his knee against the dashboard. After determining that Sims could still drive his car, Ness suggested he follow them to a nearby hospital.

Ness returned to his car, where he found Evaline sitting up, still groggy, and having trouble catching her breath. He felt his wife's head and discovered a bruise above her right ear. Although the metal of their car's left front panel had collapsed, there was still about an inch of clearance between the fender and the front tire.

What happened after that was never fully established. Joseph Koneval, a Cleveland police officer, spotted Sims' car parked alongside the road, a few feet from the point of impact. Sims was nowhere to be found. Later that morning, another motorist told police he had found the victim still sitting in his car and persuaded Sims to accompany him to a hospital for observation. Hospital staffers reported that an anonymous man had called to inquire about Sims' condition.

Sims himself was able to solve the mystery. From his hospital bed, he told police that the other driver had refused to identify himself, but that the license plate of the car was EN-1. Visited at his home by two investigators just before noon, Ness admitted his involvement in the crash and pleaded with the two officers to downplay the episode. Uncomfortable with the Safety Director's request, they shared the information with their captain, who was among police officials under investigation for improper conduct. The captain gleefully telephoned the Cleveland newspapers to share the details of Eliot Ness's crash.

Journalists found plenty of headline value in the revelation that the city's heralded Public Safety Director, an aggressive enforcer of Prohibition laws, had crashed into an innocent motorist following a night of drinking.

Three days after the crash, Ness broke his silence by calling a news conference. While admitting that he had been drinking, Ness steadfastly denied being intoxicated. He blamed the icy road surface and said he had every reason to believe Sims would follow him to the hospital. When he failed to see headlights behind him, Ness said, he circled back around to the scene of the crash, but Sims was gone.

By that time, Ness claimed, Evaline insisted that she would be all right and they drove home. Ness admitted that he phoned the hospital to inquire about Sims' condition. He further conceded that he declined to identify himself on the phone, and subsequently pressured the investigating officers, because he wanted to avoid unflattering publicity.

"It was very slippery and the thing just happened like that," Ness told reporters, snapping his fingers to reinforce the point. "I have never regretted anything more in my life. It was a very unfortunate thing all the way through."

"I remember the accident," Evaline would later tell a reporter. "It was icy. I think I was telling Eliot something about a reporter I had told off, and we were laughing. It was an ordinary thing. We just slid into the car."

Evaline said the crash took a toll on her husband, who broke his upper dental plate during the collision. "I don't think he could stand the criticism, especially when it came to his job. That's why he tried to avoid the publicity. It certainly did not reflect well on him."

No charges were ever filed, but the damage to Ness's image was irreversible. Mayor Lausche wasn't satisfied with his explanation; neither were the people of Cleveland. The fact that he was drinking into the wee hours of the morning and then trying to operate his car caused many Clevelanders to question Ness's judgment.

Lausche summoned Ness for a private meeting. There is no record of what transpired, but the outcome was immediate. The following morning, on April 30, 1942, Eliot Ness tendered his resignation as Public Safety Director. He claimed his departure was the result of his promotion to the position of National Director of the Federal Social Protection Program, under the Federal Office of Defense Health and Welfare Services. The more likely story behind the resignation was that Lausche demanded it.

"Cleveland is a different place than it was when Eliot Ness became Safety Director," wrote columnist Clayton Fritchey in saying goodbye to his friend. "Ness restored a sense of hope and pride to a beleaguered community. Cleveland was in desperate need for a lawman with the talent and integrity of Eliot Ness.

Today, policemen no longer have to tip their hats when they pass a gangster on the streets. Labor racketeers no longer parade down Euclid Avenue in limousines bearing placards deriding the public and law enforcement in general. Motorists have been taught and tamed into killing only about half as many people as they used to slaughter."

Philip Porter of the Plain Dealer was even more effusive in his praise:

"One way in which the Ness administration differed sharply from the others was that he rooted out and minimized departmental politics and when it popped up he got tough with it. He was always several jumps ahead of the chair-warmers and connivers in city government, and even to this day they can't figure him out, but have spent a good deal of their time criticizing him. As Ness enters full-time federal service, an era has ended here. The heights of law enforcement and competence which have been built up during Ness's six-year administration are so outstanding among American city experiences as to be a little amazing when you get away from town and begin to analyze and compare them. When he took office, the town was ridden with crooked police and crooked labor bosses. A dozen such were sent to prison, and scores of others scared into resignation or inactivity. There were gambling halls on every block and lush casinos in the suburbs. The little joints mostly folded and finally the big joints quit when a couple of Ness's honest cops were put in the sheriff's office. The town reached such a condition of comparative purity that about all the continual critics had to complain about was occasional bingo, strip-teasers and some policy games. We'll probably never have perfection in any municipal police administration, but we have gradually achieved something as near it as any big city is ever likely to, and we ought to be grateful to Ness for it."

The Nesses moved to Washington, D.C., where they settled into a luxurious home provided to them rent-free. Ness, now 39, tackled his new role with the same vigor he had once demonstrated in both Chicago and Cleveland.

Most of his time was spent far from home at military bases. In one sense, Eliot Ness and Al Capone were fighting the same enemy—venereal disease. Ness attacked it as a lecturer and distributor of literature at military installations. Capone's battle was a more personal one, as he drifted in and out of reality at his Miami compound.

One of Ness's assignments was to establish alliances with law enforcement authorities in communities which hosted or surrounded the military bases, in an effort to stamp out prostitution. This put Eliot Ness in a familiar situation—at odds with organized crime. In one bizarre episode, prostitutes and their supporters rallied around the site of an anti-crime speech by Ness in Peoria, Illinois, harassing the audience and displaying signs decrying Ness's actions as an affront to their personal liberties.

Labeling VD "military saboteur number one," an undaunted Ness dusted off the federal government's May Act, which imposed stiff penalties for prostitution near military bases or recruiting stations. He threatened to revoke the licenses of bars, hotels, cab services and other businesses that thrived on soldiers' paychecks if they continued to cooperate with hookers.

Prostitutes who were apprehended had two options: a jail term and fine, or enlistment in a Civilian Conservation Corps camp for alternative vocational education. Navy officials gave Ness high marks for his work, presenting him with their Meritorious Service Citation in 1943. His personnel files show that Ness also earned consistently high marks from his superiors for resourcefulness, organizational skills and initiative.

None of this could compensate for the troubles Ness was once again having on the home front.

"Eliot liked the job quite a bit and I did, too," Evaline told an interviewer in 1976. "We'd go to all these towns and he'd advise them how to get rid of their red light districts. It was funny, in a way. We met a lot of funny people in those towns, believe me, but after a while it wasn't enjoyable. It wasn't what I wanted to do with my life. Eliot realized that."

Evaline was also uncomfortable in the role of socialite. Whenever Eliot returned to Washington for extended stays, he wanted to host dinner parties for wealthy friends. The guests at these affairs were people Evaline hardly knew and with whom she had little in common; she had her own circle of friends by that time.

Her resentment over Eliot's long absences and his insensitivity to her needs deepened. In 1944, she left her husband under circumstances that neither was inclined to discuss. She rented an apartment in New York City, where she resumed her career as an artist and fashion designer. Communication between Eliot and Evaline was infrequent, at best. More than a year would pass before paperwork was completed to officially bring their marriage to an end on November 17, 1945. Court documents listed the cause as "gross neglect and extreme cruelty" on Eliot's part. Evaline ended up moving to Florida, where she developed a successful and financially rewarding career as an illustrator of children's books.

With World War II winding down and the Federal Social Protection Agency being phased out, Ness began looking for new opportunities. Among friends he had made while cutting his convivial swath through Cleveland's social scene was Janet Rex, daughter of the late Ralph Rex, majority shareholder of the Diebold Safe & Lock Company from Canton, Ohio. Impressed by Ness's reputation and his business degree from the University of Chicago, Rex made him an offer he could not refuse: step in and manage the family's business interests.

Wartime government contracts for armor plating had helped Diebold become the nation's third largest safe and vault manufacturer. On June 15, 1944, the Rexes installed Eliot Ness as chairman of the board of directors and ordered him to restructure the administratively waterlogged firm. He returned to Cleveland alone, with no fanfare.

Ness sorted through personnel files and consulted with a handful of trusted, experienced executives. He eliminated duplication up and down the corporate ladder, building resentments among some of the more entrenched employees. Ness also steered Diebold down a path of diversification. He saw the potential for using plastic, still in its infancy as an industry, in many of Diebold's products. In addition, Ness opened a separate division for the production and marketing of microfilm equipment. This became known as the Visible Records Company, a Diebold subsidiary.

During his off-hours, a new romance helped soften the emotional sting of a second failed marriage. His companion was Elisabeth Anderson Seaver, a petite and pretty brunette with dark eyes and a pleasant smile. A native of Sioux Falls, South Dakota, "Betty" graduated from the Cleveland Art Institute and became an accomplished sculptor, studying under the renowned Carl Mittes. Her work was featured in many prominent Cleveland art exhibits. A bas-relief she created still hangs over the entrance of City Hall in Sioux Falls. During World War II, Betty served as a camouflage expert at the Glenn L. Martin Aircraft Plant in Baltimore.

Like Eliot, Betty was pleasant, but withdrawn. She had recently ended a troubled marriage to an architect which left her so depressed that family members were concerned about her well-being. Betty and Eliot met through their mutual friendship with Dan Moore, the colorful Ohio Securities Commissioner, and his wife Elizabeth, who was also a sculptor.

In late 1945, Ness led Diebold's approach to a major competitor, York Safe & Lock Company of York, Pennsylvania, with a merger proposal. That deal was consummated in January 1946, with Ness becoming chiefly responsible for the York firm's thriving safe and vault business, as well as York's sales force and branch offices.

To the outside world, Eliot Ness was a dynamic business leader destined for vast wealth and prominence. Behind the scenes, there was disenchantment with his lack of attention to detail and lingering resentment by a small, but powerful, group of mid-level executives who disliked him from the start. Some of Ness's friends, both inside and outside of the company, warned him that he was a marked man. Among those who could see what was happening was Dan Moore.

Dan Tyler Moore Jr. had returned to his native Cleveland in 1937 with a physics degree from Yale and a wealth of experience in foreign affairs, politics and economics. Moore had directed the new Securities & Exchange Commission (SEC) under Joseph P. Kennedy. Upon his return to Ohio, he handed out patronage jobs for President Franklin Roosevelt and was tabbed to head the state's Securities Division. His main target was Cleveland, the "fraud capital of the United States" at that time. Moore admired the work Eliot Ness had done in Cleveland, even though the two were at opposite ends of the political spectrum.

Moore went on to direct Cleveland's regional office of the SEC and Civil Defense, then served as a civilian major with the new Office of Strategic Services, forerunner of today's Central Intelligence Agency. Among Moore's duties was to sort out the respective responsibilities of the OSS and the Federal Bureau of Investigation.

Moore was later dispatched to Egypt, ostensibly as an assistant to the Middle East's economic ministry, but in reality as a spy. He served as chief of the region's counter-intelligence during World War II, helping to foil an assassination attempt on King George of Greece and barely escaping snipers' fire in Cairo after his cover was blown.

In Egypt, and later in Turkey, Moore was closely associated with James Landis, former dean of Harvard Law School, Commissioner of the Federal Trade Commission, Chairman of the Securities and Exchange Commission, and National Director of the Office of Civil Defense. Landis had powerful influence on Middle East economic matters during the war, directing the movement of goods, the raising of crops, and the issuance of loans in connection with the U.S. war effort.

Moore and Landis parlayed their close contacts with Middle East government and business leaders into a private export/import business, the Middle East Company, and brought Eliot Ness aboard as a partner.

"This business had real possibilities," Moore explained. "Naturally, I was eager to let some of my good friends in on it, and I was probably Eliot's best friend at that time. Our troops had dropped millions of dollars in the Middle East during the war and all of that money had to be repatriated. We had a chance to cash in on that. Eliot jumped at the chance, which was a wise move, because his days at Diebold were numbered."

Ness became vice president and treasurer of the Middle East Company, while holding onto his position at Diebold, at least in title. He signed his name in a clear, confident manner, stretching the final S with a long upward flight of ink. It's the mark of a person who takes pride in finishing a job, handwriting experts say. Looking out over New York from a Middle East Company office he occupied part-time in Rockefeller Center, Ness was seen as a rising star in business circles. The January 1946 edition of Fortune magazine featured a story entitled, "There Goes Eliot Ness," excerpted as follows:

"The headwaiters at such Cleveland night spots as the Hotel Hollenden's Vogue Room and the Hotel Cleveland's Bronze Room all have tables reserved for a slimly handsome young man who may show up only a few evenings a month, but who instantly commands much attention from both sexes. He is Eliot Ness, a lakeside business headliner as the Board Chairman of Diebold, Inc. (safes, locks and office equipment) and VP of James M. Landis' Middle East Company. His table is invariably situated near the exit. Ever since his days as a special Chicago Prohibition agent in the Capone era, he has preferred to appear in a place rather than to enter it. Ness could probably be elected Mayor of Cleveland in a walkaway. Last summer, indeed, he turned down a firm offer of the Republican nomination. One unannounced reason was that he is too absorbed in his $24,000-a-year business role with Diebold to exchange it for the $15,000 political job. Ness likes to use high-flown management engineering terms in discussing what he has done at Diebold; others might say simply that he has an excellent intuitive judgment of people, plus administrative ability. At Diebold, his principal contributions thus far have been the elimination of management deadwood, the discovery and promotion of buried talent, and the revival of a discarded reorganization program. When Ness moved in, Diebold was warring with itself over what to do when the war was over. It was also having renegotiation trouble as a result of consistent overcharging. Ness promptly put through a policy of voluntary price reductions, which boosted net profits. All the new officers filling the ranks are sold on modern administrative methods and Diebold's expansion into a dozen new lines of office equipment. Most competent observers agree Ness has made an excellent start. Some of them suspend judgment on what may happen to Ness and Diebold in the tough world of the office equipment business. Ness himself says, 'I may fall flat on my face, but I'm sure having fun'."

Eliot's romance with Betty blossomed and the two were married in a quiet civil ceremony on January 31, 1946.

"We talked about a big wedding, with all our friends and family members there for a big celebration, but we both decided that we didn't want all the fuss," Eliot told friends in announcing the nuptials. "We're just eager to get on with our lives."

CHAPTER TWENTY-TWO

What Might Have Been...

In the midst of juggling his business responsibilities at Diebold and the Middle East Company with a new marriage, Ness became acquainted with an internationally-recognized hero, Claire Lee Chennault. The two hit it off from the start.

A tall Texan with rugged features and a commanding voice, Chennault earned a reputation as a daring pilot and a serious student of air tactics, as well as a zealous believer in the importance of fighter aviation. He retired from the U.S. Army Air Corps in 1937 due to physical disability and became Advisor on Aeronautical Affairs to the Chinese National Government. In 1941, he organized and trained the famous "Flying Tigers," a group of American pilots recruited to fight for the Chinese against Japanese aggressions, especially in defense of the Burma Road.

At age fifty-one, Chennault returned to active duty with the U.S. Army Air Forces as a Brigadier General. His leadership and superior tactics helped greatly to overcome the inferiority of his airmen in numbers and equipment. Chennault became a national legend in China. Upon his retirement as a Major General in 1945, he was anxious to capitalize on his relationships with China's government, military and industrial leaders. To help accomplish this goal, he turned to Eliot Ness.

Chennault convinced Ness that the Middle East Company could profit by importing silk and other Chinese goods. He was also optimistic that, through a new air freight service to be called "Chennault Airlines," Ness's group could deliver a variety of American goods to China.

Transportation was the major impediment. Air travel was restricted to the mostly government-owned Chinese National Airways, which was inefficient and congested with passenger traffic.

Due to the prolonged war with Japan, China's railways and roads had been largely obliterated. River transport was slow and of limited usefulness. Movement of commodities from the main arteries to the interior villages was accomplished by slow, arduous sampan or pack train.

China's demand for goods from abroad was sharpened by eight years of war with Japan. However, many export/import firms had shied away from China, due to economic uncertainties, volatile political affairs, customs duties, taxes and tolls imposed by provincial and city officials.

Chennault believed he could overcome these obstacles through his connections in China, combined with strong U.S. government support for businesses helping China to strengthen herself against the Soviet Union. Ness shared the general's enthusiasm, but his optimism did not rub off on Moore and Landis. In fact, Landis was already having second thoughts about the Middle East Company and laying the groundwork for a private law practice.

Moore and Landis reluctantly agreed to serve as directors, at least in a limited capacity, and provide financial support to get the new business started. In collaboration with General Chennault, they formed the Far East Company and a subsidiary, the Far East Textile Company, to deal exclusively with the China trade.

Among the seven others they persuaded to buy stock were: James C. Gruener, a prominent attorney with offices in Cleveland and Washington; General Benedict Crowell, former Assistant Secretary of War and a director of the Nickel Plate Railroad; James W. Huffman, a U.S. Senator from Ohio; and Dan Maggin, a New York financier, Director of the American Window Glass Company, and a major Diebold investor.

The Far East Company was doomed from the start. China, trying to protect her economy against outside domination, kept firm control over international trade and industry. The Chinese government bypassed private enterprise by purchasing supplies from the United Nations Rehabilitation & Relief Association. Private imports were subject to stiff, sometimes arbitrarily imposed, duties. In addition, the Far East Company faced intense competition. By July 1946, more than 100 American firms and numerous British companies were operating export/import businesses in Shanghai.

In an attempt to capitalize on a new national law requiring that the majority of stockholders in all companies be residents of China, Chennault fell back on his connections to form the Sino-American Industrial & Development Company. Chennault was one of only two Americans officially listed among the thirty-member board of directors and supervisors. Many of the other officers were current or former military leaders and successful businessmen. Chinese General Shen Yu, former field commander of the 9th War Zone in China, was elected chairman of the board. In a speech presented during the first organizational meeting, Yu told of the great esteem in which he held Chennault and his U.S. associates for their humanitarian gestures.

"On his departure for the States from Shanghai, the general emphasized to me that he would reject any offers made with the sole purpose of making profit," Yu said, according to an English translation of his remarks. "In other words, Americans who invest in this undertaking must also be willing, as the general himself is, to assist the Chinese people and to help us in the task of reconstruction... Now that the general is ready to lend a hand in improving our living conditions or environment, we are only too glad to take a part in the work for the interest of our country."

A letter Chennault sent to Ness from Shanghai that same month made no mention of such lofty goals.

"Despite pessimistic reports, I am convinced the time is ripe for action," Chennault wrote. "The Chinese need trade desperately and will work out problems and establish firm contacts with someone else if we don't take advantage of the opportunity offered."

Whatever his motivations, Chennault presented his detailed plans for Chennault Airlines to the Chinese government, then began laying the groundwork for establishment of bus service in Chengtu, a Chinese cultural and academic center. Back in the U.S., Ness obtained quotes from a Detroit firm for the purchase of fifty Ford buses. He also lined up buyers for silk and other fabrics Chennault had secured at prices that were a fraction of the amount those goods would bring in the U.S. Among the potential customers was the Macy's organization.

For the first few months, the Far East Company imported Chinese silk, musk and dye, generating modest profits for both Chennault and the American stockholders. However, Chennault soon found it difficult to obtain export permits. More silk eventually did arrive in New York, but the material was of such poor quality that the U.S. buyers Ness had found, including Macy's, rejected it.

General Chennault created an uproar in China when he negotiated a $3 million loan from the Chinese Relief and Rehabilitation Administration for the purchase of twelve huge transport planes. Some saw the plan as a ploy to set up a private American air service in China under the guise of a relief operation. The loan was eventually approved, but with two important stipulations: that the planes not carry commercial cargo, and that empty space on return trips be taken up by government non-military materials and official passengers. Chennault would still be entitled to "reasonable profit," but the prospect of capitalizing on the relief missions was eliminated.

With the Communist takeover, the government assumed responsibility for all aspects of trade in China, including the operation of a new Soviet-backed, state-controlled civil airline. Within a year, the U.S. government banned all trade with Mainland China, effectively bankrupting the Far East Company.

The venture with General Chennault now behind him, Ness concentrated his efforts on negotiating a series of contracts between the two companies he still served. The Middle East Company became sales agent for Diebold steel doors in the domestic marketplace. This relatively minor business arrangement signaled a desperate change in direction. As the export/import business collapsed, domestic distribution appeared to be the only way the Middle East Company could avoid bankruptcy.

Thomas Dunn, a skilled businessman, was brought aboard as a full-time general manager. In his first report to stockholders, Dunn painted a rosy future. "The Middle East area is becoming important to the U.S. for international security reasons, and because of raw materials vital to the U.S. economy," Dunn wrote. "The Middle East Company now has affiliated companies in all of the important Middle Eastern countries. The affiliates are financed by persons of great political and business influence in each of these countries, from a cousin of the King of Egypt to the richest industrialist in Turkey."

Moore and Landis had made in-roads in Turkey, Egypt, Lebanon, Syria, Greece, Iran, Iraq and Ethiopia. And yet, the Middle East Company earned commissions of barely over $25,000 during its first year, due to competition and unfavorable U.S. government policies. Export licenses were difficult to obtain. At the same time, the Office of Price Administration (OPA) limited the Middle East Company's ability to bring goods into the U.S., since other countries were purchasing commodities at higher prices than the OPA allowed American firms to pay.

Even more devastating to American import/export firms were some very complex developments in the international monetary system. During the Great Depression in this country, Britain had stimulated its export business by going off the gold standard. Other nations having extensive trade relations with England followed suit, tying their currencies to the British pound sterling. The outbreak of World War II transformed the sterling area from a loose federation to a very compact union controlling foreign exchange and imports. Funds could move freely within the area, but not outside except under terms of agreement.

While a sterling area country might earn dollars by exporting, it could not freely use these dollars to buy U.S. exports. Instead, the country's dollars were pooled with those of other countries in the area and rationed out to buy imports regarded by London as most essential to the war.

After the war, the U.S. government approved a $3.75 billion loan to Britain to abolish the dollar pool and liberalize exchange controls throughout the sterling area. These countries were given five years to make the transition— putting import/export companies in a desperate race against the calendar.

England's ambassadors across the globe were much more effective advocates than were the U.S. ambassadors. British officials established strong ties with government leaders and wealthy industrialists. The American ambassadors were mostly political appointees who did not stay put long enough to make the contacts necessary to help American companies gain a foothold in international trade.

Despite these obstacles, the Middle East Company remained afloat, due in large part to the officers' willingness to defer their salaries until economic conditions improved. A contract with the Charles Pfizer Company to send pharmaceuticals to Portugal, Turkey, Lebanon and Egypt gave the company a quick infusion of cash. The Middle East Company also represented a West Virginia company selling electric fans and appliances to European nations, and helped a Tennessee firm sell hosiery in Cuba.

At the same time, the company landed contracts for importing Ponderosa pine from Mexico for resale to several Cleveland area lumber yards. This was arranged through Fermin F. Nunez, a businessman whose close government ties landed him the bulk of export permits issued in his region of Mexico.

Directors of the Middle East Company saw Turkey as the most promising long-term market for American goods, due to connections Moore had established. There was an increasing demand for steel products, automotive and railroad supplies, industrial equipment and consumer goods. Moore was dispatched to Turkey to lay the groundwork for a marketing plan that became the cornerstone of the Middle East Company's efforts to lure new investors.

Moore persuaded the government leaders to approve construction of a massive hotel in Istanbul, then sold the idea to Intercontinental Hotels Corporation, a subsidiary of Pan American Airlines. In return for the rights to build the hotel, Pan Am agreed to cut the Middle East Company in on the deal as "founder and promoter," for a fee of $100,000.

Although Moore kept his partners back home apprised of developments, Ness and the others appeared to be preoccupied with their own affairs, which left Moore feeling angry, isolated and betrayed.

"I don't hold it against Eliot or any of the others personally," Moore said many years later. "I never considered Eliot a very effective businessman, and he had a lot going on at the time."

The year 1947 was one of the most eventful in Eliot Ness's life. It began with news that Andrew Volstead had died in Granite Falls, Minnesota, his faith unshaken to the end that "the law does regulate morality." A week later, Al Capone died in Florida of complications from a brain hemorrhage and bronchial pneumonia.

In late January, Eliot and Betty Ness adopted a three-year-old boy, who they named Robert Warren Ness "Parenthood was a new experience for Eliot and he enjoyed it immensely, when he could find the time," said a friend of the Nesses. "He was very frustrated that he had to travel to New York and Washington so frequently on business. He was spread too thin. He wanted to spend more time with Betty and Bobby, and they missed him, too. Betty tried to be understanding, but she felt abandoned at times."

Ness felt a growing restlessness and an unshakable desire to return to public service. He missed the challenges and the excitement of outwitting criminals and rooting out corruption or ineptitude. With those frustrations in mind, Ness shocked even his closest friends by announcing that he was putting his business career on "hold" to run in the 1947 election for Mayor of Cleveland. A number of prominent Cleveland Republicans had practically camped on the former Public Safety Director's doorstep, urging him to return to the city and campaign for mayor. Other popular Republicans had steered clear of the race because they considered the Democratic incumbent, Thomas A. Burke, unbeatable.

No one was more appalled by the decision than Dan Moore, who had just returned from Turkey when he heard the news. "He sat right here in my parlor and said, 'I'm going to give it a try,' with a smile on his face," Moore recalled. "I told him he was crazy. I knew he couldn't win and I told him that, but he didn't want to believe it."

Ralph Kelly, a political reporter for the Cleveland Plain Dealer, was among those who convinced Ness he had a chance. Kelly believed Ness's achievements as Safety Director carried more weight with voters than the problems he had with labor unions and the negative publicity stemming from the car crash and his social activities. The popular Bob Chamberlin agreed to serve as Ness's campaign chairman.

While Ness was away, Frank Lausche had resigned as mayor to seek Ohio's gubernatorial nomination. He was succeeded by Burke, a popular Democrat who had been a close friend of Ness's.

Industrial leaders welcomed the return of Eliot Ness, whose earlier battles against organized crime and racketeering in the city had benefitted them immeasurably. Donations from the business community and generous publicity from the Cleveland newspapers boosted Ness as he began his campaign. On the other hand, this support from prominent and privileged Republicans prompted Burke's forces to brand Ness as a candidate of the monied establishment.

Anyone who thought Ness had a realistic chance to win failed to recognize the power of organized labor, the apathy and short memories of Cleveland voters, and Ness's exceedingly dull campaign style. In press accounts, he was a vibrant, larger-than-life hero riding back into the city to rescue citizens from the forces of evil. In reality, he was a soft-spoken, middle-aged man who was obviously uncomfortable in the role of politician.

Charismatic in his early Cleveland days, Ness was now showing the effects of alcohol abuse, stress, and an unhealthy lifestyle, with deep lines cutting through his face, slouching shoulders and a noticeable paunch. During his speeches, he appeared nervous, stiff and uninspiring. He paid little attention to current political issues, relying instead on his faded fame as a crimefighter.

In one speech, he did make token reference to what he perceived as the issues of the day, and took a slap at Burke in the process: "I left a Cleveland that was a vibrant, spirited city interested in accomplishment and improvement... I returned to find it, by comparison, a tired and listless town; its air filled with soot and smoke; its streets dirty and in a most deplorable condition; its transportation system noisy, inadequate and approaching insolvency. The equipment of its police and fire department is poorly maintained. Its traffic moves painstakingly and with confusion. Newspapers indicate that Cleveland streets are unsafe after dark. Cleveland is going backward instead of forward."

Despite the pitch, at times Ness appeared to take his candidacy only half-seriously. Al Sutton, who had picked up where Ness left off as Public Safety Director, tried to impress upon Ness that he should avoid fraternizing with his political opponents during the campaign.

"He'd come up to my office," Sutton recalled, "and I'd say to him, 'What are you doing here? You're running for mayor and I'm working for Burke. He's about fifty feet from here. Why don't you come back after work, so we can have a drink or something?' It didn't seem to faze Eliot. I think he was just innocent and unaware of the political realities."

Ness used most of his savings to help counter the heavy campaign donations labor leaders strong armed out of rank-and-file union members for Burke. Volunteers walked through each precinct distributing "The Ness News," a tabloid that recalled Ness's accomplishments and promised changes in city government. Ness embarked on a series of handshaking tours of city streets. One pundit said he looked like a famous ex-athlete trying to relive his glory in later years as he boasted of his accomplishments as Safety Director. Posters, billboards and full-page newspaper advertisements implored Clevelanders to "Vote Yes For Ness."

"He thought he could win by standing on the street corner with Betty and shaking hands," Moore remembered. "One time I took out my pen and showed him the math, how he could shake hundreds of hands every day and still not ever see 90 percent of Cleveland's voters. Eliot didn't realize that he had to work the press, get himself some fresh publicity, and get the right people to work for him. Let's face it, politics wasn't his game."

Ness launched a series of speeches and advertisements portraying his opponent as ineffective. He also suggested Burke was beholden to union interests, and he reminded voters that Burke had been a hands-off Assistant Prosecutor who distanced himself from the Harvard Club raid. Burke could have retaliated by citing Ness's shortcomings, but he resisted. "The best politics is good government," Burke said in response to Ness's campaign tactics. "My record speaks for itself."

Just a few days before the election, Ness and Burke made a joint appearance before the Cleveland City Club, a civic organization. Burke, who spoke first after losing a coin toss, defended himself against Ness's verbal assaults by producing a thick, black stenographic book which he said contained every word Ness had uttered in the campaign.

Waving this book within inches of Ness's nose, Burke declared with vehemence, "You have made many charges in this campaign and I challenge you, as an ace investigator, to produce even one scrap of evidence to substantiate the charges."

Ness responded weakly that Burke had shown poor judgment by accepting the endorsement of a wing of the Council of Industrial Organizations known to be sympathetic to communist interests.

The voters sent a loud and clear message on November 4, when Burke won by a margin of almost two-to-one, 168,412 votes to Ness's 85,990. Ness, although disappointed by the outcome, tried to demonstrate that he was taking the defeat in stride. He telephoned Burke with congratulations and was invited to attend a victory party at the mayor's home.

Ness accepted, graciously joining in on the festivities. As the night progressed, he stunned many of those present by toasting Burke with a snide remark, "Who'd want an honest politician anyway?"

"How sad it was to see Eliot Ness, once the toast of the city, now a humbled also-ran," wrote one Cleveland newspaper columnist who attended the celebration.

A postmortem on the Ness candidacy came from Cleveland reporter John Patrick Martin, who observed that the former Safety Director had missed the boat by declining to run for mayor in 1941, during the peak of his popularity.

"We all like Eliot, and we all admired him as an honest, thorough expert in the field of law enforcement," Martin wrote in the Plain Dealer. "There was never anybody like him in Cleveland. He really captured the imagination of the public in his early years, and he was given a hero's worship unlike that given any city official within my recollection. In 1941, Ness was the most famous man in the city and the most admired."

After sacrificing his financial security and part of his reputation for the cause of public service, Ness felt rejected, humiliated and betrayed. The political campaign also greatly weakened his executive status in the business world at the same time the Middle East Company continued to self-destruct.

Fermin F. Nunez suddenly had trouble securing the Mexican supplies he had promised. The few shipments he could guarantee cost more than the Cleveland area buyers were willing to pay. Adding insult to injury, Chinese business owners who had provided flour and silk to the now-defunct Far East Company brought suit against Ness, Chennault and the Middle East Company.

The company's only hope of survival was Turkey. But before Dan Moore returned to Istanbul in a desperate attempt to save the company, he tried one last time to help his good friend.

CHAPTER TWENTY-THREE

Beginning Of The End

Dan Moore had friends in high places, including Detroit. Hearing that the city was looking for a new police administrator, Moore reached for his telephone. "Eliot was a natural for the job, a guy with all the credentials anyone could ask for, and he would have jumped at the chance," Moore said. "But no matter how much talking I did, they wouldn't bend. They said they didn't want anyone with political ambitions, since he might upset the political machinery, and Eliot had that foolish mayoral campaign in his background. They wouldn't even consider him."

Ness's foray into politics also hurt him at Diebold. The executives plotting a takeover capitalized on Ness's frequent absences to discredit him in the eyes of the stockholders and directors. A relative of the Rex family succeeded Ness as chairman of the board. The best Diebold could do for him at that point was a low-end sales position. Ness halfheartedly accepted the job, while refocusing his attention on what was left of the Middle East Company.

Eliot was drinking heavily and questioning his own self-worth. In late 1948, Eliot and Betty Ness rented a home in Cleveland, from which he commuted to his job in Canton, about forty miles away. He spent more time on the road, often drinking, than he did selling Diebold products. Ness regularly stopped in the community of Kent, where he befriended Jack Foyle, a young car dealer.

"He was a very lonesome man looking for a friend," Foyle told author Laurence Bergreen. "He was depressed by his defeat in Cleveland for mayor."

Although his financial problems were deepening, Ness paid Foyle $2,000 in cash for a new Mercury coupe, dark green, with all the extras. Almost every day, Ness stopped in Kent on his way home from work, usually around 4:00 in the afternoon, and traveled with Foyle to the Kent Hotel.

"I would have two drinks and he'd have twenty-two," Foyle recalled. "He would drink 'em like water."

Ness would often "forget his wallet," Foyle said, but on other occasions he would flash twenty-dollar bills, buy a round or two of drinks, and insist that the bartender keep the change. At the hotel lounge, Ness passed the hours reminiscing about his days in Chicago, especially about Al Capone. He complained about his treatment by Diebold and lamented the lost opportunities of his life—his unsuccessful efforts to become an FBI agent, his car crash, his failed marriages, and the humiliating election loss.

One evening, Foyle received a telephone call from the Kent Police Station, where a man claiming to be Eliot Ness had been taken following his arrest for driving under the influence of alcohol. This time, Ness really had forgotten his wallet and had no identification. The police did not believe he was Eliot Ness until Foyle arrived at the station and persuaded the officers to let him drive Ness home.

Corinne Lawson, the Nesses' housekeeper, recognized signs of alcohol abuse and denial in Eliot Ness following the mayoral election. Lawson said Ness often joked about his drinking and his battles with Al Capone, once telling her that "Old Scarface" had shot at him a few times, "but I outran the bullets."

She recalled the time she went to buy meat for the Nesses, only to be told by the butcher that their credit had been shut off due to nonpayment of a large balance. Lawson also remembered when Eliot and Betty Ness tried to buy a house in Shaker Heights. They sent a check for $3,000 to cover partial payment, but the owners returned the money, stating in an accompanying letter that neighbors did not want the Nesses to move there because the couple drank too much.

"It reached the point where some men did not like him and talked about him (behind his back)," Lawson said. "But he was liked by the ladies because he was witty. As far as I'm concerned, he was a gentleman. Eliot and Betty were both very nice people."

The Nesses kept Corinne Lawson on as their housekeeper at almost double the going rate because they appreciated her cooking, her cleaning, and her company. When the Nesses were not entertaining, Lawson said, Eliot would often sit by himself, deep in thought. "When he noticed I was present, he would 'turn on the sunshine.' He didn't want to burden others with his troubles."

By that time, Ness's closest friend and most stabilizing influence, Dan Moore, had moved with his wife and children to Istanbul to work on the hotel deal and other business prospects. Moore persuaded a Turkish company to accept shipments of streptomycin and other pharmaceuticals for repackaging and resale in Turkey. He also arranged for the importation of buses to give Istanbul its first public transportation system.

On the U.S. end, Tom Dunn put together another optimistic report to convince potential stockholders great things were in store for the Middle East Company:

"In Turkey, the company affiliated with the Middle East Company is composed of very rich Turks who have unusual influence with the Turkish government. The political influence of these individuals is extremely important because they can influence the granting of import licenses with reference to goods imported into Turkey for which payment must be made in American dollars. In this period of dollar shortages, this is extremely important because no business can be done without the obtaining of import licenses granting the payment in dollars."

Eliot Ness's name also appeared on Middle East Company correspondence, even as his effectiveness continued to slip. With Dunn aboard as a full-time general manager, the primary reason Ness remained affiliated was his potential to bring the company additional business from Diebold.

Moore invited Ness to sever his ties with Diebold and join him in Turkey. He was confident Turkish officials would hire Ness as a consultant to work out solutions to their traffic problems in several major cities, including Istanbul. However, Betty Ness had no interest in moving to Turkey and Eliot never pressed the issue with her.

The Middle East directors dispatched Ness to Washington to line up political support for the company. Ness met with administrators of the Export/Import Bank and lunched with Drew Pearson, an influential newspaper columnist whose interest in the Middle East Company could be traced to the fact that he was married to Dan Moore's sister.

On the other side of the world, Moore began to feel alienated and uneasy. As his letters to Middle East Company colleagues went unanswered, Moore feared that Dunn, Ness and the others were allowing the company to collapse. Correspondence from that era, found among hundreds of personal business papers Ness left in an obscure filing cabinet at the time of his death, suggest that Moore's concerns were justified. The Middle East Company directors failed to follow-up on business leads and refused to send Moore financial statements that would have informed him of the company's sorry financial state.

The collapse of the pharmaceutical contract was particularly frustrating to Moore. He had found an eager buyer, negotiated a price that would bring the Middle East Company considerable profit, and obtained the necessary permits to bring the materials to Turkey in exchange for American dollars. No one back in the United States hooked up with a provider—although many were available—and the Turkish company turned elsewhere.

Moore eventually signed on as a full-time employee of Intercontinental Hotels and resigned as an officer of Middle East Company. He rarely saw Eliot Ness after that, but Moore's memories remain sharp almost a half-century later:

"He was a delightful man—humorous, interesting, charming and very easy to like. People naturally gravitated toward him. He was a terrific police administrator, but he ended up trying to be something that he wasn't. I think there's a lesson in all this: if you have a tremendous gift in one area, you should abandon it with great caution. Eliot abandoned something that he was the best in the world at doing, and he suffered the consequences."

The Middle East Company continued its steady march toward insolvency. Mexico placed a steep export tax on lumber and other products for which the company had found buyers. Even the once-lucrative pharmaceutical trade with Portugal was eliminated when the Portuguese Red Cross intervened with a direct purchase arrangement. Ness, while officially listed as Vice President of the Middle East Company, had little to do with the company after Moore's resignation.

At the same time, further managerial changes at Diebold forced Ness out of that company altogether. Despite his celebrity status and his legitimate contributions to Diebold during a critical time in that company's history, Eliot Ness rates only one brief line in the corporate archives. "There seems to be some confusion about the actual years Ness was with Diebold, and there's very little information about him in the company records," said John Kristoff, Director of Public Relations at Diebold. "It's almost as if he came in, did nothing of significance, and left."

One man who had dealings with Diebold during the 1940s agreed to share his observations on the condition that he remain anonymous:

"Eliot got a raw deal. There were people there who resented the fact that Janet Rex had brought him in, out of nowhere really, and installed him as chairman of the board. It wouldn't be fair to the families for me to name any names at this point. Eliot didn't play favorites at Diebold. He just expected people to do their jobs. That went against the philosophy of a select few who were trying to milk the company for all it was worth. The fundamental difference between Eliot and the rest of them was that he really cared about Diebold and wasn't just out for himself, at least in the early stages, before he got shafted. That's why some of them were out to get him—he wouldn't 'go along to get along.' And they did get him."

Desperate for employment, Ness called on several old friends in Cleveland, expressing willingness to accept even a low-paying, menial job to support his wife and son. He took a sales position with an electronics wholesaler for a brief period of time.

Still interested in law enforcement, Ness tried to interest the Cleveland Police Department in promoting the use of a personal alarm device, sold under the brand name "Help Call," for people who were being attacked. He stood to receive a substantial commission on each unit sold, but Ness was too far ahead of his time. These alarms are now commonplace in all major American cities.

When the electronics company relocated to Chicago, Ness decided to remain in Cleveland and seek other work. He spent a few months as a clerk in a downtown bookstore, then landed a job selling frozen hamburger patties to restaurants. In time, the frozen foods business would turn many people into millionaires but, as with "Help Call," Ness was involved too early to enjoy the industry's financial rewards.

Not much has been written about Eliot Ness's activities in the early 1950s. People who knew Eliot and Betty during this period say their marriage remained strong, even as their financial plight worsened. Eliot probably spent as much time between jobs as he did employed, while Betty continued to pursue her interest in sculpture.

Both of them grew close to Bobby, a quiet, but seemingly well-adjusted boy. Despite their financial difficulties, both Eliot and Betty believed strongly enough in the value of a good education to enroll Bobby in a private school and keep close tabs on his academic progress.

Based on outward appearances, Ness was content, but people who were close to him knew better.

"Eliot was very depressed and felt victimized," said a close family acquaintance. "He went out of his way not to let others see it. Deep down inside, he felt guilty and ashamed for failing to adequately provide for his wife and son. But he also believed that he had been the victim of circumstances that were beyond his control—just plain bad luck."

CHAPTER TWENTY-FOUR

'You Should Write A Book'

G. Frank Shampanore had a dream. A short, stocky wheeler-dealer who had drifted through a series ill-fated business ventures since the early 1930s, Shampanore was sure he had a winner this time. On his drawing board was a Cleveland-based business that would earn hundreds of thousands of dollars for investors who were lucky enough to get in on the action early.

Shampanore tried to patent a process he developed to "watermark" checks and other important documents as protection against counterfeiting. Coupled with the watermarking were personal and commercial checks that bore a unique front-endorsement feature. Shampanore believed banks and other financial institutions would jump at the chance to market checks that were attractive, difficult to counterfeit, and a time-saver for cashiers.

Among those who came on board was Joseph Phelps, a tall, outgoing former semiprofessional baseball player with New Jersey roots. In the early 1950s, Phelps had promoted natural gas wells in the northeast and, in the words of a colleague, "made a lot of money for a lot of people in northern Pennsylvania." Phelps was a natural salesman, hale and hearty, with a fixed smile.

Mining interests brought Phelps and Shampanore together in Coudersport, a small village tucked in the rolling hills of north-central Pennsylvania. Also joining the team was Shampanore's young nephew, William J. Ayers, of Hackettstown, New Jersey, a mechanical designer and printer whose skills were needed to adapt Shampanore's product to the marketplace.

"The watermarking idea looked great," Ayers said during a 1995 interview. "Frank had a lot of people convinced he had a wonderful thing and I bought the whole nine yards."

Shampanore and Phelps sought an identifiable figure to demonstrate to investors that these businesses would be profitable. They shared their plan with Eliot Ness, believing that Ness could attract investors among his former business associates in Cleveland, while giving the company an air of legitimacy. The idea appealed to Ness, who was not in a position to be choosy. A $150 weekly salary was enough to support Eliot, Betty and Bobby Ness, and the stock options made the position even more enticing.

Shampanore established North Ridge Industrial Corporation as a holding company for two subsidiaries that would conduct the business: Guaranty Paper Corporation, for the watermarking and printing processes, and Fidelity Check Corporation to produce commercial and personal checks.

Although he invested little of his own money, Shampanore—by virtue of his development of the watermarking process—became board chairman and majority stockholder of North Ridge. Joe Phelps was named vice president, with Eliot Ness serving as president of the two subsidiaries.

Phelps and Ness were bubbling with enthusiasm as they began a series of meetings with potential investors. William Ayers recalled his first trip to Cleveland to begin working for North Ridge in 1955:

"Frank took me to a little room with a dinky, hand-cranked printing machine, and said, 'This is what we have to start with.' I was supposed to design and build the machines to take the watermarking process out of the laboratory and make it commercially successful. Then Frank took me to the Terminal Building, where North Ridge had an entire suite of offices, lavishly furnished with six people on staff for marketing and promoting.

"He said, 'What do you think?' I was appalled. I said, 'You better back off until we have something to sell! It's going to take about two years to build the equipment and perfect the production.' Frank didn't want to hear any of that. He said, 'That won't do. We have to show progress if we're going to get more investors.' I decided to give it my best shot."

Phelps returned to Coudersport, accompanied by Ness, and visited many of the same investors who had benefitted so handsomely from the gas well speculation just a few years earlier. Not only was Phelps well-liked and respected in Coudersport, members of the business community knew he was in line to receive a six-figure settlement from a longstanding lawsuit over some prime real estate in that region. When Phelps promised to buy back all North Ridge stock if the company failed, he erased many investors' apprehensions. Meanwhile, Phelps negotiated personal bank loans to cover some of the company's expenses.

During a trip to New York City in late 1955, Phelps and Ness met with one of Phelps' former childhood friends, Oscar Fraley, a United Press International sportswriter. After hearing the men's sales pitch during a meeting at the Waldorf-Astoria, the lanky, easygoing Fraley said he was not interested in North Ridge.

As the three enjoyed several cocktails, Phelps and Fraley reminisced about their younger days, while Ness dozed on a couch. Close to midnight, Phelps told Fraley, "You'll have to get Eliot to tell you about his experiences as a Prohibition agent in Chicago. He's the guy who dried up Al Capone. Maybe you never heard of him, but it's real gangbuster stuff: killings, raids, the whole works. It was pretty dangerous stuff."

Fraley found it difficult to believe the soft-spoken man with the pleasant smile had been such a dynamic crimefighter. For the next five hours, Ness told him of stakeouts and wiretaps, death threats and dumdum bullets, crashes through brewery doors and the extraordinary teamwork that helped bring down Al Capone.

"Eliot could talk with entertaining ease in private," Fraley recalled in a story he wrote for Coronet magazine. "Something about the relaxed atmosphere and the way we had been gabbing started him off. The next thing I knew, it was six in the morning. For hours I listened, wide-eyed and wordlessly, as Eliot talked of those deadly days in Chicago. 'Let's knock off and get some breakfast,' Eliot said, stretching and getting up from the floor, where he had been sitting with his back against the edge of a couch. 'Someday,' I suggested, 'you should write a book on your experiences. You might make some money with it.' Eliot looked up over the shoelace he was tying and it seemed to me I could detect a certain bitterness in his voice. 'I could use it,' he said."

In fact, Ness had tried to write a book about his Chicago experiences many years earlier and attempted to recruit Chicago journalists to help him, but he found no takers. The reporters viewed Ness as more of a publicity hound and saw Johnson, Wilson, Irey and the Secret Six as the true heroes of the government's attack on Al Capone.

Just before Christmas, Ness and Phelps returned to New York seeking additional investors and accepted Fraley's invitation to dine with him at a fashionable downtown restaurant. Fraley repeated his offer to collaborate on a book, but found Ness to be reluctant.

"It was a long time ago, and a lot of things happened in a short amount of time," he explained. "I'm not sure I could sort it all out."

"Listen, you've got the newspaper clippings and the souvenirs, don't you?" Fraley inquired.

"I've got a whole locker full of stuff, but you'd have a hell of a time trying to figure out what it all means. I've never taken the time to organize it."

"Just send me what you have," Fraley insisted. "I'll sort through it, get an outline together and then the thing will start to flow. At least let me see what you've got. This could really be a seller if we do it right."

Ness agreed to pile his material in a box and mail it to Fraley. He also began writing his own version of his Chicago activities, or at least as much as he could recall. His handwritten notes were disjointed, poorly-written, and brief.

Inside the box he found a veritable gold mine: case files, personal financial records, handwritten wiretap reports, newspaper and magazine articles, personal notations and more. After assuring Ness that an outline would be forthcoming in a couple of weeks, Fraley took a leave of absence from United Press International and began to put the records in some semblance of order.

Back in Cleveland, Bill Ayers was working feverishly to develop the North Ridge production facilities, while Shampanore and his associates continued to spend money faster than it was coming in. Hoping to generate business with the federal government, they opened a branch office in Washington.

"It was obvious by early 1956 that we were in a lot of trouble," Ayers remembered. "We still didn't know our capacity or what our cost was going to be in producing these checks, and yet we were advertising in bank publications and printing journals. We were getting people all excited about it, and we basically had nothing to sell."

Ayers wasn't the only one trying to persuade Shampanore to slow down. Eliot Ness, after several years of being a good soldier, confronted the company president about poor management of the business. Angered by what he perceived as insubordination, Shampanore wanted Ness out of the picture.

In July 1956, desperate to cut expenses, the officers of North Ridge Industrial Corporation moved their headquarters from Cleveland to Coudersport. The costs of maintaining offices and a fledgling production facility in Cleveland were far too high. Coudersport offered a lower wage scale, rent that was a fraction of what was being charged in Cleveland, and closer proximity to many of the North Ridge investors. The company made a token down-payment on the former Gates Grocery Store at the corner of Main and Oak streets in the center of town. Business offices were established above a Western Auto store on Main Street and over another business a half-block away on Second Street.

Eliot, Betty and Bobby Ness moved into the lower floor of a modest two-story home on Third Street, near the banks of the Allegheny River. Shampanore, Phelps and Ayers also moved with their families to Coudersport, as did Advertising Manager Rube Pollan. Ayers immediately went to work setting up a production plant, while Phelps and Ness resumed their pursuit of new investors. Stock being sold at reasonable prices was attractive to doctors, business owners and a handful of government office-holders. Many of these investors were motivated by a desire to support a venture that could benefit the community.

"We really wanted to help promote some economic activity in Coudersport," said Dr. George C. Mosch, who with his brother, Dr. Herman C. Mosch, invested $1,300 in the North Ridge Industrial Corporation and Guaranty Paper Corporation. "It also looked, at the start, like it might be a good investment. However, some of us felt that they were spending money rather foolishly. We wondered how a company that was just getting started could spend that kind of money on expensive office furnishings and things that weren't necessary."

Frank Shampanore painted a rosy picture of the business in a letter to stockholders. "We carried advertising in the October issues of the Bankers Monthly and Banking, the two leading baking magazines. The response was so great that we withdrew subsequent advertising until such time as our plants were ready for full production. Paper dealers and printers in Switzerland, West Germany, France, Belgium, Sweden, England and Canada have indicated interest in joining us in the foreign exploitation of our work."

A large spread in the local weekly newspaper, The Potter Enterprise, announced the arrival of Ness and his business partners with great fanfare:

"The annual estimated loss of $500 million to banks, depositors, and insurance companies because of check forgery will be substantially reduced, it is claimed, through use of Fidelity watermarked checks not available to individuals and companies by their local bank. Watermarked papers are available through Guaranty franchised printers, department stores and stationers... Ness's background is highly unusual for a top corporate officer. His brilliant career began as a special agent for the Justice Department, when he headed the investigation of the Al Capone and Bugs Moran mobsters that resulted in a sorely-needed cleanup of crime in Chicago."

A four-column photograph accompanying the newspaper featured the smiling faces of the six officers: Shampanore; Ness; Phelps; Carl Reidy, an attorney from Emporium, Pennsylvania; Verne Haight, one of Shampanore's colleagues, who was named executive vice president, and George McKinney, the corporation treasurer.

Coupled with the watermarking process promoted by Guaranty Paper were Fidelity Check Corporation's "four-square" checks, with the front endorsement feature and a colorful pictorial background of the buyer's choice.

The watermarking process of Guaranty Paper was said to be unique, in that it could be used on paper that was already printed, or on blank stock. Forgers of that era often printed their own checks (usually payroll duplicates), forged signatures, and had them passed by confederates in a neighborhood where many payroll checks of one company were cashed by merchants, tavern owners and other businesses. Ness and others believed their product would foil forgers around the nation.

Not everyone was convinced that Guaranty Paper was a good investment.

"Eliot saw the watermarking process as a wonderful opportunity, but some of his investors and business associates were people you weren't sure you wanted to be in business with," recalled John J. Rigas, a young Coudersport businessman at the time. Rigas is now Chief Executive Officer and President of Adelphia Cable Communications, one of the nation's largest TV cable companies.

"There were times I wanted to avoid Eliot because he kept trying to get me to invest in the company," Rigas continued. "Frankly, I didn't have the money to do it and I didn't believe in it. That wasn't Ness's fault or Joe Phelps' fault. They were both decent men. Eliot was the kind of person you couldn't help taking a liking to— an articulate man with a kind heart, a friendly smile and a warm personality. He was the kind of guy you were glad to have living in your community, even though his business ventures were so suspect."

Ness's financial plight became evident to Rigas when the personal checks he wrote to pay his TV cable bills were returned for insufficient funds. Ness also borrowed small sums of money from Rigas and other Coudersport business owners to meet the payroll at Guaranty Paper Company.

The Nesses didn't take long to work themselves into Coudersport's social fabric. Betty joined the First United Presbyterian Church, located just a block from their home. Eliot did not become an official member, but occasionally attended services. The Presbyterian minister, the Rev. Robert Loughborough, described Ness as "lonely, gracious, and not at all like the blood and thunder character Hollywood would later depict him to be."

Bobby Ness made several friends in the neighborhood, including Bill Grabe, a boy with Down's Syndrome who lived across the street. Grabe smiles as he thinks back to the excitement he felt when Eliot Ness came home from work at dusk and invited him to play baseball in the Nesses' back yard.

Betty, who was not as comfortable living in a small town as her husband and son, found others in Coudersport who shared her appreciation of art. She told one friend that Coudersport reminded her of "a Norman Rockwell painting—as wholesome, and just about as boring."

Betty made an inauspicious debut in the community. Within weeks of the family's arrival, she took Bobby down to the banks of the Allegheny River to practice some fly-casting. No sooner had she landed a dry fly on the rolling current when a fish warden pulled up and asked to see her fishing license. Like a hardened criminal, she was taken before a justice of the peace and fined $10.

"You know, Eliot just sat there and giggled throughout the whole thing. He was wonderful," Betty recalled many years later.

Some of her Coudersport acquaintances persuaded Betty to discuss her skills during a program presented to the New Century Club, a women's organization. Those who heard her presentation, entitled "Sculpturing as a Means of Personal Expression," marveled at Betty's expertise and her accomplishments in the field.

Eliot Ness often remarked to acquaintances that he felt comfortable and welcome in Coudersport, where the relaxed lifestyle and tranquility were in such stark contrast to his days in Chicago and Cleveland. At home during nights and weekends, Ness often donned a sweatshirt and gym shorts to exercise or listen to Eddie Duchin records. He also spent time reading or playing with Bobby in the yard behind their house. A highlight for Bobby was the three-block walk he and his father sometimes took to the Olympic Restaurant, a confectionary featuring homemade chocolates.

Sometimes during the day, and almost every evening after work, Ness visited one or two Coudersport tap rooms. His favorite was the Old Hickory Tavern, a large Victorian home converted to a hotel with a bar in the basement.

"He was a down-to-earth, quiet kind of guy," said Fred Anderson, a Coudersport Elementary School teacher who often saw Ness at the Old Hickory. "He was usually by himself when he came in. He wasn't unfriendly, but he didn't strike up conversations. Once he got a couple of drinks in him, he would open up and start talking about the gangster days, Al Capone, and all those exploits. He wasn't boasting, but the stories did sound a little exaggerated. We thought, if he's so important, why is he driving a beat-up old car? We never realized who he was until 'The Untouchables' came on television several years later."

Other Coudersport acquaintances reacted with polite skepticism when Ness spoke of his days in Chicago and Cleveland. Ness looked more like the aging businessman he was than the daring federal agent he claimed to have been. He was a guest speaker at a meeting of the Coudersport Rotary Club, where he detailed some of his experiences in Chicago. "Widespread public support of a law such as Prohibition is a necessary ingredient of enforceability," he told the group. "Scarcely half the people in the country were in sympathy with the Volstead Act."

"Who the heck does he think he's kidding with a story like that?" was the reaction of a local schoolteacher, Henry Staiger, as he opened the door of a friend's car following the speech, only to discover that Ness was a passenger in the back seat. Ness smiled, taking no apparent offense.

Other things about Eliot Ness did not add up to Coudersport residents. They wondered how a person of his reputation could be affiliated with a company such as North Ridge. They also found it odd that Ness showed such a strong distaste for guns, which were as common as automobiles in Coudersport.

Larry Del Grosso, who managed the liquor store in town, saw Ness frequently. "The first time he came in, he had been drinking and, out of the blue, he said, 'My name is Eliot Ness and I was one of the federal agents who put Al Capone away.' I couldn't understand how a guy like him could be for real when he was driving around in an old Ford convertible with the back window missing. He sure went through a lot of gin and scotch whiskey, which was kind of surprising for a guy who was so proud of enforcing Prohibition laws."

Economic problems were eating away at him, as North Ridge Industrial Corporation continued to self-destruct. Frank Shampanore failed in his attempts to market the products in Washington. The front-endorsement idea never did catch on, nor did Fidelity's pictorial backgrounds on personal checks. Ambitious plans to build thirty small printing plants across the country for production of watermarked checks were shelved, due to the company's financial straits.

As the rift between North Ridge officers deepened and the business moved closer to bankruptcy, Shampanore traded most of his stock for a new Mercury station wagon and fled to Odessa, Texas. There, he quietly established a small production plant and attracted some new investors for another stab at the watermarking business. Shampanore sent letters to North Ridge stockholders, attacking the integrity and commitment of Eliot Ness who, ironically, was one of the handful of people holding the company together.

With the company in turmoil, Ayers received a telegram from his uncle demanding his presence in Chicago the following day to meet with Shampanore and Charles Burns, an executive with the Franklin-Burns Company.

"I was shocked to learn that they had worked out a plan by which we were to sabotage the company and then pick it up in a sheriff's sale for 'ten cents on the dollar,' to use Frank's words," Ayers said. "I was ordered to return to Coudersport and do everything I could to cause the company to go under. I was promised all kinds of rewards for doing it."

Ayers could not bring himself to leave the North Ridge investors holding the bag, while staining the reputation of those who, in good faith, had bought into Shampanore's dream.

"I called Frank and said I wanted no part of this," Ayers recalled. "He basically told me to go to hell, and that was that."

Ayers, Ness and Phelps set about trying to make things work. They vacated the two auxiliary business offices and consolidated operations at the former grocery store. Ness drew up a detailed marketing plan filled with optimism.

"We are all aware of the remarkable improvements made in the process and the product in the last few months," Ness wrote.

"As a result, Guaranty is now in a position to rapidly develop its market."

He told of new machinery that would watermark checks, stationery and other papers with less spoilage. Ness's plan forecasted annual profits of more than $325,000, assuming that banks and corporations would embrace the watermarked checks and other paper products.

"With the market arrangements we have now, I believe we can sell and produce our product in constantly increasing volumes, at relatively low cost," he wrote. "Our operating and overhead expenses are cut to the bone and can be controlled so that they increase only as sales volumes increase. This condition should result in increasing profits as sales volume increases."

Anyone reading the Potter Enterprise of November 15, 1956, and not knowing the background of North Ridge had to assume the business was on the brink of great things. Phelps and Ness earned the unqualified support of the Coudersport Chamber of Commerce after they described the company's potential and forecasted as many as 150 new jobs at the local production plant.

"If we can obtain just one-percent of the nation's check business, our employment problem will be solved," Ness told the business group. "We have something wonderful, I think, but our problem is letting the world know we have it. Tell your friends to ask for our checks and, with local support as the beginning, we can go on in ever-widening circles to reach the four corners of the nation."

Ness and Phelps boasted of the National Sheriffs' Association endorsement their North Ridge products had received, thanks in large part to the promotional work of association member Harold Holcomb, Sheriff of Potter County, Pennsylvania.

While Ness and Phelps promoted, Bill Ayers tried to make the pieces fit together. Orders were coming in, but not in sufficient volume to make the business profitable. As hard as that trio worked to keep the business alive, G. Frank Shampanore was doing his best to destroy it. Shampanore's poison pen letters continued to arrive in the mailboxes of stockholders, community leaders and, eventually, rank-and-file employees of the Guaranty Paper Company plant in Coudersport.

Despite Shampanore's long-distance attacks, Ness retained the unswerving loyalty and respect of the plant employees. Each morning, he and Joe Phelps met at the coffee counter in Mackey's Restaurant to discuss business, often interrupted by small talk with local business owners and politicians who filed in and out.

CHAPTER TWENTY-FIVE

Symbol of Courage & Decency

Eliot Ness visited the small office of family physician Dr. George C. Mosch in late 1956 for a physical examination. Dr. Mosch found the 53-year-old patient to be in generally good health, but he was concerned about a slight heart murmur. Mosch prescribed a mild tranquilizer, Miltown, and referred Ness to Dr. Kurt Zinter, an internal medicine specialist and cardiologist in Wellsville, New York, about thirty miles away.

Dr. Zinter's examination revealed that the former crimefighter was suffering from inactive rheumatic valvular disease. Eliot was cautioned to avoid exertion and continue taking a sedative. He never mentioned the diagnosis to his friends or business partners, and it's possible he never told Betty.

One afternoon, Ness was deeply involved in preparations for an audit of North Ridge Industrial Corporation books when he received a phone call from Oscar Fraley, informing him the Julian Messner Publishing Company had offered a contract for their book, based on Fraley's outline and some sample chapters. Ness would receive a $1,000 advance, to be followed by royalties after the book went on sale.

Fraley agreed to visit Coudersport in two or three weeks and work with Ness on the manuscript. While he awaited the writer's arrival, Ness consulted with his wife and several of his Coudersport acquaintances for advice on the book.

"He was actually surprised that the publishing world was interested in his story," said one of those friends, Jack Dorfeld. "I remember him saying that he was a little upset that Fraley insisted on making his Chicago days sound so dramatic, and so much more thrilling than they really were. That bugged Eliot. The thing is, though, Eliot didn't have a clear recollection of all that did happen way back then. I think he and Fraley were both under a lot of pressure to make things up, or liven things up, so they could make some quick money. I know that the Eliot Ness I read about in that book wasn't the Eliot Ness I knew—far from it."

"I don't believe Eliot actually wanted the book to be published, but he needed the money and I think he wanted to recover some of his forgotten fame," said Bill Ayers, who also offered advice on the manuscript before Fraley's arrival. "He was many times on the verge of chucking the whole project because the book was making him out to be a hero, which he honestly didn't consider himself to be. I still get a little upset when he's depicted as the John Wayne type. That wasn't Eliot's style at all. He was very mild-mannered."

Among others assisting were Walter Taylor, editor of the Potter Enterprise, and Dorothy Wilkinson, who had the unenviable task of tending to North Ridge affairs as a combination secretary/silk screen artist at the Guaranty Paper plant. When Ness visited the home of Dorothy and her husband, Lewis Wilkinson, he often arrived with a bottle of liquor in one hand and a stack of Guaranty Paper check registries in the other. He used the back of the registries to scratch out notes for the manuscript. Mrs. Wilkinson told interviewer John Graves that, during the informal hours she spent helping Ness with his book, she found him to be literate and intelligent, although he occasionally had difficulty finding the right words to use.

Betty Ness persuaded her husband to remove one of the anecdotes he and Fraley had written about the time Ness raided a brothel and arrested several prostitutes. While the paddy wagon was going around a corner, or so the story went, the back doors flew open and several of the women tumbled out onto the street. Betty felt very strongly about the impropriety of prostitution and did not think it appropriate for Eliot to make light of it.

The intensive work sessions between Ness and Fraley were sometimes exercises in futility. Meeting in Fraley's small room at the Hotel Crittenden or at Mackey's Restaurant, they worked their way through huge piles of materials. Sometimes, when Fraley questioned Ness about inconsistencies or contradictions, a frustrated Ness would pound his head with his palm. Alcohol and the passage of time had dimmed his memory, and he had to struggle with the fact that newspaper accounts of his law enforcement career in Chicago were incomplete and, more often than not, inaccurate.

At times, he would leave for a walk on the snow-covered streets of Coudersport and return with more of the details having fallen into place. Fraley recalled, "He would start out at a half-run and then, in a few minutes, slow to a lazy, sauntering walk which allowed him to inspect anything in his sight. Little escaped him. His eyes probed the contents of a dusty store window, noticed a misspelled word on a billboard, or spotted an acquaintance through the murky window of a restaurant. Quickly noticeable on these monotony-breaking journeys was the friendly warmth which drew people to him. Eliot had not been in Coudersport long, yet it seemed that he knew everybody in town. Nor was it a case of being recognized as a celebrity. He was, their attitude said, a welcome neighbor."

Despite Fraley's encouragement, Ness expressed skepticism about the book's sales potential. Fraley, on the other hand, was so optimistic that he tried to persuade Ness to commit to a second book collaboration, focusing on his accomplishments in Cleveland. Neither of them could have known that *The Untouchables* would provide the seed from which the legend of Eliot Ness would grow.

During their lengthy conversations, Ness failed to mention many important aspects of his life, from his failed marriages to his unsuccessful political campaign. Fraley later told a journalist he never knew of these developments until long after Ness was dead. He did tell Fraley of his hard-luck career in business, which strengthened Fraley's resolve to help a man for whom he felt a genuine fondness. Ness conceded that he was desperate to complete the book project as an insurance policy against the total collapse of North Ridge Industrial Corporation.

With only a handful of orders for checks arriving, Ayers expanded Guaranty Paper Company's operations to include commercial printing of non-watermarked products, such as letterheads, envelopes and post cards for local businesses. For several months, these small print jobs provided the bulk of the income to meet payroll and other expenses. Phelps was drawing no salary, while Ness, Ayers, and Advertising Director Rube Pollan were receiving only modest paychecks. Treasurer Verne Haight was also on hand, tending to business and secretly keeping Shampanore apprised of developments.

On March 14, 1957, Shampanore sent letters to Ness and Ayers demanding their resignations "in the interest of economy and the welfare of the stockholders," and accusing them of everything from theft and disloyalty to mismanagement and incompetence. Ayers decided the time had come for his uncle to answer for his actions. He summoned all of the people who still had an interest in North Ridge Industrial Corporation for a board of directors' meeting.

Almost four decades later, Ayers still has the minutes of that tension-filled meeting.

"This is the first time in my life that I've felt as if I'm on trial," an angry, but controlled, Eliot Ness told the directors. "I've been involved in gathering evidence on gangsters, putting crooked cops and union thugs behind bars. I thought I had seen everything, but the behavior and movements of G. F. Shampanore are something new to me. I plan to sue him for libel, unless it appears that doing so would cause serious damage to this company."

Ness said Shampanore's actions were destroying morale, scaring away investors, and causing those who already invested money to believe that they had been swindled. He wondered aloud how Shampanore could try to make his own nephew a scapegoat for the company's failures.

"He (Ayers), and no one else, has made our product saleable," Ness said. "He's the greatest influence for good that we have. So, if Bill Ayers leaves, I leave, too. It's quite obvious that Mr Shampanore is trying to destroy this company."

An appreciative and disillusioned Ayers then stood to drop his bombshell: Shampanore's application for a patent on the highly-touted watermarking process had been rejected several months earlier. The United States Patent Office determined that Shampanore's "magic formula" was similar to products already developed in England and California.

Shampanore failed to inform stockholders of this critical blow to the company's prospects for success. He finally came clean in a letter to Ayers, informing his nephew that, with new partners, he was moving forward with plans to open a watermarking operation in Texas:

"North Ridge has only three things of value—the formula, the one-sided check, and your machine. I can take a pinch of salt and an ounce of vanilla and it's a different formula. I assigned the patent application to North Ridge, but it has been rejected. I am setting up a new company and letting North Ridge go down the drain, salvaging what stockholders we see fit to favor."

Directors and other investors in the room sat in stunned silence after Ayers read the letter aloud.

"They say blood is thicker than water and it hurts me to say this, but I put ninety percent of the blame on Frank Shampanore and his grandiose ideas, combined with very poor business management," Ayers said. "By the time Eliot Ness had any real authority to operate the business, it was pretty much destroyed. Spending money before we had anything to produce was wrong."

Even if the watermarking formula could have been patented, it was of marginal value, due to its limited permanency and its tendency to bleed into the paper upon which it was printed. Carl Lindahl, a linotype operator at a competing Coudersport print shop, said a frustrated Eliot Ness once approached him with Guaranty's latest watermarking examples, desperately seeking help. The brown smudges he held in his hand looked nothing like the distinct, commercially-appealing marks that had been made on previous products.

As it turned out, Hammermill Paper Company, which had a near-monopoly on the type of stock used by Guaranty Paper Company, had changed the chemical composition of its paper, further diminishing the effectiveness of the watermarking process.

Ness's health continued to deteriorate. A week after the directors' meeting, he complained of feeling weak upon arriving as guest speaker at a meeting of the Coudersport Parent-Teacher

Association and nearly collapsed. Once he felt better, Ness delivered a very effective speech on the problems of juvenile delinquency.

Three days later, while walking up the stairs to attend services at the First United Presbyterian Church, Ness became dizzy and had to sit. The Reverend Robert Loughborough, who was among those who attended to Ness, jokingly said, "Well, Eliot, I guess you'd go to any extreme to avoid hearing one of my sermons."

On April 16, Ness appeared before Dr. Mosch for another physical examination, which revealed that he was suffering from high blood pressure. At that time, hypertension was usually treated with a tranquilizer, in the belief that reducing a patient's level of stress could lower his blood pressure. Dr. Mosch gave Ness another prescription and advised him to return for follow-up examinations.

In late April, Fraley supplied Ness with galley proofs for The Untouchables and sent a $1,000 check as Ness's share of an advance. Anxious to derive additional income from the venture as soon as possible, Ness barely reviewed the proofs and mailed them back to Fraley. The book was scheduled to appear in the fall, but Eliot Ness would never see the finished product.

Late in the afternoon of Thursday, May 16, 1957, he and Phelps were involved in an exhaustive review of financial reports. They stopped after Phelps complained of a slight headache, and arranged to resume their work at Ness's house a short time later. Ness slipped on his jacket and gathered his briefcase for the five-minute walk from the office to his home. The two headed down the steps together, pausing briefly to inform Ayers of their plans.

It was an uncommonly muggy spring day in Coudersport. Ness and Phelps progressed to the center of town, where they separated to run some errands. Ness stopped at the Rexall Drug Store to fill his prescription. Then he walked a half-block to the offices of The Potter Enterprise, where editor Walter Taylor declined an invitation to join Ness for a quick drink.

Ness's final stop was at the liquor store, where he bought a bottle of scotch. He hurried along the tall maple trees that lined the sidewalk, removing his coat and folding it over his arm as he walked. Beads of perspiration formed on his forehead and his pace quickened as he neared his home.

He dabbed his brow with a cloth handkerchief and headed for the kitchen, peering through a doorway at Bobby, who was in the living room. Twisting the cold water faucet, he reached for the latch of a cupboard above the sink, pulled out a glass and collapsed, the glass shattering in the sink as Ness fell shoulder-first to the floor. Betty, who was out in the yard tending to her flower beds, heard the glass breaking and noticed that the water was running for a long time. Receiving no response after calling Eliot's name, she hurried inside to find her husband's lifeless body crumpled on the floor next to the sink.

Bobby stood a few feet away, frightened by the desperate, helpless tone in his mother's voice as she cried out in panic. She felt Eliot's neck, praying that she might detect a pulse, then scrambled for the telephone to summon Dr. Mosch. Betty was just hanging up the phone when Joe Phelps arrived.

Choking back tears, he checked Ness's body, then calmly told Betty there was nothing a doctor could do. Betty rested her head on his shoulder, sobbing. Dr. Mosch arrived moments later. Eliot Ness was pronounced dead at 5:00 p.m.

Bobby Ness said his father appeared to be in pain as he arrived home, an observation which was also made by neighbors Ellen Grabe and Winifred Grover, who spotted Ness as he approached his house.

Walter Taylor, the newspaper editor, was the next to arrive, in his capacity as Deputy Coroner. After conferring briefly with Dr. Mosch, Taylor telephoned Potter County Coroner George Grabe, a funeral director who lived across the street from the Nesses. Both Taylor and Grabe concurred with Dr. Mosch that Ness had, from all appearances, died of a heart attack. They agreed that no autopsy would be necessary. Taylor then ran the three blocks back to the newspaper office and placed a call to Associated Press to tell the world Eliot Ness was dead.

On Saturday, May 18, a brief funeral service was held at Grabe Funeral Home. Several of Ness's business associates were among the fifty people attending. "Here's the only man I ever met who had no larceny in his heart," said Joe Phelps, tears welling in his eyes as he stood over the open casket. "Eliot was in a different league."

Ness's body was cremated. During a memorial service held at the Presbyterian Church of the Covenant's Christ Chapel in Cleveland, about 100 former colleagues, friends and family members heard the Rev. Harry B. Taylor praise Ness for "his community interest, his public service, his courage and integrity, his youthful and vital spirit, his warmth and understanding, and his concern for people."

The sun shone through the blue stained-glass window behind the pulpit where the pastor stood. White and yellow flowers formed a semicircle in front. Among those paying their respects were Robert W. Chamberlin, who had recently retired as a decorated Brigadier General with the U.S. Army; and former Mayor Edward Blythin, then a Common Pleas Court judge. A Cleveland City Police Department Honor Guard stood in formation outside the church.

In the Potter Enterprise, Walter Taylor offered this eulogy from a Coudersport perspective:

"What kind of man was this amiable, gray-eyed six-footer with the soft voice, who walked from side to side as he hurried along the street? Eliot Ness was kind of a walking contradiction, an understatement, a giggler, a 'man you knew from somewhere,' a man you'd pick out if you were looking for a fellow elbow-bender, a face in the crowd. This nemesis of syndicated crime was a fall guy for every small bore rafter who came along. For a wayfarer seeking a 'quarter for a bite,' Ness was the easiest of marks. He was unobtrusive and little known in the community to which he came as a corporation president. No son had a better father and no wife a better husband. They told me so. Few people in town knew the dimensions of the man who had been euchred into taking over direction of a shaky industrial complex. If Ness did nothing to set himself apart from an assortment of men whose luster as self-appointed saviors of an industry-starved town had begun to wear thin, it wasn't because he was unaware of the facts of life. Within a few short months, he found himself in the eyes of many in the community tarred with the same brush. But his unerring talent for getting things done blinded the former federal agent to anything but the job at hand. That the business is coming apart at the seams cannot be attributed to either bad faith or bad management on his part."

Chicago newspapers did not even note the passing of Eliot Ness. However, in Cleveland, obituaries recalled Ness as a committed, effective public servant.

"His death at 54 is untimely and unexpected," reported the Cleveland Press. "It will come as a shock both to the countless Clevelanders who knew him personally, and to those to whom he was, as Safety Director, a symbol of courage and decency."

Former Cleveland Mayor Harold Burton, then a United States Supreme Court Justice, was among the dozens of former Ness associates sending telegrams to Betty. "I have lost a great and good friend," he wrote. "The nation has lost a valuable citizen.

In a Cleveland Plain Dealer story, Burton praised Ness as "a courageous, competent public official with the utmost integrity, completely devoted to duty."

Among the many ironies of Eliot Ness's life was the breakdown of his finances at the time of his death. He owned no real estate and left to his widow only a rusty 1952 Ford convertible, valued at roughly $200; approximately $275 in a checking account; thousands of shares of worthless stock in North Ridge Industrial Corporation; and $200 out of the original $1,000 paid out as an advance for the book. In his wallet were two uncashable paychecks from Guaranty Paper.

Within weeks of Ness's death, Sheriff Harold Holcomb posted a foreclosure notice on the door at the Guaranty Paper Company. Internal Revenue Service field officers seized the company's checking account at Citizens Safe Deposit & Trust Company, while Coudersport's First National Bank foreclosed on loans made for equipment.

Fact and rumor have always mingled freely in what is said of North Ridge, Guaranty, Fidelity, and the whole cast of characters. A planned federal investigation of the corporation's failure was either abandoned or quashed. Joe Phelps sued North Ridge on behalf of the betrayed stockholders, but there was never a trial. After paying off his personal guarantees of the North Ridge stock to his friends, Phelps left Coudersport in October 1957 and became an industrial real estate salesman in southern New Jersey.

Shampanore's watermarking operating in Texas collapsed and he retired from the business world with little to show for all of his ventures.

Bill Ayers stayed in Coudersport to clean up the mess. Taking over payments on a printing press the bank was about to seize and securing small loans from friends, he opened up "Tool Craft," a small print shop and mail order business for his own tools, just across Main Street from the old Guaranty Paper shop.

"I was not going to leave Coudersport under a cloud," Ayers said. "I was the only one left to take the blame, and I had nothing to be ashamed of. No one set out to intentionally beat anybody else out of money. We honestly thought we had a good product. We were probably all guilty of being gullible and over-enthusiastic."

Ayers' new business struggled until John Rigas, the cable television pioneer, approached him with a plan to produce coupon booklets for customers to use in paying their cable bills. A quarter-century later, when Ayers sold his "T-C Specialties" (short for Tool Craft) printing business, it was the world's largest producer of coupon payment books.

CHAPTER TWENTY-SIX

Eliot Ness, The Myth

Oscar Fraley was able to insert an epilogue in *The Untouchables*, informing readers that Eliot Ness had died, just before the book was published in November 1957, retailing for $3.95 in hardback.

Ness was right about one thing—*The Untouchables* was not a big seller. However, the story did capture the interest of producers from CBS-TV's Desilu Studios. In April 1959, the exaggerated exploits of Eliot Ness were the basis of a two-part dramatization on "Desilu Playhouse." Mae Capone, her son Sonny, and Al's sister Mafalda were so incensed about the distortions that they filed a $1 million defamation suit against Desilu and the show's sponsor, Westinghouse Electric. The suit was dismissed, but it did draw attention to the program's shortcomings. Nevertheless, solid ratings convinced the producers that "The Untouchables" could be expanded into a weekly, hour-long network series for the American Broadcast Company.

ABC hired Walter Winchell to provide the documentary-style narration for the black & white, gritty episodes. Each show featured one gun battle after another, pitting Ness and his G-men against the evil-doers in any number of settings. The program's theme music was as tough as its premise. Faced with the task of creating a new action-packed installment each week, the writers plunged into pure fantasy. Theirs was the first TV show to use blood squibs, taut storytelling and some of the big-screen effects that are common on television today.

Few gave "The Untouchables" much chance to survive, but the American television audience was drawn by the show's frequent, sometimes crudely graphic, bursts of violence and bloodshed. Americans believed they were getting an authentic look at the Prohibition era.

The show was not popular with everyone. Even after Eliot Ness's death, J. Edgar Hoover remained paranoid about the celebrated lawman. He ordered FBI staffers to watch "The Untouchables" each week and summarize every plot, in case the FBI was misrepresented in any way. Hoover also tried, unsuccessfully, to persuade Desi Arnaz, whose Desilu Productions owned the show, to change the plots so that the Prohibition Bureau's role was diminished and the FBI's profile boosted. Hoover fumed when episodes showed Ness solving a crime that fell under the FBI's regular jurisdiction.

Over a period of four seasons, 114 episodes aired, starring Robert Stack as a Ness character who was all-knowing and always-triumphant. Stack's resounding macho voice was a plus, but he wasn't the first choice for the job. Van Heflin and Van Johnson were both approached, and neither was interested in the part. Stack's trim and taciturn rendition of Ness was off-base in some respects, but no one challenged his representation of Ness's intelligence, courage and honesty.

The program may have lasted longer, but it offended the nation's Italian population, who complained that it reinforced negative stereotypes. That growing outcry and the backlash being heard from local ABC affiliates as a result of viewer complaints about excessive violence forced Desilu to drop the series. The program ended the same way it began—in a hail of bullets. It resurfaced briefly in 1962 as two movies, "The Scarface Mob" and "Alcatraz Express," which were actually re-edited episodes of the television series.

Robert Stack, already a movie star in the late 1950s, catapulted to fame in his role as Eliot Ness.

"ABC saw it as something to carry the garbage for their big programs, The Pat Boone Show and Adventures in Paradise," Stack said in an interview. "It looked better on the screen dark, so we shot mostly night scenes. I sometimes stumbled home at four or five in the morning. It was a killer schedule, but 'The Untouchables' had a special quality, a motion picture technique on TV. I was proud to be associated with it."

The filming itself presented some element of danger. Stack recalled the time a 1930 Buick he was driving lost its brakes and smashed through a wall at the end of the sound stage. He escaped serious injury, but was shaken. "We had some crude props and special effects." Stack noted. "Splinters of glass were flying everywhere. The timing devices on explosive charges were out of the 19th century. You had to count the seconds and run."

Stack, who never met Eliot Ness, won an Emmy Award for his work on "The Untouchables," but insists he never wanted to steal the thunder from the man he portrayed. "Capone owned the cops; he owned Chicago. So when Ness made war on him with his six other guys, they were considered dead meat. You had to be pretty brave or at least a little strange to do that. In Paris, they all recognized me as Mr. Ness, and that was kind of exciting. It wasn't me they liked, it was the character I played. Why should they know Robert Stack? The character was interesting; who played it didn't mean a darned thing."

Among his most cherished souvenirs is a 1952 personal check for ten dollars written out to "Cash" by Eliot Ness to cover a losing bet on a sports event. The check, given to Stack by a Hollywood acquaintance more than a decade later, had bounced due to insufficient funds. Stack said the check is a symbolic reminder of Ness's integrity.

"Here's a guy who could have been wealthy if he would have accepted the bribes he was offered, but he stood for something greater, and what kind of thanks did he get? He couldn't even cover a ten-dollar check. I consider Ness a hero. Heroes are driven by their own drum to do the things they have to do. I have known brave men in my life, and there is a commonality to the way they do things."

During an episode of "This Is Your Life," Stack was introduced to Betty Ness.

"She walked out and I took her hand and kissed it," Stack remembered. "After, they asked why, and I said, 'I don't know. I didn't know what to do.' She was a charming woman. She said it was surprising how much of her husband I happened to capture. That meant a lot to me."

Betty Ness confirmed that assessment during a newspaper interview. "I like Robert Stack in Eliot's role on TV, and so does Bobby," Betty said. "All but one thing—Stack is so grim-faced through it all, and you know Eliot wasn't like that. Much of the stuff they have used would have come as a surprise to Eliot. It's pure fabrication. I hope to establish, as time goes on, that he was just a real good guy who did other things besides going around smashing stills and shooting at people. Eliot was a restless man and an innovator. He was concerned about juvenile delinquency and civil rights long before they became headlines in the newspaper... He lived his life with a constant concern for others and a goal of making their lives better. There wasn't a dull moment in my life married to him."

Even Oscar Fraley was taken aback by the television adaptation of the Eliot Ness character he helped to produce. "As a popular TV series, 'The Untouchables' suddenly turned the gentleman I knew, who died a non-entity, into a national figure," Fraley wrote. "Eliot Ness really was two men. In public he was the Ness of television: talking little, but with authority, and using short, terse phrases. In private, with a few close friends, he was the 'other' Eliot Ness, with a bubbling sense of humor and ready smile. At these times, he would kick off his shoes and sprawl casually on the floor. Then the words rushed out in a smooth flood which mixed wit, perception and warmth."

To his dying day, Fraley made no excuses for his role in creating the Eliot Ness myth. "Any personal and possibly selfish reasons aside, it makes for a warm feeling to know that the man who was nobody in his final years finally came into his own through the publication of our book."

The Untouchables myth lives on even today in the form of reruns from the old program and an hour-long syndicated show, also called "The Untouchables," which recently aired on about fifty stations nationwide.

Other Hollywood adaptations have further distorted Ness's image. In the summer of 1987 with great fanfare, Paramount Pictures released a $25 million movie, "The Untouchables," directed by Brian De Palma and starring Kevin Costner as Eliot Ness.

Scriptwriter David Mamet was careful to specify that the movie was "inspired" by the book written by Fraley and Ness, and even that was a stretch. Episodes such as a hotel lobby confrontation between Ness and Capone never took place. The film's scene of Ness throwing Frank "The Enforcer" Nitti off a roof was not only fictional, but illogical. The real Nitti had committed suicide not long after learning that he would be serving a second prison term for tax evasion and had been betrayed by surviving members of Capone's organization.

Kevin Costner had a sincere desire to emulate Ness's personality and mannerisms, within the confines of the script. For advice, he turned to Al "Wallpaper" Wolff.

"They wanted me to be an advisor when they did 'The Untouchables' TV series, but I didn't want to, because I knew it would be phony," Wolff explained. "I told Costner that Ness was passive. I told him how to walk like Ness. Ness walked slowly. When I watched the TV show, I just laughed at how phony it was, but parts of the movie were pretty real, even though there was a lot of Hollywood thrown in. Costner did a good job—I was a good teacher."

Until Al Wolff's advice was sought by producers from Paramount Pictures, even his family was unaware that he had been one of the Untouchables. "Stories about my government work were between me and Uncle Sam, and some of them still are," he explained. "I don't want to mention names, 'cause they have children and grandchildren and I don't want to put a tag on them."

After the 1987 movie made Ness famous among a new generation of Americans, Robert Stack resurrected his Eliot Ness character in a fictional made-for-TV movie for CBS, entitled "Eliot Ness: Welcome to Detroit." He followed that with another two-hour TV movie, "The Return of Eliot Ness," which aired on NBC in 1991. Stack also narrated an episode of the current NBC show, "Unsolved Mysteries," focusing on the inability of Ness and other Cleveland law enforcement authorities to solve the serial killings by the Mad Butcher.

Betty Ness received some modest royalties from sales of *The Untouchables,* but the checks, usually for less than $50, were not nearly enough for her to support herself and Bobby. There is one story circulating that, on the advice of friends in Cleveland, she sold all rights to royalties from book sales and screen adaptations for a mere $1,000.

Betty was a troubled woman during the years immediately following her husband's death. In late 1957, she and Bobby returned to the Cleveland area and visited Corinne Lawson, the Nesses' former housekeeper. Lawson agreed to let them live in her home while Betty looked for a job that would allow her to afford a small apartment. Their stay with Lawson lasted for more than a year, during which time Betty's own alcohol problems, largely hidden from her Coudersport acquaintances, became all too apparent to Corinne Lawson.

"I would find bottles under her bed and everywhere," Lawson said. "But she and Mr. Ness had done so much for me and had been so nice that I didn't care about that."

Betty went to work as a clerk for a clothing boutique on Cleveland's Carnegie Avenue. Later, she worked as a medical records specialist for a Cleveland hospital. Eventually, she and Bobby moved into an apartment at Cleveland Heights, just east of the city, and Betty was hired to teach pottery-making. Some of the pieces she produced early in her career are showcased as part of the Cowan Pottery Studios collection, which is on display at the Rocky River Public Library near Cleveland.

After Bobby was grown and married, Betty moved to San Juan Capistrano, California, to live with relatives.

Robert Warren Ness kept the ashes of his father in an unopened box at his Cleveland Heights home. Bobby and his wife, who were childless, visited Coudersport briefly in the early 1970s. He died of leukemia on August 31, 1976.

Elisabeth Anderson Ness died on November 4, 1977, at her California home at the age of 71. An obituary in the Cleveland Plain Dealer stated that she had been suffering from cancer for the past several years.

There are no markers to memorialize Eliot, Betty or Bobby Ness. Their ashes can be found in the Cleveland area garage of Bobby's widow, Sharon Darkovich, who said she doesn't know what to do with them.

Epilogue

Souvenirs of Eliot Ness are everywhere, from the Cleveland Police Historical Museum, where the public can view his Smith & Wesson revolver and countless photos and newspaper clippings, to liquor store manager Larry Del Grosso's closet, where a pair of Ness's gym trunks, picked up at a yard sale, hang as a reminder of Del Grosso's conversations with a man who became a celebrity.

Rebecca McFarland, a librarian who serves on the Board of Trustees for the Cleveland Police Historical Museum, tries to preserve Ness's memory with a slide show and well-researched speech about his Cleveland days.

Most recently, Arts & Entertainment Television Network produced an hour-long documentary about Ness for that cable service's popular "Biography" series.

Joe Phelps, visiting Coudersport in 1965, sat at a front table of Mackey's Restaurant and noticed a newspaper story stating that Al Capone's son, Sonny, had been arrested for shoplifting two bottles of aspirin and a package of batteries from a Miami Beach convenience store. "Everybody has a little larceny in them," was the quote from Sonny Capone, who had changed his name to Albert Francis.

"Not everybody, Sonny," Phelps said after reading the blurb aloud to his lunch partner. Phelps went on to tell his acquaintance about the man with whom he had spent so many mornings at the same counter almost a decade earlier.

Ness himself sometimes looked back incredulously at his own life. "Hell, I'm just like anyone else," he once said. "There were certain things I had to do and I did them. Of course, I'll admit that when there was action at hand I did feel a certain sense of exhilaration; maybe even exultation. But, many a time after it was over and I realized what had happened or how close a call it had been, I broke out in a cold sweat."

Bill Ayers, who knew Eliot Ness better than anybody alive today, wrote:

"The real test of a man's moral fiber is to be found in his everyday life. Eliot Ness attacked every menial problem with the me zeal that he must have used to attack the overwhelming dds facing him in battles against crime. He refused to accept defeat in situations where a lesser man would give in. I have never known an individual who lived by a stricter code. Eliot was uncompromising in his principles, both in his crime-fighting days and in his business dealings, even to his own personal loss. They say all men have a price. Well, whatever his price was, it was so high that nobody could pay it. Eliot Ness was a man to talk and laugh with, to drink with, and share the joys and sorrows that make up life. In his place, he left a legend that, like most legends, is an unfit memorial."

Sources

Books

Capone: The Life And World Of Al Capone, by John Kobler (Putnam, 1971)

Four Against The Mob, by Oscar Fraley (Award Books, 1976)

Cleveland Murders, Oliver Weld Bayer, Editor (Duell, Sloan & Pearce, 1947)

Cleveland: Confused City On A Seesaw, by Phillip W. Porter (Ohio State University Press, 1976)

The FBI Story, by Don Whitehead (Muller, 1957)

Al Capone: The Biography Of A Self-Made Man, by Fred D. Pasley (Ives Washburn, 1930)

The Untouchables, by Eliot Ness and Oscar Fraley (Julian Messner Company, 1957)

Torso: Eliot Ness And The Hunt For The Mad Butcher Of Kingsbury Run, by Steven Nickel (John F. Blair, Publisher, 1989)

The Tax Dodgers, by Elmer L. Irey and William J. Slocum (Greenberg, 1948)

The Bootleggers, by Kenneth Allsop (Arlington House, 1961)

The Dry & Lawless Years, by John H. Lyle (Prentice-Hall, 1960)

Brotherhood of Evil: The Mafia, by Frederic Sondern (Gollancz, 1959)

Chicago: The Second City, by A. J. Liebling (Knopf, 1952)

Barbarians In Our Midst, by Virgil W. Peterson (Little, Brown, 1952) e Case Against Prohibition, by Charles A. Windle (Iconoclast, 1927)

The Gold Coast And The Slum: A Sociological Study of Chicago's Near North Side, by Harvey W. Zorbaugh (University of Chicago, 1929)

The Gang, by Frederic M. Thrasher (University of Chicago, 1928)

Gem Of The Prairie: An Informal History Of The Chicago Underworld, by Herbert Asbury (Alfred A. Knopf, 1940)

The Lawless Decade, by Paul Sann (Crown Publishers, 1957)

Big Bill Of Chicago, by Lloyd Wendt and Herman Koga (Bobbs-Merrill Company, 1953)

The Mob's Man, by James D. Horan (Hale, 1960)

Scarface Al And The Crime Crusaders, by Dennis Hoffman (Southern Illinois University Press, 1993)

Murder, Inc., by Burton B. Turkus and Sid Feder (Gollancz, 1952)

The Last Untouchable, By Paul Robsky and Oscar Fraley (River City Press, 1962)

Periodicals

"The Real Eliot Ness," by Steven Nickel, American History Illustrated, October 1987

"The Last Untouchable: A New Movie Flushes Out An Old Eliot Ness G-Man From Undercover," by Civia Tamarkin, People Weekly, July 18, 1987

"The Mob At The Movies," by Tom Mathews, Newsweek, June 22, 1987

"Al Capone: Chicago's Untouchable Mobster," American History Illustrated, October 1987

"Reliving A Massacre," Newsweek, January 29, 1979

"Browsing In Gangland," by Joseph Epstein, Commenta[ry], January 1972

"The Real Eliot Ness," by Oscar Fraley, Coronet, January 1972

"Eliot Ness To Millions," by Taris Savell, Grit, July 9, 198.

"Eliot Ness In Coudersport," by Bob Merten (transcript of speech presented to Coudersport, Pa., Rotary Club on May 10, 1993)

"The FBI's TV Files," by William P. Barrett, Rolling Stone, April 21, 1988

"In The American Grain," by Richard Schickel, Time, June 8, 1987

"Stack Is Back As Mr. Untouchable," by Timothy Carlson, TV Guide, November 9, 1991

"The First Untouchable Of Them All," by Laura Shapiro and Ray Sawhill, Newsweek, June 26, 1987

"Meet The Real Gangbuster: Eliot Ness," by John H. Graves, Potter County Leader, June 24, 1987

"As I Knew Eliot Ness," by William J. Ayers, Potter Enterprise, November 24, 1971

"Eliot Ness's Last Days," by Walter Taylor, Potter Enterprise, March 22, 1961

"There Goes Eliot Ness," Fortune, January 1946

"The Capone I Knew," by Ray Brennan, True Detective, June 1947

"Radio-Directed Mobile Police," by Eliot Ness, American City, November 1939

"Evaline Ness, Rising Star In The Illustration Firmament," American Artist, January 1956

"Cleveland Vs. The Crooks," by Stanley High, Reader's Digest, February 1939